RIGHTS OF HINDU AND MUSLIM WOMEN

RIGHTS OF HINDU AND MUSLIM WOMEN

Edited by
NEERA BHARIHOKE

SERIALS PUBLICATIONS
NEW DELHI

First Published - 2019

ISBN: 978-81-8387-135-8

Published by

SERIALS PUBLICATIONS
4830/24, Prahlad Street, Ansari Road
Darya Ganj, New Delhi-110002 (India)
Phone : 23245225
Fax : 91-11-23272135
E-mail: serials@satyam.net.in

CONTENTS

PREFACE

Indian Constitution guarantees equal rights to women and men, but strong patriarchal traditions continue which view daughter as a liability, wife as an object of subordination, mother as an aide of family burdened with house maintenance and daughter-in-law as a typical housewife who is suppressed and shackled by the age-old customs and traditions. Subjugation of women is deep-rooted to such an extent that it goes largely unseen, unexamined and unquestioned.

Women perform primary task of maintaining welfare and comfort of their families. Women have also been active income-generating members of the family. Their contribution in areas of agriculture and economic activity is visible in rural life too. But they are thoroughly deprived of resources like education, health care services, access and freedom to adopt family planning processes. These are essential supplements to execute the various tasks and responsibilities of women in domestic as well as economic region. Perception of women having lower social status results in her labour and work being undermined, unappreciated, unvalued and unacknowledged.

Present issue of the journal highlights the rights which exist in favour of women but are not enforced. At times, women, despite being equipped with the rights, lack the will or power to use them. The articles in the issue draw the attention towards the availability or at times the lack of the rights in particular quarters of activity of women. Gross violation and contravention of rights available to women are not paid any attention by the implementation agencies. Articles also draw attention to economic view point and the impact of use or non-use of the rights by women. A foretaste of the research articles contributed by few authors highlights the atrocities and lacunae in the system.

There was a time when rights and women were considered to be antonyms of each other and incapable of co-existence. A combination of two was viewed as a mismatched amalgamation. With time, role and responsibilities of women has attained new perimeters and perception. The woman of today is portrayed as a persona with rights, powers and privileges. Transformation of a woman's role from subjugation to liberation is often acclaimed to be an endowment of the modernization of the society. Educational and occupational blueprints have also changed and amplified resulting in women entering the provinces, which were considered to be dominated by men. Women issues have received remarkable attention in the legislative arena too. Laws have been enacted to ensure her protection and empowerment in her family and home as well as in her job place.

Rights have emerged in favour of women, at times by social change or by change in perception of society or by enactment of laws. But existence or possession of rights is a hollow and meaningless notion unless these rights are exercised. Gender inequalities imbibed in our social structure place hindrances on the way of women to put into effect these rights. Rights signify empowerment. The truth is that the power and autonomy to exercise these rights is women empowerment. Women empowerment can be achieved only by granting women the primary rights of expression, autonomy and decision-making.

DR. NEERA BHARIHOKE

WOMEN RIGHTS IN INDIAN SOCIETY: AN ANTHROPOLOGICAL OBSERVATION

*Samar Kumar Biswas** &
*Somenath Bhattacharjee***

I

INTRODUCTION

The subject of human rights is gaining much importance in the present day world scenario. Today the wave of new world order exploitative attitude, consumerism and greed of a few refuting the needs of many. The right of life is the essence of human rights. Basically it refers to those elemental rights which any human deserves to have honoured in order to survive, enjoy well being and flourish or fulfill him or herself simply by virtue of human being. There are several attributes of human rights. The most important are right to individual dignity, right to equality, right to culture and religious freedom, right to life, right to justice, right to respect and privacy, right to earning and employment, right to property and right to women and child. Anthropology being the wholistic study of man deals with the social and cultural aspects of human life. Women are the reproducing unit of the world. The continuation of generation and continuation

* Lecturer, Department of Anthropology, North Bengal University, Darjeeling 734013, West Bengal.
** Research Scholar, Department of Anthropology, North Bengal University, Darjeeling 734013, West Bengal, *e-mail: smrkbis@yahoo.co.in.*

of cultural heritage is taking place through the women. Thus in this new world order of human rights the position and perspective of women as a whole must be analyzed from its own anthropological dimension.

In early prehistoric period the human being dealt their livelihood as like other animal. Then they were totally parasite on nature. There were no preponderant concept of family, marriage, permanent settlement, economy and they dealt a nomadic life and the livelihood almost continued with simple technological implements. But after the glacial period there occurred a lot of climatic change and the mean temperature of the earth gradually got increased. The post glacial period provided a number of bio-cultural changes to the concerned ancestors of modern human being. The human being slowly started to find permanent settlement and livelihood through the domestication and food production. The neolithic period was the determinant of the same. In that period there was no concept of division of labour. A number of new technological implements came to their livelihood. They started to produce surplus production. Due to these progresses specification of work was started. The females were mostly confined to look after the domestic courses, and the outer world affairs was the matter of the males and ultimately this practice was incorporated into the social system. In this way the authority and succession over the technological implements and the control of food and food resource as well as surpluses confined to the hand of the male which resulted that the women had to depend on their male counterparts for their livelihood. Thus the necessities of livelihood as well as economy slowly went under the authority of the male and as a result they started to occupy the higher social position in comparison to the female and the right of livelihood of the women got confined into the hand of the male altogether.

There is unquestionably a great deal of variety in the status and role of women in various cultures. However in considering culture as a whole, it is universally true that women occupy a secondary status. Sherry Ortner (1974) speaks of three factors by which the position of women in a society can be measured, these are –

(i) Statements of cultural ideology which explicitly devalue women, their product and their role.

(ii) Symbolic devices such as the concept of defilement associated with women.

(iii) The exclusion of women from participation in the area believed to be most powerful in the particular society whether religious or secular.

In every human society women bear and rise up the children. The only way a home could exist was if there was a division of labour. In simple societies it was based upon needs and biological factors. Freed from biological imperatives the young males could roam from the home to the place of hunt. Women foraged too but they were constrained by the necessities of carrying and nursing babies and stayed closer to or at the home. The horizons of the women thus become more limited and seem to have cast the role of the female as a member of a private sphere a domestic world. For this purpose the discussion has been primarily confined on the rights of women in Tribal and Hindus in Indian society.

Status of Women from Prehistoric to Developing Society

Women in Middle Palaeolithic: The findings from the Shanidar cave reveals that at least women and children and occasionally elderly man remained close to the hearth fire while younger males engage din activities that took them away from the cave. The findings of neanderthal skeleton of a young girl in Siberia reveals that she was buried in skin clothing with jewelry of bone and shell whose grave was surrounded by antlers and horns. No doubt this woman so honoured had a high status in society.

Women in Upper Palaeolithic: About 25000 years ago a symbolic representation of women in the portable art of upper palaeolithic period in Western Europe was found. The most important one is the cult of 'venus' which are the rough portrayals of females in which the sexual and secondary sexual characteristics are greatly exaggerated with swelling breasts, tapering legs which altogether symbolizes that the women are the productive unit of nature and they can nourish the descendents through her physical capability. It shows the natural fertility of mother earth as represented by the females in the society. Along with the venus cult there were abstract female figurines, mother goddesses and agriculture paintings and sculptures.

Power and Authority of Women in Simple society: Power is defined as the ability to make others conform to one's wishes while authority is defined as the legitimization of power by the society. Most likely any woman has a degree of power commensurate with network of people with whom she has influenced. In patrilocal societies it is recognized that the women is being removed from her family and that her children will belong to her husbands group. Often the woman's family will be compensated in advance by a gift of bride wealth for this loss of labour or personnel. When both sets of kin had a financial investment in a marriage they were mutually interested in its success, because returning or forfeiting the bride wealth constituted a hardship. Consequently a woman could appeal to her relatives by marriage among which she lived if she felt herself excessively abused by her husband or other women in group. Women are valued for their abilities as workers and producers of children. For example in Samoan society a woman who had produced children outside his marriage is considered a more desirable wife because she has already proven her reproductive capacity. Here a woman can find herself among a group of co-wives. Her status in such a group increases as her sons grow in age and in influence. In matrilocal societies the women had their own status and position in comparison to the men. They mostly are the decision making authority in the family, here her brother has a key role to play.

Women in developing societies: These societies have generally been colonial possession which have recently found themselves independent or are forced by recent industrial development. Here the women have to play active role both in the family and outside of their family. Due to middle class income holding they have to make themselves directly involved in the source of earning. Her status in the family depends on the amount of her earning. Here they have to play a desirable role in the family altogether (Kessler, 1976:12-50).

II

ROLE STATUS AND AUTHORITY OF WOMEN FROM EARLY TO MODERN INDIAN SOCIETY

The concept of women has been best described in an ancient Sanskrit saying- *"yatra nari pujante tatra devo ramante"*. Women have been given the ascription of mother goddess and she is considered as the source of 'shakti'. Status of women in any society is a significant pointer to the level of culture of that society. Sex inequality denotes a condition where prevailing social norms, values and stereo types ascribe to women an inferior status to that of men and debar them from taking equal part in social, economic, political and cultural life of the community. In almost all societies women have been given inferior and unequal social position in the society. There are ample evidences to suggest that women have been subordinated, subjugated and exploited in the society. In order to study the position of women the entire scenario has been divided into three broad period's viz. the first period-from 800 BC to 1800 AD described as the pre colonial period. The second period-from 1800 AD to 1947 described as the pre independence period. The third period-from 1947 to till date described as the post independence period.

Normative Structure of Traditional Indian Society: The Vedic texts and the Dharmashastras are said to constitute the norms for Brahmanism and the religious practices for the upper castes. *Arthashastra* of Kautilya and *Manusmriti* broadly covering the period from 400 BC to 500 AD are sources for getting insights into the normative structure determining the behaviour of women. It has been usually believed that except early Vedic period women was given a subordinate position to men. The women's place was by and large regarded as being in the home. During the period of *Puran* and *Smriti* the women were much respected and it was considered absurd to condemn a woman if she was empowered and ravished. The *Agnipuran* also asserted that a woman was not polluted by forcible assault or conception. Such cases were considered as an accidental circumstances and the victim would be readmitted to her previous position after the birth of the child. Dowry system was rather unknown to the Indian society. A man who committed adultery with a woman of low caste shall be put to death so harsh were the laws against persons who committed crime against women. Woman is counted as *shakti* in Indian mythology. The *tantras* universally propounded the profound and revolutionary concepts of equality of the sexes when western countries were still slumbering in the dark ages. The glory and greatness of Indian womanhood is reflected in the unknown, unsung and unhonoured tales in our national heritage. The virtues and vigour has been brought to the fore in the murale of Ajanta, Ellora and other caves and in the sculpture of Khajuraho, Konark, Rajasthan and South Indian temples.

Women in Caste System : In order to property estimate the position of women in ancient society a brief reference to the stratification system as expressed through varna and caste system is necessary. Features like caste system endogamy as a mechanism of recruiting and retaining control over the labour and sexuality of women concepts of purity and pollution segregating groups and also regulating mobility of women are very crucial. The other very important feature of caste system is its control over women's labour. India being primarily depended on agriculture, for instance, women can engage themselves in water regulation, transplantation of crops weeding but not ploughing. With upward mobility of the group women are immediately withdrawn from the outside work. The linking of women and Shudras together is one more evidences of the low position of women. Prescriptions and prohibitions for Shudras and women were the same on many occasions. The caste system not only provided a legitimization to feudal relation of production but ideologically also provided justification for the subordination of women.

Women in Pre-Colonial Period: The birth of a daughter which was not a source of anxiety during the Vedic period became a source of disaster for father during the post Vedic period. Education of women which was an accepted norm during the Vedic period slowly began to be neglected and latter on girls were totally denied any access to education. *Upanayana* or the sacred thread ceremony which was performed to initiate a person into the Vedic studies was prohibited in the case of women and Shudras by the Manav codes the closing the door for any formal education of the women. By 8th century AD the marriageable age for girls was lowered to 9 to 10 years which not only gave a final blow to any effort at educating women but began the sinister practice of prepuberty marriages. In the medieval period she was even expected to die either on the same pyre with her husband or follow him and become 'sati'. Treatment of the widow thus at times bordered on the inhumane and callous levels. It is to be mentioned here that particularly after the establishment of class society and the rise of private property in the post Vedic period women's position in the society declines.

Women in Pre-Independence Period: In this period the country passed through complex economic and political developments due to the working of merchants, industrial and political capital. The imperial system initiated the capitalist mode of production but retained many pre capitalist institutions like the caste system and inhuman socio- religious practices. During this period there were two major movements which affected the position of women. These were the social reform movement of the 19th century and the nationalist movement of 20th century. Both these movements raised the question of equal status of women. Specially the role of *Arya Samaj, Brahma Samaj* must be mentioned in this concern and the pioneers of these movements were Raja Ram Mohan Roy, Ishwar Chandra Vidyasagar, Annie Besant etc. The prime important movements were Sati Outlawed (1825), Widow Remarriage (1856), III Treatment of Widows, Child Marriage, Denial of Property Rights and Education of Women. The Child Marriage Restraint Act or Shudras Act prohibited marriages below the age of 14 years for a girl. The middle class women entry into the world of work appears more significantly after the Second World War. A few women did take up some professions like law, medicine, teaching etc. But their number was very few.

Women in Post-Independence Period: Middle class educated women particularly in large urban agglomerations, who are working and moving freely, generate an impression that Indian women's status has substantially improved. Moreover there is evidence of capable, efficient, powerful women at times with political clout, which reinforces this impression. But on the other hand in small towns or rural areas on in city slums, women still suffer from social and economic oppression. In small towns and villages upper caste women even today are confined to home bound activities and involved in responsibilities and interests limited only to their kith and kin. She is expected to look after domestic chores and her typical roles are those of a housewife and mother. Her role in the outside world has not yet been accepted in the same manner as men's. Women are generally treated as unpaid family workers. Free India adopted a path of development based on mixed economy with a great emphasis on industrialization. It accepted the pattern of dual sectors viz. public and private. In this concern poverty and unemployment have the worst effect on woman. It is now recognised that the policy of economic development which relies heavily on advanced technology, multination collaborations, export promotion and encouragement to private sectors paves the way for a higher degree of concentration of capital and extremely exploitative relations of productions have a very serious implications for women (Desai and Krishnaraj,1987: 10-25).

III

SOCIAL, ECONOMIC AND POLITICAL DEPRIVATION OF WOMEN IN NON TRIBAL INDIA

Social Position of Women in India after Independence and Contemporary Period: Middle class educated women particularly in large urban agglomerations, who are working and moving freely, generate an impression that Indian women's status has improved substantially. But in small towns and villages upper caste women even today are confined to home bound activities and involved in responsibilities and interests limited only to their kith and kin. Particularly the 'sati' was the common practice among the varna Hindus and among them the widow remarriage was strictly prohibited. By the turn of the century pioneers like Vidyasagar, Ram Mohan Roy abolished the discrimination against women and the concerned British Government passed a number of laws to protect the atrocities against women. Among them most important were-

In 1825-Sati Outlawed.

In 1856-Widow Remarriage made legal.

In 1870-Special Marriage Act passed to allow inter community marriages.

In 1921-Women got the right to vote in Madras province.

In 1937-Women got limited right to property.

It is only from the beginning of the present century that the legal status of women has come to be considered objectively in various legal systems. It is affirmed not only to bring about equality of status but also provide equal opportunity for women. Woman's physical structure and performance of maternal functions place her at a disadvantageous position in the struggle for subsistence and her physical well being becomes an object of public interest and care in order to preserve the strength and vigour of the race. Domestic environment is very important parameter for deciding the status of women at home and in the society. Through self help groups the interactions in meetings help to develop friendship, express solidarity with the problem of others, nurture leadership and enhance one's own capacity as steeping towards development. Women find a new identity through S.H.G. The group affiliation is a strengthening bond and a powerful tool to resolve their problems. Presently the self help group enhance equality of status of women as participants, decision makers and beneficiaries in the democratic, economic, social and cultural spheres of life. But the needs and application is far from any proportionate distribution and in rural areas still now the women and entire female folk have to suffer from economic deprivation and exploitation both from the male within their household or in their society.

Table 1
Educational level of Household population

Category	*Male*	*Female*	*Total*
Illiterate	25.3	48.6	36.9
Below primary school	21.1	17.1	19.2
Above primary school	18.4	14.5	16.5
Middle school complete	13.0	8.1	10.6
High school complete	10.7	6.0	8.4
Higher secondary complete	11.2	5.6	8.4
Person	212185	204870	417055

Source: NFHS -2, 1998-99.

The situation of women's educational involvement differs quite high than that of the males and in the feature of higher education they are lagging quite behind in comparison to that of the males (Seth, 2001: 115-153) (See table 1 and 2).

Economic position of women: Industrial capitalism transplanted on Indian soil by colonial rule created major discontinuity for the Indian economy. Along with the

Table 2
Per centage of Girl's Enrollment to total Enrollment

Year	*Primary*	*Middle*	*Secondary / Higher secondary*	*Higher education (degree and above)*
1950-51	28.1	16.1	13.3	10.0
1960-61	32.6	23.9	20.5	16.0
1970-71	37.4	29.3	25.0	20.0
1980-81	38.6	32.9	29.6	26.7
1990-91	41.5	36.7	32.9	33.3
2000-01	43.7	40.9	38.6	39.4
2002-03	46.8	43.9	41.3	40.1

Source: NSSO, 2005

agriculture every household carried on work on spinning and weaving, artisan, craft production. Unlike the insecure craftism of feudal Europe, the Indian craftsmen and women enjoyed economic security though not necessarily prosperity because they supplied the needs of the village on a customary basis. In addition many women were engaged in different independent occupations, food processing crafts, trade and were paid in cash or kind. After 1901 technological changes, foreign competition, changes in demand, legislative actions designed to protect women were all acting in combination. Between 1911 to 1961 the worker rate had fallen for male 8 per cent and for female 18 per cent. In the newly formed industries total employment grew to a level of 1500 thousand but the share of female workers was only 86 thousand which gives the ratio of male to female 70:4. In the service sector the female work force decreased by 1, 89,000 while that of males increased by 32, 37,000 and opportunities for males were greater in the better paid administrative, defense and professional jobs. Mainly during 1961 to 1981 the reduction of female workforce occurred due to their substitution by male labours. There were several other causes also like- technological changes altered the occupational structure; growing unemployment and sluggish growth of income per capita resulting in insufficient opportunities for potential female workers (Seth, 2001: 189-230). The working involvement of the women in labour force and their growth of employment opportunity give us a more dismal picture as stated below-

Table 3
Person in Labour Force

Year	*T/R/U*	*Male*	*Female*
1993-1994	T	85.4	42.0
	R	87.6	48.8
	U	79.1	23.4
1999-2000	T	83.5	38.5
	R	85.4	45.6
	U	78.6	20.9

Source: 38th, 50th, 55th survey of NSSO on Employment and Unemployment situation in India

Table 4
Trends in Growth of Employment

Year	*Total*		*Rural*		*Urban*	
	M	*F*	*M*	*F*	*M*	*F*
1983-1993/94	2.2	1.7	2.0	1.5	2.8	3.2
1993-94/1999-00	1.9	0.9	1.6	0.8	2.6	1.5

Source: 38th, 50th, 55th survey of NSSO on Employment and Unemployment situation in India

The household industry has only 25 occupational groups where as the non household industries number more than 10,000. The most important structural feature of female non agricultural work force is its heavy concentration in household production relative to men and their inferior position in the modern non household sectors. Even in the non household sector such as in trade, business, professions they rarely have the status of employers. The rural women has to play multiple but complex role as mother, housewife, farmer, trader, worker etc. She therefore has to work 13-14 hours per day with a very little share in family food and nutrition.

Table 5
Share of Women in workforce in Rural and Urban Areas

Rural / Urban	*Sector*	*1993-1994*	*1999-2000*
R	Agriculture	39.4	38.7
	Mining	24.3	20.8
U	Manufacture	35.8	35.5
	Electric Gas Water	15.9	0.0
R	Construction	13.5	11.5
	Trade/Hotel	17.6	13.5
A	Transport/ Storage	2.5	1.6
	Other Service	21.4	24.3
	Non Agriculture	22.9	21.3
L	All Sector	35.8	34.6
U	Agriculture	42.36	39.73
R	Mining	11.02	9.85
	Manufacture	21.57	20.92
B	Electric Gas Water	6.28	5.79
	Construction	13.75	11.94
A	Trade/Hotel	10.91	12.38
	Transport/ Storage	3.47	4.08
N	Other Service	26.23	28.58
	Non Agriculture	18.20	17.79
	All sector	21.18	19.71

Source: NSSO, 2005

Mostly in rural India the agriculture is the prime economic outfit. In the rural India a landless women primarily sustain their livelihood by working as a wage labourer and agriculture farmer. Many a time they are attached to landlords family and mostly deprived by male folk; a near landless women having a small bit of land which are dry and uncultivable, poor irrigation facility, lack of resource and lack of cattle wealth impair them in cultivating their land; a small peasant women work in the family farms and farms of the others as wage labourers to add something to the low income of the family; even a rich peasant women have to depend on his male members of the family for proper observation of the work and his share over the produced crops. The wage rate in agricultural occupation gives a more detail data-

Table 6
Wage Rate in Agricultural Occupation 2004-2005 (in Rs.)

Occupation	Wages of Men	Wages of Women
Ploughing	72.28	41.58
Sowing	66.09	46.17
Weeding	57.79	46.73
Transplanting	62.06	50.98
Harvesting	61.95	50.99
Winnowing	54.93	42.69
Threshing	59.15	46.63
Picking	54.60	41.49
Herdsman	41.51	31.68
Well Digging	84.17	47.09
Crushing	60.62	42.73

Source: Ministry of Labour, Govt. of India

It has been seen among the Rajbansi Stone crushers (an unorganized occupational group) of Balasan river bed in Darjeeling district that the women work along with their male as a production unit, but most of the earning go to the hand of the male and they spend it without any concern of their female. As a result the women have a mere purchasing capacity and in most of the cases they have to face a lot of difficulties. Beside this in most of cases they have to depend on their male members for decision making (Field Study, 2004-2007).

Political position of women: Till the end of the 19th century women in India were crushed under the weight of evil customs like infanticide, child marriage and even sati. But from the early nineteenth century due to the movement of social reformists these social evils were started to get eradicated very frequently. The demand for franchise before independence was pressed for by the elite woman who were conscious of their political rights and who were influenced by the democratic values and ideals. A deputation of women meets the then viceroy Montague in 1917 to demand the right to vote for women. The government of India Act 1919 lay down that the question of franchise could be settled by the provinces. By 1926 women secured equal position in franchise so far as the election to the provisional legislatures was concerned. The political authority is the prime status which empowers a nation and even a social group. In Indian society the male has their own dominance to confine the political status within their own hand and own authority. Just after independence till the eighties the women were far away from the male in seeking the electoral franchise, the table shows the details.

Table 7
Per centage of Voters

Year	*Total voting per centage*	*Per centage of male voters per centage*	*Per centage of female voters*
1957	47.74	55.77	38.77
1962	54.76	62.05	46.63
1967	61.33	66.73	55.48
1971	55.35	61.00	49.15
1977	60.49	65.63	54.96
1980	56.92	62.15	51.22

Source: Election Commission of India

Female turnout in states like Orissa, Madhya Pradesh, Rajasthan, Uttar Pradesh and Assam is relatively very low due to their traditional customary conservatism and own caste biasness. Even during the first forty years of independence the scenario of ministry rank reveals the clear picture that women were kept aside from the mainstream political field in Indian perspective.

Table 8
Female Ministerial Ranks

Year	*Cabinet Minister*	*Deputy Minister*	*Minister of State*
1957	-	3	-
1962	2	5	2
1967	1	3	2
1971	1	2	2
1977	1	-	3
1980	2	2	2
1985	1	-	4

Source: Election Commission of India.

Table 9
Female Members from 1st to 13th Lok Sabha

Lok Sabha Session	*Total Seats*	*No. of women elected*	*Per centage*
1st (1952-'57)	499	22	4.40
2nd ('57-'62)	500	27	5.40
3rd ('62-'67)	503	34	6.70
4th ('67-'70)	523	31	5.90
5th ('71-'77)	521	22	4.20
6th ('77-'79)	544	19	3.40
7th ('80-'84)	544	28	5.10
8th ('84-'89)	544	44	8.10
9th ('89-'91)	517	27	5.20
10th ('91-'96)	544	39	7.16
11th ('96-'97)	544	40	7.35
12th ('98)	544	44	8.10
13th ('99)	543	48	8.83

Source: Election Commission of India

Many factors are important in the election of women candidates such as literacy, family background, familial financial position, involvement in politics, local conditions, campaign strategy, pull within party and politics. Many active women leaders and members of political parties feel that the main reason why the women are reluctant to the contest the elections is the deliberate discrimination on the part of men who lead political parties and impose a decisive influence in the selection of party candidates. But the 73rd and 74th amendment of the Indian constitution provided 33 per cent for women in panchayat and urban local bodies and it served as a major breakthrough to provide equal political status for women.

IV

STATUS OF WOMEN IN TRIBAL INDIA

In the tribal society there is no visible distinction between the men and women. Tribes in general do not have any market preference for boys and girls. Among the matrilineal Garos and Khasis a girl is an asset and the potential heiress of the family. In tribal societies girls and boys enjoy considerable freedom in their movement. Among many tribes boys and girls can freely dance with each other. The institution of dormitory for young boys and girls was widely distributed in tribal India. These dormitories function as a singular institution for preparing the boys and girls for adulthood. Here they not only enjoy a free sexual training but they also learn various skills of dance, song and the tribal lore which are necessary to function as a member of society. After marriage there have been some changes in the roles of the tribal girls. A good hard working wife is considered as an asset in tribal society. In her new home she also enjoys considerable freedom in her movement. In tribal society a wife enjoys an almost equal status with her husband. Among patrilineal tribe the bride is under the control of her mother-in-law and other co- wives if they are senior to them. Initially a mother- in –law is supposed to treat her son's wife as her own daughter and should guide her in all works. A mother is considered superior to other women. A barren woman is not usually mal treated and in such a case her husband is free to marry again without divorcing his barren wife. The wife being a working hand is considered as an economic asset. The management and economy of the household lies in the shoulder of the wives of Jenu Kuruba (See Pfeffer and Behera, 1999:168-179). She sells and buys in the weekly market. While borrowing money, paddy, poultry on repaying the debt all the transaction played between the money lenders wife and the loners' wife, while the husband is a mere observer here. Among the north eastern tribe like the Meches the women are compared with the mother earth (Biswas, Field Study, 2006). They symbolizes that the first drop of monsoon makes the earth fertile while the first menarche of a women shows her status of fertility; thus the women and the earth are both determined as the symbol of production and the livelihood of the earth is on a continuation due to their reproducing capability.

Role in Economy: It is usually observed among many tribes that working mothers carry their babies even to the fields. So the other members back at home remain undisturbed. At the middle age mother gets her own daughter to help her all domestic matter like issues on work in the field and selection of mate for her daughter and so on. Motherhood confirms a special status to a tribal women and she is treated like a fruit bearing tree as like the Muria where a women must be treated with care and respect. In the tribal societies a widow is not debarred from any activity normally done by a married woman. She works in the family and also in the field without any stigma. Marrying a divorced women or widow is not tabooed. A widow is free to remarry and if she is young and industrious she has hardly any difficulty to find a male. Among some tribes a widow marries her deceased husband's younger brother. A Garo widow is automatically get married to her youngest daughter's husband and it is with her permission the husband may have sexual intercourse to the younger wife. The social position of aged women in tribal communities is not altogether very problematic. An old lady continue to work for her family as best her health permit. She looks after the small babies and does such kind of jobs for which she is capable. An old tribal woman is not under care in her family, sometime the old women officiates over the family and other social matters and they are continued to be honoured by all even at their older ages. Among the Gaddis both the male and female share equal status in their occupational pursuits (See Pfeffer and Behera, 1999:115-142). Among the Jenukurubas both boys and girls were given full freedom in the matter of choosing their life partner. The practice of dowry was totally unheard. Even today pre puberty marriages are very rare because they basically belief that marrying a girl before her attainment of puberty is inappropriate. Marriage is obligatory in tribal societies. A large number of marriages have taken place by mutual content like among the Santal, Munda where a girl may has ran away by with a boy of her own community. On that case marriage is solemnized later through proper rights, rituals and payment of proper bride price. Selection of spouses is left completely to the choice of the partners concerned and here the girl play a more important role than the boys. In social matters the tribal woman enjoys considerable freedom of movement and choice compared to their non tribal counterpart. She has her own status and decision making capability within her own community. It is to be mentioned here that among the Khasis the marriage of the youngest daughter is negotiated but the other daughter may marry according to their choice. The bride price is high for girls who is thrifty, strong, hard working and know the art and craft for household management. Among the tribals a woman can divorce her husband if she is impotent or cannot provide her food or treat her badly. Among matrilineal Garo, a woman may ask her husband to leave her home if she is not satisfied with him. The girl has every right to divorce the boy after forceful marriage if she is not up to her choice.

In the tribal societies besides working in the household the concerned women also have to work in the field. After marriage the young wife takes care of her husband, her child and shoulders all the household responsibility including agriculture, cattle, poultry and everything belonging to her husband. Women even incur the lone and repay it to the money lenders, sell the forest products in the local market. The women folk among the Bondas (See Pfeffer and Behera, 1999:180-189) work as a bonded labour named as Goti. The tribal women perform an important role in the concerned economic life. The Birhor of Hazaribagh district (See Pfeffer and Behera, 1999: 226-230) are involved in the collection of roots, tubers and fruits which constitute their food at certain season which is essentially considered as the job of the women. They accompany the males when they go out for hunting and trapping small game, mainly rabbits and jungle fowl. Women play a major role in the making and marketing of rope. Husbands go to the market for collection while the wives stayed at their home. Besides household activities the wives also visit the adjacent market with their rope made products. Even per day a woman cover 7-8 villages traversing a distance of 18-20 miles in both ways.

The tribal women enjoy more social freedom because of their heavy demand in the economic life. In the plain land tribes the women are engaged in the field of agriculture and they are indispensable. The property is owned both by male and female folk and the women spent their income with out any advices from the men folk. The Jenukurubas are a hunting–gathering tribe. In the food gathering stage women and men together used to produce food. Women use to collect tubers fruits flower, fire wood and water. Among them men and women hunt together. The roles of father and mother are not sharply differentiated, both sexes sharing responsibility for the caring of children. Women in the said tribe are equal partner with men in shifting cultivation. Women participated in major agricultural activities and trade. Today almost all of their women work as an agricultural wage labourer. The women's participation in the economic activities is universal among the tribals. Among the Khasis the husband may seek his wife's or her mother's advice in regard to the familial matters. Among the Santal every head of their household care for his wife's opinion in the family matter. Traditionally Santal women are equal with the men both in rights and privilege. They are equally respected and are equally responsible for making the Santal society as a whole. The Totos, a primitive tribe of West Bengal reside in Toto Para village of Jalpaiguri district. It has been observed that the women enjoy every aspects of their life along with the men. A woman can choose her life partner; even she can divorce her husband if she is not satisfied. The women have the right to opine their view regarding familial and interfamilial conflicts to their traditional village panchayat. Though conflict in Toto society is rarely noticed (Biswas, Field Study, 2004 and 2006). Among the Meches of Ballalguri in Jalpaiguri district and the Rabhas of Bochamari in Cooch Behar district, it has been observed that the women have the right in every aspect, they can choose their life partner or they can divorce him if she is not satisfied or if he is lazy. Except political issues they have the freedom to take decision regarding their family course, economy and other involvement (Biswas, Field Study, 2003, 2004 and 2006).

Among the Drukpas of Buxa duar in Jalpaiguri district, the women can enjoy full freedom in economic pursuits and they inherit the lions share. Even today their inheritance of property and residence is matrilineal. They have the right to select their life partner and in this context they do not depend on their guardian's opinion. They have the authority to divorce and remarriage if their earlier relation is troublesome (Biswas, Field Study, 2007).

Role in Political Field: The tribals have the notion, politics and organisation of groups where the activities are taken by males where as the works relating to home and children are carried out by female and even in the matrilineal tribes the property is dealt in the hand of female. When it comes to the question of decision making the men come in forefront. The girl may select her life partner but it is the male or the head of the family who finalises the matching. Even in the case of matrilineal Khasis it is maternal uncle who is the competent authority. Decision regarding social matters such as the violation of social norms, ex-communication, compromises etc. it is the male who decide in the council. The tribal women in India hardly play any fore front role in their political matters as it is exclusively under the control of men. The women are excluded from the political sphere but as a counter balance they have their own dominance in the religious and economic perspectives. Like others the village panchayat of the Totos is constituted by the male members where women have no scope to represent (Biswas, Field Study, 2004 and 2006). Except in village panchayat, the Drukpa society provides prime importance to their women folk in every decision making. The women have the right to seek justice from their village panchayat (Biswas, Field Study, 2007).

Role in Religion Sphere: Religion is a part of the nature. Tribals worship trees and animals and believe in ancestral worship. The entire family or the village as a whole go to the groove and offer prayer as well as make offerings. In this ceremonies the age and sex has no bar in the participation. In the realm of religious practices and rituals the women have a very limited but important role. A tribal woman cannot hold the office of the priest. There are even certain restrictions over their visit to the sacred places and to worship traditional deities and ancestors. Among the Bondas the women are strictly kept at a distance from all religious activities and they are not allowed to touch the things which are used for the worshipping the deities. The sacred objects and places are not to be touched by women as she is considered impure because of menstruation. Among the Toda and Kota the women are debarred from crossing the temple. Santal women generally do not get the place of honour in rituals, but in some rare occasion it has been seen that the women take part in preparing the puja materials in the houses or at jaher. Despite that the concerned women folk in tribal societies are engaged in organizing the religious festivals and help the male to culminate the required materials needed to perform the rituals. Here the worship is done for the entire familial welfare and for the welfare of the entire village. Especially the prayer is being done to increase the reproductive aspects and fertility status of the concerned women folk. Among Totos, Rabhas, Meches and Drukpas the women folk except the priest hood, enjoy participation and play an important role in their religious festivals. Though sometime the women have to follow the taboos during their mourning and other pollution period (Field Study, Biswas, 2003, 2004, 2006 and 2007).

CONCLUSION

The status of women in the non tribal Indian society is dealing with a number of contemporary issues. Mainly in urban and industrial societies the technology based economic pursuit shifts over the authority of machinery to the male and the women have to depend on the production of male. Naturally a very little amount of the entire production is authorized in the hand of the female and from there she can hardly manage her expenditure. On the other hand in rural agriculture based societies the production of crops and the concerned working involvement related with the production is totally under the dominance of male and the female is a mere secondary helping hand for them. Thus the economy and economic authority is shifted to the hand of male and as a result the education and political authority also get confined to the male dominance because these are the driving forces of the society. Mainly from the economic, political and educational perspectives the women status in non tribal India is quite lower than the male as a whole. On the other hand the tribal population provides an almost equalitarian status to their women folk. Women in tribal society are treated as an economic asset and they treat the women as the symbol of fertility and nature. Even in their daily familial affair the concerned women have a very crucial role to play. In the economic perspective the concerned tribal women plays a crucial role because they maintain their household activities and along with that they are involved in cottage based work with the help of forest based resources and other raw materials. So in the tribal society both the men and women play an equalitarian role to maintain their familial integration and its source of economic pursuit as a whole. Thus among the tribals the women are recognised as a part of resource which treats them to achieve the honour and prestige in their domain of daily life. Here the women are treated as mother and nature which provides them prestige and status in the society and any kind of offence against the women folk is strictly punishable.

Thus in comparison to the tribal and non tribal society the rights of women are existing in an opposite pole and the tribal people are bearing the traditional cultural heritage of our country which provide an equalitarian status to the women in their society and maintain familial and societal integrity as a whole. In the present era of modernization and globalisation there are augment documentation of equality of women and protection of their rights. But from the overall observation it is clear that the right of human being is mostly confined in authority of resource and the technological devices which are controlling the resources. On the other hand these technological authorities could be gained through political or educational access. Thus until the women folk in Indian society are provided with adequate educational skills or political access, till then, they are far from the achievement of controlling economic and livelihood resources as well as operation of technological implements of their own purposes. The division of labour on the basis of sex is fundamental in human society but by naming it, the women folk in the Indian society have been confined to their household territory. In concluding remarks it is to be mentioned here that to provide actual women right in Indian society the division of labour on the basis of sex would have to be abolished and the activities of livelihood be shared by the concerned family members altogether. It can create the opportunity that the women would also have the chance to gain accesses over natural resource by implying their educational knowledge and to control over the resources through political authority.

ACKNOWLEDGEMENT

Acknowledging to the Department of Anthroplogy, North Bengal University.

REFERENCES

Ahuja, R. (1999), *Indian Social System*, Rawat Publications, New Delhi.

Bailey, F. G. (1966), *Tribe, Caste and Nation: A Study of Political Activity and Political Changes in Highland and Orissa*, Manchester United Press, Manchester.

Barman, M. (2002), *Persecution of Women Widows and Witches*, Indian Anthropological Society, Calcutta.

Bhasin, M. K. and M. Bhasin (1999), *Women's Status and Fertility Among Transhuman Gaddis of Himachal Pradesh*, G.Pfeffer and D.K. Behera (eds) *Contemporary Societies: Tribal Studies*, Vol. 1, p. 115-142. Concept Publishing House, New Delhi.

Biswas, S. K. and S. Bhattacharjee (2005), The Stone Crushing Women of Balasan River Bed An Appeal From Humanitarian Perspective, *South Asian Journal of Human Rights*. Vol. 1 (1-2), January-December, 2005. Serials Publications, New Delhi.

Biswas, S. K. and S. Bhattacharjee (2006), *Effect of Land Alienation: A Study Between a Scheduled Caste and a Primitive Tribal Group* in S. H. Samel (ed.) *Rights of Dalits*, Serials Publications, New Delhi.

Biswas, S. K. and S. Bhattacharjee (2006), *"Impact of Globalization on A Tribal Community", Journal of Social Anthropology*, June 2006, Vol. 3, No. 1. Serials Publications, New Delhi.

Channa, K. (ed.) (1988), *Socialisation, Education and Women, Explorations in Gender Identity*, Orient Longmans, New Delhi.

Chapman, J. K. and Gates, M (ed.) (1976), *The Victimization of Women*, Sage Publications, California.

Choudhury, N. C. (1977), *Munda Social Structure*, Ava Press, Kolkata.

Das, A. K. and M. K. Raha (1967), *The Rabhas of West Bengal*, Temple Press, Calcutta.

Desai, N. and Thakkar, U. (2001), *Women in Indian Society*, National Book Trust, India.

Desai, N. and Patel, Y. (1990), *Indian Women Change and Challenge in the Inter national Decade1975-1985*, Popular Prakashan, Mumbai.

Desai, N. and Krishnaraj, M. (eds) (1987), *Women and Society in India*. Ajanta Publications, Delhi.

Dube, L. (2001), *Anthropological Explorations in Gender, Intersecting fields*, Sage Publication, Delhi.

Ghadially, R. (1988), *Women in Indian Society*, Sage Publication, New Delhi.

Ghotaskar, S. (ed.) (1992), *Struggles of Women at Work*, Vikas Publishing House, New Delhi.

Gisbert, P. (1978), *Tribal India*, Rawat Publication, Jaipur.

Green, J. (ed.) (2003), *Albert Einstein Selected Writings*, Left Word Books, New Delhi.

Jha, U.S. and P. Pujari (eds) (1996), *Indian Women Today: Tradition Modernity and Challenge,* Kaniska Publisher, New Delhi.

Kaushik, S. (1997), *Knocking at the Male Bastion: Women in Politics*, National Commission for Women, New Delhi.

Kessler, E. S. (1976), *Women an Anthropological View*, Rinenhart and Winston, New York.

Leonard, E. B. (1982), *Women, Crime and Society*, Longman, New York.

Majumder, B. (1991), *Toto Folk Tales*, Asiatic Society, Calcutta.

Mukherjee, B. M. (1999), *Status of Elderly Persons in Birhor Tribe of Madhya Pradesh*, G. Pfeffer and D. K. Behera (eds) *Contemporary Societies: Tribal Studies*, Vol.1, p. 226-230. Concept Publishing House, New Delhi.

Naik, T. B. (1957), *The Bhills*, Bharatiya Adim Jati Sevak Sangh, New Delhi.

Nayar, S. and Mankekar, K. (eds) (2005), *Women Pioneers in India's Renaissance*, National Book Trust, India.

Playfair, A. (1909), *The Garos*, David and Nutt, London.

Roy, K. (2001), *Women in Early Indian Societies*, Manohar Publishers, New Delhi.

Roy, P. (1999) *Social Life of Bonda*, G. Pfeffer and D. K. Behera (eds) *Contemporary Societies: Tribal Studies*, Vol. 1, p. 180-189. Concept Publishing House, New Delhi.

Sanyal, C. C. (1973), *The Meches and The Totos: Two Sub Himalayan Tribes of North Bengal*, University of North Bengal, Darjeeling.

Seth, M. (2001), *Women and Development, The Indian Experience*, Sage Publications, New Delhi.

Vidyarthi, L. P. and B. K. Rai, (1977), *The Tribal Culture of India*, Concept Publishing, New Delhi.

Wilson, E. (1977), *Women and the Welfare State*, Tavistock, London.

RIGHTS AND ISSUES OF EMPOWERMENT OF WOMEN IN INDIA– A CROSS CULTURAL ANALYSIS

*T. Subramanyam Naidu** & *G. Palanisamy***

THE MEANING OF EMPOWERMENT

The most conspicuous feature of the term empowerment is that it contains within it the word 'power'. So obviously, empowerment is about power and about changing the balance of power.

Empowerment of women is the keynote of women's movement now-a-days. Empowerment contains the word 'power' which is exercised in economic, social and political relations between individuals and groups. Power may be defined as control over resources and ideology. This definition makes it clear that women in general are relatively powerless because they do not have control over resources and hence have little or no decision making power, yet the decision taken, affects their lives every day.

THE CONCEPT OF EMPOWERMENT

Women's empowerment is relatively a new concept in the realm of development. It is a process, which changes the

* Dean, School of Social Sciences and International Studies, Pondicherry Central University, Pondicherry- 605014, INDIA, *email: tsnaidu_52@yahoo.com*

** Research Associate, Department of Anthropology, Pondicherry Central University, Pondicherry- 605014, INDIA, *email: vgpsamy@gmail.com*

existing power relations in favor of the poor and marginalized, among the women. It is a long-term process that requires changes in the behavior and attitudes of women and men and the ideas that societies hold about gender.

Various strategies have been adopted for bringing about this complex process, among which one of the most frequently used, is the collectivization of women, mobilization of their small savings and provision of micro credit. Self Help Groups or women's groups organized for this purpose by Government and non Governmental agencies all over India.

The empowerment of women can be defined as "global access to resources, power and decision-making". This is an essential requirement to attain gender equality i.e: the process required for the realignment of power in decision making at the household, institutional and at all levels of the society. The ultimate goal is equitable partnership between women and men, built on the strengths of shared knowledge of the energy, skills and creativity.

The movement for women's empowerment was launched in 1996 for taking women with dignity and equality into the next century. The objective of the movement were gender equality, gender justice, social security, elimination of all types of discrimination against women and integration of women into economic development and mainstream of economy.

The concept of empowerment is related to the concept of freedom. Empowerment is equipping one to improve the living condition (Devadas *et al.*; 1988). It does not identify power of women in terms of domination over others, but in terms of the capacity of women to enhance their ability to gain control over the crucial material and non-material resources and thus minimize their risks. Empowerment approach recognizes the triple role of women namely production, reproduction and community management which manifests itself through the formation and organization of groups (FAO, 1990).

THE PROCESS OF EMPOWERMENT

Implicit in participation is empowerment or transfer of power to the people. Empowering is development of skills and abilities of people to enable them to manage better, negotiate with existing development delivery systems. Some see it as more fundamental and as essentially concerned with enabling people, to decide upon and undertake actions, which they believe are essential to their development. The empowerment process encompasses several mutually reinforcing components but begins with and is supported by economic independence, which implies access to and control over production resources. A second component of empowerment is knowledge and awareness the third is self-image and the final is autonomy.

The women in India have been identified as a disadvantageous group. They form a weaker section and are subject to excessive male domination. For this reason they seldom get a chance to develop their health, personality and participation in development programmes within and outside their home environment. The women form a great-untapped reservoir of human energy that comes out from within the treasure of unlimited human resources as against limited natural resources. The natural and material resources in India are very much limited in respect of its overwhelming population and therefore this country greatly depends on maximum utilization of human resources. India cannot afford to keep the womenfolk aside from making their participation in the process of development. Moreover, the condition of women will not improve unless they get opportunities and make use of such occasions to earn experience, increase skill and efficiency and prove their ability in discharging their social responsibilities.

The situation of women as it exists is one of low status of women that are powerless, endangered by development, suppressed by poverty and oppressed by patriarchy. Traditions structures have failed to make room for them as equal partners in the decision-making processes; nor has the system ensured that their interests and concerns are reflected in development plans and local programme.

They are ignorant, unaware and ill informed about how they could live better lives with less drudgery, morbidity and fear of violence. Even though nature has endowed them with superior biological strength, the environment stifles their development. At every age more women die than warranted to keep the sex ratio adverse in most parts of the country.

The issues of empowerment of women moved centre stage during the last three decades of the second millennium mainly through the efforts of the United Nations by declaring 1975 as the Women's year for the abolition of discrimination against women in centuries where it still exists. The resolution by the United Nations of the International Women's year urged: "to strive for equality between men and women; to promote a higher role of women in the economic, political, social and cultural life of countries; to promote their active participation in the struggle for the development of friendship and co-operation between nations for peace and social process". The decade 1975-82 as the women's decade. This period coincided with the 6th Plan period in India when the approach was shifted from welfare to development and further efforts during the subsequent Plans culminated in the farming of a National Policy for Empowerment of Women approved by the Cabinet on 20th March 2001. However despite constitutional guarantee of equality and justice, legislative support of a plethora of Acts and introduction of policies and programmes, the goals of gender equality and justice, empowerment of women still remains a distant dream for Indian women.

NATIONAL POLICY OF EMPOWERMENT OF WOMEN

The national policy of empowerment of women has set certain clear cut goals and objectives. The goal of this policy is to bring about the advancement and empowerment of women. The policy will be widely disseminated so as to encourage active participation of all stakeholders for achieving its goals. Specifically, the objectives of this policy include:

- Creating an environment through positive economic and social policies for full development of women to enable them to realize their full potential.
- The de-jure and de-facto enjoyment of all human rights and fundamental freedom by women on equal basis with men in all spheres–political, economic, social, cultural and civil.
- Equal access to participation and decision making of women in social, political and economic life of the nation.
- Equal access of women to healthcare, quality education at all levels. Career and vocational guidance, employment, equal remuneration, occupational health and safety, social security and public office etc.
- Strengthening legal systems aimed at elimination of all forms of discrimination against women.
- Changing societal attitudes and community practices by active participation and involvement of both men and women.
- Mainstreaming a gender perspective in the development process.
- Elimination of discrimination and all forms of violence against women and the girl child; and
- Building and strengthening partnerships with civil society, particularly women's organization.

The national policy on empowerment of women in its introduction states, the principle of gender equality is enshrined in the Indian Constitution in its Preamble,

Fundamental Rights, Fundamental duties and Directive Principles. The Constitution not only grants equality to women but also empowers the state to adopt measures of positive discrimination in favour of women. Within the frame work of a democratic polity, our laws, development policies, plans and programmes have aimed at women's advancement in different spheres. From the fifth Five Year Plan (1974-78) onwards has been a marked shift in the approach to women's issues from the welfare to development. In recent years, the Empowerment of women has been recognized as the central issued in determining the status of women. The National Commission for women was set up by the Act of Parliament in 1990 to safeguard the rights and legal entitlements of women. The 73rd and 74th Amendments (1993) to the constitution of India has provided for reservation of seats in the local bodies of Panchayats and Municipalities for women, laying a strong foundation for their participation in decision making at the local levels.

EMPOWERMENT OF INDIAN WOMEN

Empowerment of women involves many things – economic opportunity, property rights, political representation, social equality, personal rights and so on. The process of empowerment is taking place that so many levels that is quite difficult to guage the actual nature and extent of empowerment in improving status of women. Certainly the process is entangled in struggles of civil society against the state and under the weight of historical practice and ongoing debates over the appropriate role of ideologies.

The Human Development Index as calculated by the UNDP is based on three major components life expectancy at birth, literacy and per capita purchasing power. Among the 174 countries ranked, India gets the 128th rank. Gender Development Index is also available for 143 countries in which India ranks 108.

Indian scenario presents a dismal picture on several key indicators contributing to human development. The first alarming signal is the sex ratio adverse to women. As per the 2001 Census the sex ratio is 933 and it is further disappointing that in the 0-6 years group, the sex ratio is only 927. The table 1 provides the details of sex ratio from the year 1901 to 2001. The data shows that there is a steady decrease in the female sex ratio.

Table 1
Sex Ratio in India in 100 years

Years	*Sex Ratio*
1901	972
1911	964
1921	955
1931	950
1941	945
1951	946
1961	941
1971	930
1981	934
1991	927
2001	933

Source: Census of India 2001

We have very high infant mortality rate of 70 per 1000 liver birth. The under 5 mortality rate is also high at 98 per 1000 liver births. The maternal mortality rate is too high at 410 per one lakh. The percentage of children immunized is not satisfactory at 72 per cent of BCG, 69 per cent for DPT and Polio, 55 per cent for measles and 73 per cent for TT. As many as 33 per cent infants are stunted and 18 per cent are wasting.

The poor health of women coupled with low literacy profiles adversely affects their work participation rate and the resulting standard of living. Hence our Human Development Index continues to be at the lower running of the ladder (Seethalakshmi, 2002).

Women are the bearers of the next generation, the caregivers in the family. But they suffer every deprivation. They are the beasts of burden, attending to all domestic chores, fetching fuel, fodder and water, generally from long distances, working from dawn to dusk on family farms or enterprises with no reward, no asset and no recognition in the system of national accounts. Even when they do bring in some income, they spend it all, on the family and struggle to battle in poverty. Often they also finance the husband's "leisure activities" like alcohol only to be beaten when he is drunk.

EMPOWERMENT OF WOMEN AND EDUCATION

Education is the corner stone of women's empowerment because it enables them to respond to opportunities, to challenge their traditional roles and to change their traditional roles and to change their lives. Education of women benefits the whole society. It has a more significant impact on poverty and development than men's education. It is also the most influential factor in improving the child's health and reducing infant mortality. It also has an effect on family size. The more years of education a woman has, the higher is the degree of her independence. Education would actually accord women certain advantages in areas where women have historically lacked access or differential rights. Education would empower women to achieve many social, psychological, economic and political dreams which are denied to her traditionally.

The policy of the government of India for empowerment and development of women lays emphasis on removal of women's illiteracy and obstacles inhibiting their access to elementary education, women's participation in vocational, technical and professional education at different levels. The government also lays stress on non-discrimination, thus seeking to eliminate sex stereotyping in vocational and professional courses. It actively promotes women's studies as a part of various courses and encourages educational institutions to take up programmes to further women's development and to promote women's participation in non-traditional occupations in existing and emerging technologies.

Equal access to education for women and girls will be ensured. Special measures will be taken to eliminate discrimination, universalize education, eradicate illiteracy, create a gender sensitive education system, increase enrolment and retention rates of girls and improve the quality of education to facilitate life-long learning as well as development of occupational/vocational/technical skills by women. Reducing the gender gap in secondary and higher education would be a focus area. Sectoral time targets in existing policies will be achieved with a special focus on girls and women, particularly those belonging to weaker sections including the scheduled castes/scheduled tribes/other backward classes/minorities. Gender sensitive curriculam would be developed at all levels of educational system in order to address sex stereotyping as one of the causes of gender discrimination.

The education of women and girl continues to be an area of major emphasis in the programmes and projects of the Indira Gandhi National Open University. The women's enrolment in universities/colleges is currently 39.94 per cent. Besides there are five exclusive women's universities and 1,578 women's colleges of which 219 were opened during the last three years. The University Grants Commission has a number of schemes for promoting women's education under which the following are provided for:

- Setting up of centers and cells for women studies
- Technology course for women universities are under graduate courses in engineering and technology
- Part-time Research Associate ships for women
- Special scheme for construction of women's hostels
- Financial assistance to women's colleges (52 years old) for purchase of books, journals and equipment and

- Day-care centers in universities

There is no easy or quick fix to the problems related to empowerment of women in India. The real solution lies in a holistic approach that deals with all the major interrelated issues of economic welfare, social justice, education, health, religions and customary traditions.

Despite all our plans, female adult literacy in the country has just touched 54 per cent in 2001. This leaves 46 per cent of our women illiterate and unaware of their rights. It is true that education opens up new vistas to women but education alone does not solve problems. For the mass of our women, it cannot be education of the traditional kin. What they need is training in vocations skills, coupled with a basic knowledge related to their local situations. Special incentives to encourage the education of girls in regular schools particularly, in our rural areas and urban slums are an urgent necessity.

EMPOWERMENT AND PATRIARCHAL SYSTEM

The Constitution of India guarantees equality of opportunity and status to women and men. It directs that women shall not only have equal rights and privileges with men but also that the State shall make provisions-both general and special for the welfare of women. Despite the above constitutional guarantee, women in India who constitute nearly half the population are still subjected to many disadvantages, disabilities and inequalities in our male-dominated society.

For women in India, life is not all that easy. They have access to education and jobs, but there are limits placed. Women are lawyers, journalists in politics, in business, in academia. Women filmmakers are making a mark in their field. But these are very few exceptions and do not have to confront the problems that the majority of women face by virtue of unequal laws that place them in a secondary status. Women have had to fight heavily on patriarchal system that continues to govern the country. This is manifest in the demand that people must accept, without question, what the power-that-be decide is best for "the people". The nature of patriarchy is to rule by dictat, not by reasoned debate. It is the antithesis of democracy.

EMPOWERMENT RIGHTS

India, like any other developing country has a large unorganized sector where the majority of women workers are found. This sector has been largely neglected in so far as provision of support services and social security benefits are concerned. Even the basic laws, like the Minimum Wages Act, Equal Remuneration Act, Maternity Benefits Act, etc. have not benefited them. The enforcement machinery of the Labour Departments has totally failed to give this sector the support and the protection that it deserves. Unskilled, immobile and tied down to family chores, the profile of women workers relative to men is significantly lower by all parameters – in terms of proportion to total workers, work participation, work share in the organized sector as well as number of working days in a year. Efforts made so far, for skill development of women have been far too inadequate. In the new economic regime of competition, survival would be difficult without the right skills to avail of new employment opportunities. Training institutions and programmes need to be effectively oriented to impart appropriate training in areas, which offer employment/earning opportunities for women both in urban and rural areas.

Eighty percent of our women are rural based and it is their lives that truly represent the reality of India. Their needs are different from those of women in urban areas where education and more comfortable living are seen. Their prime requirements are not labour saving devices and processed food, but a roof over their heads, proper sanitation, protected water supply, health and children services, adequate nourishment and guaranteed employment. Balancing services and programmes to cover both these sections in which discrimination against women is the common basic fact and the real challenge. Generalizations become superfluous, centralized plans become inoperative and borrowed solutions become catastrophic.

EMPOWERMENT INTERVENTIONS

The situation requires urgent interventions. Budgets must reflect women's needs National Plans must be decentralized to respond to their special problems. If things are to improve for them urgent steps to achieve empowerment through security and better quality of life and capacity building have to be initiated. It is critical to set goals for various sectors with time bound action Plans to achieve them.

The central and state governments have over the years initiated several programmes to change the mindset of rural women with incentives to enable them women to live in dignity. Religious heads and law courts have also responded to this critical need to change attitudes in families and bring about a shift from the 'son preference' syndrome. More action would be necessary in this direction with media campaigns to remove gender bias.

Participation in the freedom struggle brought political awakening to our women. Reservations in the local bodies have ensured women's entry into the political process at the grass root levels. There is now a demand to carry these reservations forward into the Assemblies and to Parliament in order to empower women and bring them into leadership positions. But empowerment is more than political participation. Women have to be equipped to help themselves, they have to be made aware to their rights and enable to discover their own potential (Mahila Sashaktikaran, Adhiveshan, 2002).

RURAL SCENARIO

The rural scenario is still one where the womenfolk in general remain at the periphery. With heavy responsibilities of tending their families and the farms, it is doubtful if they would have the time, despite their inclination to attend meetings of the Gram Sabha where all adult women are members. What is more, certain factors like caste, feudalism, apathy and family status do come in the way. Though we have given an equal status to women and rightly so, it is yet to be seen if, they are really motivated to contribute their mite in such meetings.

EMPOWERMENT THROUGH SELF HELP GROUPS

The global conference on Women's Empowerment, 1988, highlighted empowerment as the surest way of making women "partners in development". Development on the other hand should ultimately become a process of empowerment. Empowerment is an active process enabling women to realize their full identity and power in all spheres of life. As the Food and Agriculture Organization (FAO, 1990) has rightly put it, empowerment of women at the grass roots has emerged as the most recent approach to women in development (Devadas and Sithalakshmi, 1996).

The basic strategy for bringing the women into the mainstream of socio-economic development should consist of fuller facilities for their education, health care and employment. Endowed with learning and wisdom, good physique and job skills, women should be in a position to contribute effectively to the development of the family, the community and the society.

The Government has taken up the theme of women's empowerment as one of the main agenda items to tackle rural poverty and socio-economic issues. The women have taken up self-help movement through savings as a mass movement-a path chosen by the women to shape their future destiny. Development agenda of the State/Union Territory in the last few years has been to place the people, especially women in the forefront has enabled formation of a large number of Self Help Groups throughout the length and breadth of the states/union territories.

Governments have worked out special programmes for the sustenance of these groups through a number of training programmes, exposure visits and regular capacity building programmes. The socio-economic survey and skill level of these groups is being monitored on a quarterly basis to plan out improved and more effective programme to support these groups.

Recently, Government has taken special efforts to assist the Self Help Group women in marketing their products without any middlemen. Government is extending a greater support to the Self Help Group by allocating special funds.

Empowerment of women is a crucial factor in the eradication of poverty as the women are the key contributors to the economy and in combating poverty through both remunerative and non-remunerative work at home in the community and in the work place.

THE ECONOMIC PERSPECTIVE OF EMPOWERMENT OF WOMEN

Gender Bias: Cultural traditional and economic necessity have always meant a significant role for women in agriculture. In India, it is not uncommon that women do not have control over the land. Even, where women constitute a larger share of agricultural produce but there are cultural constraints to easy communication between men and women because almost all extension workers are men. Therefore, the role of agricultural extension workers is very significant. Besides, cultural norms have to be addressed before we tackle other dimensions.

In animal husbandry women have a multiple role. UN estimated 75 million women as against 5 million men are engaged in the Indian dairy sector. Their activities vary widely ranging from care of animals, grazing, fodder collection, banning of animal shed to process milk and livestock products. Though women play a significant role in livestock management and production women's control over livestock and its products is negligible. Though women work in every sphere of the farm sector they are not recognized as farmers. Consequently, they remain outside all agricultural development programmes and services.

Not only do women perform more tasks, their work is also more arduous than that undertaken by men. Both transplanting and weeding require women to spend the whole day and work in muddy soil with their hands. Moreover, they work the entire day under the intensely hot sun while men's work, such as ploughing and watering the fields is invariably carried out early in the morning. Women's work, unlike men's does not involve implements and is based largely on human energy, it is considered unskilled and hence less productive.

Women work longer hours and their work is more arduous than men's. Women's contribution to agriculture – whether it is subsistence farming or commercial agriculture – when measured in terms of the number of tasks performed and time spent, is greater than men. "The extent of women's contribution is aptly highlighted by a micro study conducted in the Indian Himalayas which found that on a one-hectare farm, a pair of bullock's works 1.064 hours, a man 1,212 hours and a woman 3,845 hours in a year".

Women's participation in income generating activities is believed to increase their status and decision making power with employment. They do not remain as 'object' of social change, but become 'agents' of social change. They cease to be only 'consumers' of economic goods and services but true 'producers'. They participate in social reproduction as well as reproduction of labour for the next generation.

The economic contribution is related to their status and role in the family and in the society. If a woman is not economically self-dependent, she can never claim an equal status with man. The problem of poverty cannot be tackled without providing opportunities of productive employment to women. Even where there is a male earner, women's earning forms a major part of the income of poor household. Moreover, women contribute a large share of what they earn to basic family maintenance than men; increases in women's income translates more directly into better child health, nutrition and family well being.

Women's participation in the labour force also brings about changes in awareness and attitudes, which may have long-term benefits such as access to health and education programmes, reduction in birth rates, thrift and savings etc., Economic independence of women will create far reaching social changes and prove as a necessary weapon for them to face injustice and discrimination.

One of the pre-requisites to promote empowerment of women is promotion of organizations among women. Women can be organized through a variety of means namely through formation of co-operatives, Mahila Mandals, Self Help Groups and the like. Through collective action, women can be empowered socially, economically and politically. Organizational behavior of the women's group was the major influencing factor contributing to the success of the economic pursuits.

The goal of poverty reduction and empowerment of women can be effectively achieved if poor women could organize into groups for community participation as well as for use of their rights in various services related to their economic and social well-being (Deepti Aggarwal, 2001).

NUTRITION AND HEALTH EMPOWERMENT

Nutritional well-being is a sustainable force for health and development and for maximization of human genetic potential. In fact, the measurement of national development is by nutrition and health indicators like neo-natal mortality rate, infant mortality rate, mortality under-5 years, maternal mortality rate, crude death rate and life expectancy at birth. The nutritional status of the community has therefore been recognized as an important indicator of national development. In other words, malnutrition is an impediment in national development and hence assumes the status of national problem and not merely a sectoral problem.

Mere economic development or even the adequacies of food at household levels are no guarantee for a stable and satisfactory nutritional status. At the same time, however, the overall development strategy of a country is likely to have a pronounced bearing on what nutritional planning can accomplish. Therefore, the task is not merely in terms of formulating a nutrition policy but also in terms of locating and grounding it in the overall development strategy of the country.

For nutrition to improve many factors are necessary. A recent study by the United Nations which confirmed that there is no one formula to follow had this is to say about some of the factors that are essential: nutrition and economic growth, nutrition and the status of women, nutrition and social sector spending (UNICEF, 1998).

The present health scenario in India depicts the enormous efforts made by its government with the assistance of International agencies, in promoting the health of its population and is particular women and children. Various programme interventions in the form of maternal and child health services through the years have come to stay to protect the health of the mother and child.

In India, women in reproductive age and children below 5 years of age comprise 62 per cent of the total population. The table 2 provides India's population by age and sex. .

They are the most vulnerable group in the society. Naturally they need better health care and attention. Hence the health care services directed to the women and the Government of India gives children priority. Significant gaps in health care infrastructure, health personnel and health services have been observed when there was a maximum need in a country where more than one third of population is below poverty line. These gaps are bound to widen, if appropriate steps are not initiated to bridge them.

Table 2
India's Population by Age & Sex

Age	*Male*	*Female*	*Total*
0-14	175,228,164	165,190,951	340,419,115
15-64	324,699,562	301,821,383	626,520,945
65 and older	23,925,371	23,138,386	47,063,757
Grand Total	523,853,097	490,150,720	1,014,003,817

Source: Census of India 2001

The global concerns about the health of women and children of the developing countries have drawn greater attention during the recent past. The Cairo International conference on "Population and Development" (1994), formalized and growing international consensus for improving reproductive health, including family planning for human welfare and development. This consensus proves a new vision of population policy, which recognizes a crucial distinction between the overall goals of population policy and the reproductive and child health programme. The goal of this programme is to reduce unwanted fertility safely and to provide high quality health services, thereby responding to the needs of individual, as well as to stabilize the population growth. The reproductive and child health approach is adopted to strengthen the existing infra-structural interventions in order to promote the health of women and children. This is an effort to build the nation. The adoption of reproductive and child health approach by the Government in 1996 is a step in the right direction to ensure greater health care of mothers and children.

It has been rightly pointed out that every effort by the Government to provide services is not only to be appreciated but also should be rightly and judiciously utilized through effective community participation. Still, much needs to be done to ensure safe motherhood and child survival.

Thus the history of development of maternal and child health service interventions show the enormous impact to ensure the health of mothers and children. However the infant mortality rate (74) and the maternal mortality rate (3.6) besides morbidity are still high. The low utilization of related services interferes with the health of mother and children. There is an imminent need to identify the factors that inferred with the utilization of maternal and child health services in order to develop appropriate strategies to overcome the hurdles and enhance their utilization (Sangeetha, 1998).

Promotion of village level women's organization is now being recognized as an important step towards the improvement of women's nutrition and health status. Self Help Groups do have s significant role to play in the lives of women.

POLITICAL EMPOWERMENT OF WOMEN

The concept of political participation of women is broader than the one covering women's participation only in the electoral and administrative processes. It includes the whole gamut of voluntary activities with a bearing on the political processes, including voting, support of political groups and communication with legislator, dissemination of political views and opinions among the electorate and other related activities.

Political empowerment of women in India has limited application mainly because of various dubious considerations of social, economic and political variables. Broadly, political participation of women is severely limited due to a nexus of traditional factors; these are the domination of Indian politics by consideration of caste, class, religion, feudal and family status etc., all of which are essentially patriarchal forces that work in favour of men against women. Consequently, women are still left on the periphery of the political process and political participation remains in contesting elections and also capture of some seats of power and influence.

There are several socio-economic constraints by which women have been marginalized. The number of women in leadership position at the local village, district and national level is still not commensurate with their number in society. In India, limited adult franchise was granted to women in 1937, since then, women have been participating in political process as voters as candidates contesting the elections involved in deliberations both in State Assemblies and Parliament and also through holding public office at different levels in the judiciary (Ashok Kumar, 2000).

Women's participation in formal elections is to a great extent dependent on the mobilization efforts of the political parties, general awareness among the community of the importance of exercising franchise and the overall political culture.

If we have a look at the past history of the women's political participation, we find that no serious efforts appear to have been made to mobilize women as a political pressure group by any political party. In addition, over the years, the number of women contestants in parliamentary elections has not increased. Political parties seem uniformly reluctant to field women candidates. The high cost of the electioneering is another deterrent to most women candidates. Because of these factors there is an increasing tendency among women to contest elections as independent candidates.

RESERVATION FOR WOMEN

With the Panchayati Raj institutions getting constitutional status by way of the 73rd Amendment Act, it is hoped that the women will have a greater participation in the Panchayati Raj institutions. The 73rd Amendment Act provides for reservation of one-third of seats for women and these seats may be allotted by rotation to different constituencies in a Panchayat. Similar reservations have been made in respect of the office of the Chairman also. Consequently, wherever elections to Panchayati Raj institutions were held after 1993, wards or constituencies were reserved for women (Sweta Mishra, 1995).

The outcome of these elections in terms of women's participation has been very encouraging. Elections in Karnataka, Orissa, Andhra Pradesh and West Bengal earlier had witnessed appreciable number of women turnout as voters as well as candidates. Not merely for the reserved constituencies, but even for the general constituencies, women had contested with great confidence. In many states, the percentage of women who got elected to Panchayati Raj institutions exceeded the reserved positions. Thus, it can be said that in all these above instances, the participation of women went beyond expectations.

ROLE OF NON-GOVERNMENTAL ORGANIZATIONS

Voluntary action stimulated and promoted by Non Governmental organizations engaged in development play a significant role at the grass roots level in the Indian social milieu; the success of rural development depends upon the active participation of the people through self-help organizations. The Non Governmental Organizations involve people in the developmental process and relate themselves to work with people. This means that their main plan is the generation of self-confidence and self-help through self help Groups and independence among the people of the community in which they operate. They substantiate the efforts of government with regard to provision of social welfare through rural development programmes planned for this purpose.

Non Governmental Organizations acts as 'creators', 'preservers' and destroyers' of evils in rural areas. They create awareness among people, create livelihood and opportunities for people with their co-operation, preserve what is needful to their environment, cultural base, appropriate technologies and scientific practices, etc and destroy the evils like alcoholism, superstitions and other social ills.

In recent years, the Non Governmental Organizations have acquired greater importance and significance than ever before because the administration has not been able to reach the people especially the poor and weaker sections to the desired level. In this context, the fact that the Non Governmental Organizations are the appropriate agencies for creating the right type of climate for change and development cannot be disputed.

DISCUSSION

Gandhiji said that women are the companions of men, gifted with equal mental capacities. She has the right to participate in the minute detail of the activities of life and she has right of freedom and liberty with man. But today in India with special reference to the village, we see that by sheer force of a vicious customs even the most ignorant and worthless men have been enjoying superiority over women which do not deserve and ought not to have. We can however see that the trends have changed to a great extent with more and more women coming out and competing with men in many spheres. We can see today women in all sphere of life with no exception. But majority of these women are from urban areas and only handful are from villages. If this trend has to change, social empowerment of women is a must. Of course this is visible in the matters of fewer rules of socio cultural segregation too. Widows are in most cases today not treated or shunned as inauspicious the way they used to be, two generations ago, however this could be seen in urban only. In villages we still see the prevalence of certain age old taboos and there should be a social change order by which Indian women especially from the rural areas stand as a monumental example of social and cultural emancipation, worth enough of the whole world to take an example.

Human Development directly correlated to people participation and development not only by-passed women but also made them victims of it. Participation leads to empowerment supported by economic and social dependents. It is now recognized that women hold the key to sustainable development. Empowerment of women socially is the most important aspect that our policy makers should have in mind before embarking upon any scheme, programme, meant for the rural folk.

Looking to the present status of women in agriculture, it is the utmost need to revamp the entire approach towards women farmers to cater to their existing needs. For this, there is no way but to develop the human resources. Hence, empowerment of women is the need of the day, as it is the surest way of making women "partners in development" and bringing them in the mainstream of development, not only as 'beneficiaries' but as 'contributors'.

The traditional social structure, equal norms and value systems continue to place Indian women in a situation of disadvantage in terms of role relationship, decision making and sharing of responsibility. Their social status is still shrouded by a variety of institutional complexes, connections and myths. "The emancipation of women will not be handed over on a silver-plate by some party or political movement" (Fatima Beevi: 1991). In order to strive for equality, women must express their will to achieve it. Women must fight back for their participation and respond to the demands of progress. No social change can occur without talking about women. Any social change that does not include a change in the position of women is fertile and is ultimately bound to fail. President A.P.J. Abdul Kalam in one of his speeches mentioned that the "empowering of women is a prerequisite for crating a good nation, when women are empowered, society with stability is assured. Empowerment of women is essential as their thoughts and their value system is lead to the development of a good family, good society and ultimately a good nation". Therefore the empowerment woman is very important not only for the growth and development of the family/society but also to the nation as a whole.

REFERENCES

Ashokumar, (2000), *Political participation of Women: Role of Women in the Twenty First Century*. New Delhi, Anmol Publications Pvt. Ltd, p.63-65.

Deepti Agarwal, (2001), "Empowerment of Rural Women", *Intensive Agriculture*, March-April, p.4.

Devadas, R. P. and Sithalakshmi, 1996. *Unpublished M.Phil and M.Sc. Thesis,* Avinashilingam Deemed University, Coimbatore.

Devadas, R. P., Lakshmi Santha Rajagopal and A. Ramathilagam, 1988. "Home Science Education and Women's Empowerment", Paper Presented for the *Association of Women in Development Conference. Global Empowerment of Women*, Washington.

FAO, (1990), "Gender issues in Fisheries and Aquaculture Including Proc", *Workshop on Enhanced Women's Participation in Fisheries Development*, pp. 36-58.

Fatima Beevi, (1991), "Forward" *The Women of Indian Republic*, Ashis Publishing House, New Delhi.

Mahila Sashaktikaran Adhiveshan, (2002), "Empowerment of Women A Background Paper", Women for Equality, Pease and Progess – International Decade for Women, All India Mahila Congress, October 1st, pp.156-15.

Sangeetha, P., (1998), *The Empowerment of Women in India*. Sage Publications, New Delhi, pp. 54 & 134.

Sithalakshmi S., (2002), "Contribution of Home Science Towards Women's Empowerment", Paper Presented during KVK National Workshop, Avinashilingam University, Coimbatore, p.1.

Swe ta Mishra and S. N. Mishra, (1995) "Women and Political Process in India", *Kurukshetra*, August, p.42.

UNICEF, (1998) "Malnutrition: Causes, Consequences and Solutions", The State of the World's Children, p.7.

REPRODUCTIVE RIGHTS & REPRODUCTIVE HEALTH OF WORKING WOMEN IN URBAN SLUMS: AN ISSUE OF CONCERN

*Nidhi Kotwal** & *Sonal Sharma*

INTRODUCTION

The poor health of Indian women is a concern on both national and individual levels. Indian women, particularly those in the North, fare poorly. The consequences of women's unfavorable status in India include discrimination in the allocation of household resources, such as food and in access to health care and education as well as marriage at young ages.

Due to poverty and illiteracy, the knowledge factor of the Indian women regarding reproductive health and reproductive rights is pathetic. According to the various surveys conducted by the Government and other non-Government Organizations (NGO's) their knowledge regarding reproductive health care is futile and very limited. No doubt, non-working women are unaware, even workingwomen in slum areas (maids, labour class etc) are affected by various myths regarding reproductive health care. They not only have scanty information but also lack in the sources concerned with reproductive care. They consider their aspect as a matter of shame and neglect it. World Health

* Lecturer P. G. Dept. CRM & E. Govt.College for Women, Parade. Jammu.

Organization (WHO) and United Nations Children's Emergency Fund (UNICEF) 2006, concluded that 100, 000 Indian women die each year from pregnancy related causes; maternal mortality and morbidity are two health concerns that are related to high levels of fertility. India has a high maternal mortality ratio-approximately 453 deaths per 1000, 000 births in 1993. Mukherjee *et al.*, (2004), conducted a study, in "Motilal Nehru Camp" slum of South-Delhi. All currently married women aged 15 to 49 years available in the slum were interviewed. Data collected on specific contraceptive behavior of the women were analyzed. Age at marriage and age at first cohabitation with husband has increased only marginally while age at first childbirth has decreased over a time period of 30-35 years. Contraceptive use for the study population was 51.3 per cent (201/392). Adoption of permanent contraception became more common than temporary ones only after having three children and then peaked after having five children. Use of spacing method at one child was only 9.4 per cent (15/53). For each number of living children, women with more number of sons were more likely to use a contraceptive than with no or less number of living sons. A Main source of IUDs and permanent sterilization was public health sector for condoms and oral pills however chemists and private doctors were preferred. The health status as well as health services provision was poor in the slum.

In most countries, the neglect of women's reproductive rights severely limits their opportunities in public and private life, including opportunities for education and economic and political empowerment. The ability of women to control their own fertility forms an important basis for the enjoyment of the other rights. Shared responsibility between women & men in matters related to sexual and reproductive behaviour is also essential to improving women's health. (Singh & Prakash 2006).

J&K is one of the most educationally backward states in India. According 2001 census, the literacy rate by sex has increased from 44 per cent for males and 20 per cent for females in 1981. To 66 per cent for males and 42 per cent females in 2001. In J & K 50 per cent urban females and 22% rural females are economically active. (Director of Census Operation, J & K 2001). The more women are counted in the labour force but most are still relegated to unpaid family labour or low paid jobs. The review of literature revealed that very little information is available on reproductive health of women in urban slums in J&K.

To know the awareness of reproductive health & reproductive rights among women in urban slums, the present study was undertaken with the objective to study the awareness of reproductive Health & Rights among working women in the age of 20-45 years, in urban slum areas of the Jammu City.

RESEARCH METHODOLOGY

The Present study was conducted in urban slum areas of Jammu City. A sample of 100 working women in the age group of 20-45 years were selected from four different slum areas in Trikuta Nagar, Shastri Nagar, Sainik Colony and Subash Nagar.From the selected areas 25 workingwomen were selected purposively from each area and finally a sample of 100 respondents was prepared. The data was collected in the month of April-May 2006. A rapport was first built with the respondents. An interview schedule was formulated for data collection. It included questions regarding Safe Motherhood Family Planning, Abortions, AIDS/HIV/STDs, Menarche, Menopause and Reproductive rights. Though the schedule was prepared in English, all questions were put in a conversation style. Respondents were contacted by home visits. Minimum of 2 visits were made for each respondent. To analyze the data, collected information was classified in the light of objectives set forth for the study. The classified data was coded, tabulated and per cent calculated for the same.

RESULTS AND DISCUSSIONS

All the women were illiterate. Lack of education, compelled them to join low paid sectors. Most (45%) of the respondents were engaged as part time housemaids. They served in more than one family and in each house, worked for a specific period only. Thirty Five per cent of the women worked as informal women laborers and were engaged in carrying heavy weight of bricks, water, cement etc to the work place. Fifteen per cent of them worked as vegetable vendors and 5% worked in warehouses and in ration shops. Their work was to clean and pack cereals and pulses. Fifty eight per cent of the women belonged to small families having a size of 4–6 members and 42% belonged to large families with 7-9 members. All the respondents belonged to nuclear families. Majority (52%) of the respondents had income of Rs.800 to 1000 per month depending upon the work availability. Majority, 80% of the husbands were engaged as laborers, 7% as masons, 3% as gardeners and 10% were not working. It was difficult for the women to manage their expenses and were hence compelled to enter into profession. The respondents resided in a typical slum area. Their houses consisted of temporary huts (Jhompadi's). Majority of the respondents (75%) lived in Kuccha houses made of wooden planks, cane, mud etc. The roofs were thatched and covered with black polythene sheets, (25%) of the respondents lived in semi pucca houses where the walls were made of bricks. Majority (82%) of the women lived in small huts with single room. All the family members lived in the same room without any proper ventilation and in poor hygienic conditions. All respondents used tap water supplied by municipality at different parts of street or temples. Toilet facilities were poor. The huts were lined with narrow pathways and open garbage.

SAFE MOTHERHOOD

Table 1 depicts that majority (74%) of the respondents had their first pregnancy between the age of 14-16 years. The

Table 1
Respondents Age During First Pregnancy

Responses	*Respondents(n=100)*
A. 10 – 12 Years	4
B. 12-14 Years	22
C. 14-16 Years	74

respondents were not aware of the side effects of early motherhood. The main reason behind the early pregnancy was that their marriages were settled at the age of 6-7 years and afterwards when they attained menarche they were shifted to their in-law's home. A study conducted by Santhya and Jejeebhoy (2003) revealed that women undergo pregnancy at ages 15-19 years over one in five give birth by 17 years.

Table 2
Effects of Early Child Bearing

Responses	*Respondents(n=100)*
A. No Ill Effect On Mother/ Child	87
B. Premature Baby is Born	13
C. Nutritional Deficiency In Mother	7
D. Death of Mother	6

*Multiple Responses

It is clear from the Table 2 that majority (87%) of the respondents believed that early child bearing does not have any ill effect on the mother or child's health. They were of the opinion that early child bearing leads to easy delivery. Thirteen per cent of the respondents were of the opinion that it leads to birth of premature babies, 7% were of their opinion that it leads to nutritional deficiencies in mother and 6% believed that it might result in death of the mother.

Table 3 depicts that the respondents did not experience any serious complications during pregnancy. The most common problems faced by them during pregnancy were, tiredness (65%), followed by nausea (22%), hypertension and B. P. (7% and 5% respectively). Only 19% women had complications during delivery (forceps delivery) and 5% had post delivery complications. Dr. Parikh found similar results in 1996 among women in Bombay slum.

Table 3
Complications During Pregnancy

Complications	*Respondents(n=100)*
1. Pregnancy Related Complications	
(a) Tiredness	65
(b) Nausea	22
(c) Hypertension	7
(d) B. P.	5
(e) Any Other	1
2. Complication During Delivery	19
3. Post Delivery Complications	5

*Multiple Responses

Table 4
Immunisation Schedule During Pregnancy

Responses	*Respondents(n = 100)*
A. No	83
B. Yes	17

It is clear from the table No.4 that majority (83%) of the respondents did not follow the immunization schedule during pregnancy and were not protected against vaccine preventable diseases because they were not aware of it. Only 17% of them immunized themselves during their pregnancy period from the local hospital.

Table No 5 depicts that women were reluctant to seek health care especially gynecological health care for several reasons. Women tend to be inhibited from discussing gynecological problems with physicians' especially male physicians. The women visited doctor only when accompanied by their husbands. Women perceived problems as normal aspects of womanhood and 17% of the women went to doctors only in extreme conditions. Another reason for not seeking medical help was the cost of treatment, so 85% of the women resorted to home remedies and 83% were dependent on local dais. This kind of attitude leads to delay in treatment and the infection may flare up and cause irreversible damage, leading to serious reproductive consequence for the women.

Table 5
Health Seeking Behaviour

Responses	*Respondents (N = 100)*
Home Remedies	85
Local Dais	83
Visit To Doctor	17

A similar study conducted by Citizens council (Baroda 1998), found that women resorted to home remedies at morbidity stages. In a study by NFHS in J&K 42%births were attended by health attendants including doctors and nurses. Traditional birth attended and rest by friends and relatives attend one half of births.

DIET DUIRNG PREGNANCY

The urban slum-working women adhered to a variety of prenatal and postnatal beliefs and practices such as pregnant women must work hard and eat less to have less pain during childbirth. Instead of taking extra calories and nutrients, they took less diet because of the two reasons, Financial Problem and Ignorance regarding special diets during pregnancy. The respondents were not aware that poor diet during pregnancy affects the mother's health.

FAMILY PLANNING

Table 6
Knowledge of Contraceptive Methods

Methods	*Respondents (n=-100)*
A. Condoms	30
B. IUD	10
C. Pills	70
D. Sterilization	80

* Multiple Responses

Table 6 reveals that the respondents were aware of contraceptive methods like sterilization, oral pills (*Saheli, MalaD*) and condoms. But they did not use these methods. The respondents did not know that condoms are provided free of cost by the Government Agencies.. Majority (80%) of the women believed that sterilization would ruin women 's health. Most of the women stated that "*Bacche Ishwar Ki Den hain. Inhe paida hone se rokne par paap chadta hain. Aur jitne zyada kamane wale haath hon utna accha hai*. (Children are gifts of God, if we try to stop their birth by any mean we'll be cursed. More children mean more financial help). They came to know about the methods of family planning from their friends, colleagues, radio and T.V. Pareek and Rao in their study, pointed out that the knowledge and use of contraceptive methods for child spacing were uncommon in couples.

ABORTION

Table 7
Safe Abortion

Responses	*Respondents(n=100)*
A. Not Aware	62
B. When Conducted By Dais	30
C. By Doctor	8

It is depicted from the above table no.7 that majority (62%) of the respondents were not aware about the safe abortions. Thirty per cent of the respondents believed that the abortion was safe when it was conducted by dais at home. They stated that dais provided them home remedies like *Gram Karha* (a concoction made of herbs), which helps in their abortion in a very simple and easy manner, they believed that doctors would use different kind of instruments which would lead to infections and further complications. The respondents believed that once the instruments "*Gande Auzaar*" are used on them they will not be able to conceive in future.

Table 8
Legal Abortion

Responses	*Respondents(n=100)*
A. Not Aware	62
B. When There Is Complication During Pregnancy.	28
C. When There Is Retarded Growth Of Foetus	10

Table 8 shows that majority (62%) of the respondents were unaware about legal abortion. Twenty eight per cent were of the opinion that abortion was legal when there was complication during pregnancy and 10% when there is retarded growth of foetus. Many respondents said that abortion was illegal if it was done without the consent of the mother. All the respondents viewed that *aborting a girl child was a great crime*.

HIV/AIDS/STDS

Table 9
Knowledge of Working Slum Women Regarding Hiv/ Aids / Stds

Responses	*Knowledge of Hiv / Aids / Stds*		
Not Aware	*Heard of Hiv /* Aids/ Stds	*Mode of Transmission*	*Prevention*
	40	83	73
Aware	60	17	27

Table 9 reveals that only 60% of the respondents had heard of these terms but did not know the full form of HIV/AIDS/STDS. They had heard about these words through, Electronic media (Radio, T.V.) Similar results are found by Lahiri in 2002. Where he found that television was the greatest sources for providing information reg. AIDS/HIV/STDs. Eighty-three per cent of the respondents were ignorant of the mode of transmission of HIV/AIDS/STDs. They had misconceptions that insect bite, cat scratches, touch, shaking hands, staying together, second hand clothes, using the same vessels were the causative factors of AIDS/HIV/STDs. Similar study was conducted by Oladepo D etal, in (2002) whereby women perceived that AIDS could be spread by kissing, hugging and shaking hands. Seventy-three per cent of females were ignorant of the preventions of HIV/AIDS/STDs. Misconception about curability of HIV/AIDS was found among the respondents, who believed that this can be cured. The seriousness of the disease was known to a very few.

MENARCHE/MENSTRUAL PROBLEMS/ MENOPAUSE

Table 10
Experience when Menarche Attained

Responses	*Respondents (n=100)*
A. Aggressive	40
B. Depressed	35
C. Fearful	25

Most (42%) of the respondents attained menarche at the age of 15-16 years, 32% attained menarche at the age of 13-14 years and 26% of them at a very early age of 11-12 years. Table 12 reveals that 40%of the respondents felt aggressive, depressed (35%) and fearful (25%) when they attained menarche. The women had these experiences because they did not have prior knowledge regarding menstruation. They expressed that there was no one in the family for guided them. A similar study was conducted by Rakesh (1988) where by he revealed that parents especially the mother do not educate their daughters about various aspects of menstruation such as ages of onset, its duration and healthy practices during menstruation. That's why the girl faced bad experience when they attained menarche

Table 11
Menstrual Problems

Problems	*Respondents(n=100)*
A. Low Backaches	69
B. Dysmenorrhoea	23
C. Metorrhagia	13
D. Polymenorrhea	7

* Multiple Responses

It is depicted from the Table 13 that majority 69% of the respondents reported low back pain (*Kumar dukhti hai*), 23% reported symptoms suggestive of dysmenorrhoea (*Mahavari Mein sara vakht dukhta hai*). 13% reported of metorrhegia (*Vakt pe* mahavari nahi aati) and 7% reported polymenorrhea (*Jaldi mahavari aa jati hai*). Mulgaonkar 1996 among women in a Bombay slum found similar results.

Menopause: All the respondents had no idea regarding menopause. The respondents wondered when they came to know that the age of 45-50 years women stops menstruating and not capable of reproducing young ones.

SUMMARY AND CONCLUSION

Woman's health is seen only as means to achieve other social goals rather than end in itself. Woman's needs are either unsaved or are undeserved and women suffer from several problems with the key aspect of sexuality and reproductive health such as reproductive tract infections (RTI), infertility, morbidity due to childbirth and violence against girls and women. Women's reproductive health is to a large extent influenced by their subordinate social and economic status and by gender related inequalities, which, overtly or covertly, impede their access to care.

The present study "Awareness of reproductive health and rights among working women of urban slum areas" was conducted in Jammu City, with an aim to know the awareness of urban slum women regarding reproductive health (Safe motherhood, family planning, abortion, HIV/AIDs/STDs, menstruation, menopause,) and reproductive rights. The sample comprised of 100 working women in different urban-slum areas in Trikuta Nagar, Shastri Nagar, Sainik Colony and Subash Nagar. Purposive random sampling was used to select the sample. An interview schedule was used to elicit the information.

Regarding safe motherhood, all slum women had a history of marginal nutrition coupled with spaced pregnancies. Majority (74%) of the women had their first pregnancy between the ages of 14-16 years. They were not aware about the ill effects of early child bearing. Women had normal complications during pregnancy, 19% of them had complication during delivery and 5% had post delivery complications. Eighty-three per cent of the women did not follow the immunization schedule during pregnancy. Seventeen per cent them visited doctors only in extreme conditions and 55% of them resorted to home remedies.

Majority (84%) of the respondents had knowledge about family planning. The women knew about contraceptive methods, condoms (30%), IUD (10%), pills (70%) and sterilization (80%), but they did not adopt these methods. They used traditional methods for birth spacing for family planning because they had misconceptions that these contraceptives were expensive and unsafe

Majority (62%) of the women were unaware about safe and unsafe abortion. Thirty-eight per cent of women knew about abortions and believed that this should be done by trained dais by providing them home remedies. Otherwise it leads complications during next pregnancy (20%). According to 38% of the women abortion was illegal if done without the consent of mother. All of the respondents viewed that aborting a girl child was a great crime.

Regarding HIV/AIDs/STDs, 60% of the women had never heard of these terms. The women were ignorant of mode of transmission and curability. They thought that insect bites, dog bites, cat scratches, kissing, hugging, sharing clothes and sharing vessels etc was the causative factors for HIV/Aids/STDs. Only 17% of women reported sexual intercourse as a mode of transmission. It was found that women did not have prior knowledge regarding menarche (when a girl first menstruates) because there was no one in their family to guide them. These women complained about menstrual problems like low backache (69%), dysmenorrhoea (23%), metorrhagia (13%) and polymenorrhea (7%). These women also practiced certain taboos related to menstruation, which was passed on to them from one generation to another (mothers, aunts and story tellers). During menstruation, women abstained from worshipping (75%), touching pickles (60%), carrying heavy loads (20%), and having sex (40%) No food fads or beliefs related to menstruation were followed. Women were ignorant about menopause. The slum women were unaware about reproductive rights.

It can be concluded that there were many areas regarding reproductive health where the slum women had insufficient knowledge. Many efforts should be made in this field for the dissemination of awareness regarding reproductive rights among slum women. Community support and participation are essential to facilitate the planning and delivery of health care services. Enhancement of overall literacy rate can also change the concept of reproductive health. Women should be provided education free of cost in their convenient time. Intervention programme concerning reproductive health and rights should be carried out frequently in slum areas.

REFERENCES

Barker, G. (1998), Need for more Research in Violence Against Women, Personal Communication. pp. 38-48 (unpublished).

Gar. Sharma, S. N. and Sahay, R. (2001), Socio-cultural Aspects of Menstruation in an Urban Slum in Delhi. *Journal on Reproductive Health matters* 9(3); 17-19.

Jejeeboy, S. (2000), Adolescent Sexual and Reproductive Behaviour: A Review of the Evidence from India. pp. 26-28. Rawat Publications, Jaipur.

Mulgaonkar, Veena B. (1996), Reproductive Health of Women in Urban Slums of Bombay. Social Change. India *Journal of Community Medicine*, 26 (3 and 4) 137-156.

Rao, V. (2004), Women and Society, Himalaya Publishing House, New Delhi. pp. 122.

Roy, A. (2003), Development of Women, An Assessment, pp. 62-90, Rajat Publications, New Delhi.

Singh, B. and Prakash, S. (2006), Women Education and Women Rights in India. pp. 220-261, Vista International Publishers, New Delhi.

Stephenson, R. and Zoe, M. (2004), Maternal Health Care Services: Use among Rural-urban Migrants in Mumbai. *Asia-Pacific Journal,* 19(1): 39-60.

Tripathy, N. (2003), Women in Informal Sector. pp. 2-82, Discovery Publishing House, New Delhi.

UNFPA (1995): Guidelines on Reproductive Health.

VIOLENCE AGAINST WOMEN AND PREVENTIVE MEASURES

*Kuljit Kaur**

INTRODUCTION

"I am the woman who holds up sky
The rainbow runs through my eyes
The sun makes a path to my womb
My thoughts are in the shape of clouds
But my words are yet to come."

This quotation may remind us that in law and in life the agony of discrimination against women is a poignant reality. The *Beijing Declaration* and *Platform of Action* and the *Universal Declaration of Human Rights* proclaim the equality of sexes. But promising words of the countries are yet to enact and revise their domestic laws to protect the women from violence all around.[1]

Violence against women is a manifestation of the historically unequal power relations between men and women, which have led to domination over and discrimination against women by men and to the prevention of women's full advancement. Violence against women throughout the life cycle derives essentially from cultural patterns, in particular the harmful effects of certain traditional or customary practices and all acts of extremism linked to race, sex, language or

* Head, Department of Laws, Guru Nanak Dev University, Amritsar-143 005.

religion that perpetuate the lower status accorded to women in the family, the workplace, the community and society. Violence is exacerbated by social pressures, notably the shame of denouncing certain acts that have been perpetrated against women.

Acts of threats of violence, whether occurring within the home or in the community, or condoned by the State, instill fear and insecurity in women's lives and are obstacles to the achievement of equality and for development and peace. The fear of violence, including harassment, is a permanent constraint on the mobility of women and limits their access to resources and basic activities. High social, health and economic costs to the individual and society are associated with violence against women. Violence is one of the crucial social mechanisms by which women are forced into a subordinate position compared with men. In many cases, violence against women and girls occurs in the family or within the home, where violence is often tolerated. The neglect, physical and sexual abuse, and rape of girl children and women by family members and other members of the household, as well as incidences of spousal and non-spousal abuse, often go unreported and are thus difficult to detect. Even when such violence is reported, there is often a failure to protect victims or punish perpetrators.

Women's lack of access to legal information, aid or protection; the lack of laws that effectively prohibit violence against women; failure to reform existing laws; inadequate efforts on the part of public authorities to promote awareness of and enforce existing laws; and the absence of educational and other means to address the causes and consequences of violence. Images in the media of violence in particular those that depict rape or sexual slavery as well as the use of women and girls as sex objects, including pornography, are factors contributing to the continued prevalence of such violence adversely influencing the community at large, in particular children and young people.

KINDS/FORMS OF VIOLENCE

The term "violence against women" means any act of gender-based violence that results in, or is likely to result in, physical, sexual or psychological harm or suffering to women, including threats of such acts, coercion or arbitrary deprivation of liberty, whether occurring in public or private life:

- Physical, sexual and psychological violence occurring in the family, including battering, sexual abuse of female children in the household, dowry-related violence, marital rape, female genital mutilation and other traditional practices harmful to women, non-spousal violence and violence related to exploitation;
- Physical, sexual and psychological violence occurring within the general community, including rape, sexual abuse, sexual harassment and intimidation at work, in educational institutions and elsewhere, trafficking in women and forced prostitution;
- Physical, sexual and psychological violence perpetrated or condoned by the State, wherever it occurs.
- Other acts of violence against women include violation of the human rights of women in situations of armed conflict, in particular murder, systematic rape, sexual slavery and forced pregnancy.
- Acts of violence also include forced sterilization and forced abortion, coercive/forced use of contraceptives, female infanticide and prenatal sex selection.
- Some groups of women, such as women belonging to minority groups, indigenous women, refugee women, women migrants, including women migrant workers, women in poverty living in rural or remote communities, destitute women, women in institutions or in detention, female children, women with disabilities, elderly women, displaced women, repatriated women, women living in poverty and women in situations of armed conflict, foreign occupation, wars of aggression, civil wars, terrorism,

including hostage-taking are also particularly vulnerable to violence.

- The effective suppression of trafficking in women and girls for the sex trade is a matter of pressing international concern. The use of women in international prostitution and trafficking networks has become a major focus of international organized crime. Women and girls who are victims of this international trade are at an increased risk of further violence, as well as unwanted pregnancy and sexually transmitted infection, including infection with HIV/AIDS.

MEASURES TO PREVENT AND ELIMINATE VIOLENCE AGAINST WOMEN

Actions to be taken By Governments

(1) *Exercise of due diligence* to prevent, investigate and, in accordance with national legislation, punish acts of violence against women, whether those acts are perpetrated by the State or by private persons;

(2) *Enact and/ or reinforce* penal, civil, labour and administrative sanctions in domestic legislation to punish and redress the wrongs done to women and girls who are subjected to any form of violence, whether in the home, the workplace, the community or society;

(3) *Adopt and/ or implement* and periodically review and analyse legislation to ensure its effectiveness in eliminating violence against women, emphasizing the prevention of violence and the prosecution of offenders; take measures to ensure the protection of women subjected to violence, access to just and effective remedies, including compensation and indemnification and healing of victims, and rehabilitation of perpetrators;

(4) *Work actively to ratify and/ or implement* international human rights norms and instruments as they relate to violence against women, including those contained in the *Universal Declaration of Human Rights*[2], [21] the

International Covenant on Civil and Political Rights,[3] [13] the *International Covenant on Economic, Social and Cultural Rights*, [13] and the *Convention against Torture and Other Cruel, Inhuman or Degrading Treatment or Punishment*;[4]. [22]

(5) *Implement the Convention on the Elimination* of All Forms of Discrimination against Women, taking into account general recommendation 19, adopted by the Committee on the Elimination of Discrimination against Women at its eleventh session;[5] [23]

(6) *Promote an active and visible policy of mainstreaming a gender perspective* in all policies and programmes related to violence against women; actively encourage, support and implement measures and programmes aimed at increasing the knowledge and understanding of the causes, consequences and mechanisms of violence against women among those responsible for implementing these policies, such as law enforcement officers, police personnel and judicial, medical and social workers, as well as those who deal with minority, migration and refugee issues, and develop strategies to ensure that the revictimization of women victims of violence does not occur because of gender-insensitive laws or judicial or enforcement practices;

(7) *Provide women* who are subjected to violence with access to the mechanisms of justice and, as provided for by national legislation, to just and effective remedies for the harm they have suffered and inform women of their rights in seeking redress through such mechanisms;

(8) *Enforce legislation* against the perpetrators of practices and acts of violence against women, such as female genital mutilation, female infanticide, prenatal sex selection and dowry-related violence, and give vigorous support to the efforts of non-governmental and community organizations to eliminate such practices;

(9) *Adopt all appropriate measures*, especially in the field of education, to modify the social and cultural patterns

of conduct of men and women, and to eliminate prejudices, customary practices and all other practices based on the idea of the inferiority or superiority of either of the sexes and on stereotyped roles for men and women;

(10) *Create or strengthen institutional mechanisms* so that women and girls can report acts of violence against them in a safe and confidential environment, free from the fear or penalties or retaliation, and file charges;

(11) *Ensure that women with disabilities* have access to information and services in the field of violence;

(12) *Create, improve or develop as appropriate, and fund the training programmes* for judicial, legal, medical, social, educational and police and immigrant personnel, in order to avoid the abuse of power leading to violence against women and sensitize such personnel to the nature of gender-based acts and threats of violence so that fair treatment of female victims can be assured;

(13) *Adopt laws, where necessary, and reinforce existing laws that punish* police, security forces or any other agents of the State who engage in acts of violence against women in the course of the performance of their duties; review existing legislation and take effective measures against the perpetrators of such violence;

(14) *Allocate adequate resources* within the government budget and mobilize community resources for activities related to the elimination of violence against women, including resources for the implementation of plans of action at all appropriate levels;

Local governments, community organizations, non-governmental organizations, educational institutions, the public and private sectors, particularly enterprises, and the mass media should also assist the Govt. in taking the following Actions::

(1) *Provide well-funded shelters and relief support* for girls and women subjected to violence, as well as medical, psychological and other counselling services and free or

low-cost legal aid, where it is needed, as well as appropriate assistance to enable them to find a means of subsistence;

(2) *Establish linguistically and culturally accessible services* for migrant women and girls, including women migrant workers, who are victims of gender-based violence;

(3) *Support initiatives of women's organizations and non-governmental organizations all over the world to raise awareness* on the issue of violence and to contribute to its elimination;

(4) *Organize, support and fund community-based education and training campaigns to raise awareness* about violence and mobilize local communities to use appropriate gender-sensitive traditional and innovative methods of conflict resolution;

(5) *Recognize, support and promote the fundamental role of intermediate institutions,* such as primary health-care centers, family-planning centers, existing school health services, mother and baby protection services, centres for migrant families and so forth in the field of information and education related to abuse;

(6) *Organize and fund information campaigns and educational and training programmes* in order to sensitize girls and boys and women and men to the personal and social detrimental effects of violence in the family, community and society; teach them how to communicate without violence and promote training for victims and potential victims so that they can protect themselves and others against such violence;

(7) *Disseminate information on the assistance* available to women and families who are victims of violence;

(8) *Provide, fund and encourage counselling and rehabilitation programmes* for the perpetrators of violence and promote research to further efforts concerning such counselling and rehabilitation so as to prevent the recurrence of such violence;

(9) *Raise awareness of the responsibility of the media in promoting non-stereotyped images of women and men,* as well as in eliminating patterns of media presentation that generate violence, and encourage those responsible for media content to establish professional guidelines and codes of conduct; also raise awareness of the important role of the media in informing and educating people about the causes and effects of violence against women and in stimulating public debate on the topic.

(10) *Develop counselling, healing and support programmes for* girls, adolescents and young women who have been or are involved in abusive relationships, particularly those who live in homes or institutions where abuse occurs;

(11) *Take special measures to eliminate violence against women,* particularly those in vulnerable situations, such as young women, refugee, displaced and internally displaced women, women with disabilities and women migrant workers, including enforcing any existing legislation and developing, as appropriate, new legislation for women migrant workers in both sending and receiving countries.

CONCLUSION

Equality, partnership between women and men and respect for human dignity must permeate at all stages of the socialization process. Educational systems should promote self-respect, mutual respect, and cooperation between women and men. Experience in a number of countries shows that women and men can be mobilized to overcome violence in all its forms and that effective public measures can be taken to address both the causes and the consequences of violence. Men's groups mobilizing against gender violence are necessary allies for change. Governments and other actors should promote an active and visible policy of mainstreaming a gender perspective in all policies and programmes so that before decisions are taken an analysis may be made of their effects on women and men, respectively.

REFERENCES

UN, Fourth World Conference on Women, Beijing,China, Sept. 1995.

General Assembly Resolution 217-A (iii) of 10, December 1948.

Both the Covenants were adopted by the General Assembly on 16, December 1966.

General Assembly Resolution 2106 [xx], dated 21, December 1965.

RURAL WOMEN'S EMPOWERMENT, RIGHTS AND AWARENESS: AN EMPIRICAL STUDY FROM ORISSA*

*Reetuparna Das***

INTRODUCTION

The waves of feminism of the eighteenth century have originated from the West and have gradually spread its message to the women of the developing countries (Jha and Pujari, 1998).This has become aptly significant in the realm of today's gendered dimensions of development, when there has been a considerable interface between the international influence and the national policy-making in the development front. Thus, gender equity has emerged as pronounced and pervasive, which is strongly reflected in the United Nations (UN) International Development agenda since the 1990s (NIPCCD, 2005; Kaushik, 1997).

Due to the growing 'feminization of poverty' indicating the fact of women constituting about 70 per cent of the world's poor population (UNDP, 1995; Banerji and Sen, 2000), the alleviation of poverty of women has become a priority concern throughout the world. And therefore, the enactment of the

---

* Revised version of the paper presented in the national seminar organized by the Department of Political Science, Central University of Hyderabad in 2006.

** ICSSR Doctoral Fellow in Anthropology, N.K.C.Centre for Development Studies, Bhubaneswar, Orissa; regd. under Sambalpur University, Sambalpur, Orissa.

women's rights at the international level as well as national level (Kuriakose, 2005; Kapur, 1996; Medhi, 1996) has enabled the actors of the civil society with a stronger footing to improve the impoverished socio-economic conditions and status of women, especially of rural women. This is how rural women have stepped into the challenges of the twenty-first century (Lewellen, 2002; Schuurman, 2001).

RURAL WOMEN'S RIGHTS

Whenever the issue of women's rights and proper implementation and follow-up of these rights come up, the efforts at the global level more often than not have proved to leave a positive impact. In fact, the concern for women's rights has never been confined to any single nation, but rather their enactments have been possible only due to the pressure of the collective global movements. Specified laws for rural women, however, have not yet been formulated in India.

A simple recapitulation of the major entitlements enshrined in the international conventions to safeguard rural women's rights and empower them, reveal immense relevance of these for Indian rural women, *inter alia*: (i) right to equal access to institutional credit, training and appropriate technology to support and promote their productive activities; (ii) right to participate equally in the decision-making processes of the family; (iii) right to protection against domestic violence – as passed by the UN General Assembly in 1994; (iv) affirmation of the rights to land and other resources by the national government, in order to defy customary practices that prohibit or limit their access to these resources; (v) right to participate in development planning; (vi) right to have equal access to the basic necessities of life like health and nutrition, education and employment. Above all, the most important is the 'Convention on the Elimination of all forms of Discrimination Against Women' or CEDAW that came into force in 1981. This Convention has recognized a wide range of rights to improve the situation of women including the rural ones. Besides, there is a rising concern at the UN level which has started to make serious analyses of conditions of rural women notwithstanding the intensified impacts of global commercialization.

RATIONALE OF THE STUDY

In India more than 70 per cent of the population is rural, half of which is comprised of females (Registrar General and Census Commissioner, 2004:1-18). So, here female population is constituted mostly of rural women who represent two-thirds of the nation's population living below the poverty line (Mohanty, 2004). They constitute the backbone of the rural economy in India, but ironically are also those 90 per cent of the women labourers who suffer in the informal sector (Madhubala, 1992). So, no wonder that they are targeted as the major beneficiaries under the 'National Policy for Empowerment of Women, 2001'.

This illuminates the basic necessity for their empowerment and for protection of their due rights. And the quest for an inevitable question arises here: if the rights of these women are truly safeguarded in the real life situation. The question becomes especially important as several legal provisions and conventions have been already made to protect the rights of women. And there has been a strong concern for maximizing the benefits and minimizing the possible adverse effects specifically for rural women (Report of the UN General Assembly, 2001)[1].

STUDY AREA AND THE PEOPLE: A SOCIO-ECONOMIC PROFILE

Orissa as a state of India's eastern zone, is a backward one with its 47 per cent households below the poverty line and shows high rates of ST and SC population- 22.13 per cent and 16.53 per cent respectively (Government of Orissa, 2005). The situation is grimmer in the western part of the state. This part experiences extreme climatic conditions including high temperature and low rainfall, and its landscape is prominently featured by hilly tracts. The district of Balangir lies in this part, covering about 23.76 per cent of the total area of the state (*ibid*). This district is quite infamous for its multifarious socio-economic disadvantages like severe drought, abject poverty and starvation death. Here rural women are severely marginalized by poor economic status, low literacy and poor health condition.

The BPL census reveals that, around 60 per cent of the families in Balangir live below the poverty line (XIM/CENDERET/WORC, 2002) and most of these BPL families reside in villages. Table 1 shows the population profile with the rural-urban break-up of the district. It is interesting to note here that, the sex ratio of 991 (approximate) of the rural population of the district is quite higher than that of the state level of 972 as well as the national level of 933. Majority of the villages in this district are multi-ethnic by composition. There are different Scheduled Castes (SC) and Scheduled Tribes (ST), besides Other Backward Castes (OBC) and General Castes (GC).

OBJECTIVES AND METHODOLOGICAL STRATEGY

This study underlies the following basic objectives:

1. Find out through the local women self-help groups (hereinafter WSHGs), the level of awareness and practice of the rural women's due rights.
2. Broadly delineate some pragmatic suggestions as development measures in order to ensure the positive effects and mitigate the negative ones.

To serve the purpose of this study a single block, viz. Balangir block of the district was randomly selected. Owing to the ethnic composition all the WSHGs under the study block, these were broadly categorized into four types: SC WSHGs, ST WSHGs, OC (other castes except SC and ST) WSHGs and mixed WSHGs (the mixed compositions of all or any two of the earlier three ethnic categories). Following this, 10 groups each from these ethnic categories were selected through simple random sampling and thus, total 40 WSHGs

Table 1
Population Profile of Balangir and Orissa (Census 2001)

	Total Population		Rural Population		Urban Population		Sex Ratio		
	Rural Population	*Urban Population*	*Male*	*Female*	*Male*	*Female*	*Total*	*Rural*	*Urban*
Balangir (District)	1182871	154323	594182	588689	79803	74520	984	991	934
Orissa	31287422	5517238	15748970	15538452	2911600	2605638	972	987	895

Source: Statistical Abstract 2005 (pp 1-6), Govt. of Orissa.
Note: Sex Ratio = Number of females per 1000 males.

Table 2
Brief Profile of the Study Women Self-Help Groups

Ethnic Category	*Formed by*		*Total Members'*	*Average Age (year)*	*Average BPL Status (%)*	*Average Literacy Rate (%)*
	Govt.	*Non-Govt.*				
SC Groups	6(60.00)	4(40.00)	61	38	62.29	50.24
ST Groups	10(100.00)	0(0.00)	53	36	60.37	13.69
OC Groups	4(40.00)	6(60.00)	58	41	75.86	30.57
Mixed Groups	6(60.00)	4(40.00)	52	41	76.92	31.63
Total	26(65.00)	14(35.00)	224	39	68.86	31.53

Source: Fieldwork 2005-'06; Balangir ICDS Office.
Note: SC = Scheduled Caste; ST = Scheduled Tribe; OC = Other Caste; Mixed Group = A group comprised of members of all or any two of the first three ethnic categories; figure in parenthesis indicates per centage.

of 15 villages under 11 Gram Panchayats were studied. Table 2 reflects a brief profile of these groups. The anthropological research techniques used were: structured and unstructured interview, structured and unstructured focus group discussion, and informal discussion. To avail data on the awareness and practice of rights, 50 per cent members of each sample group were randomly selected, personally interviewed and have been evaluated through ordinal scoring technique. Secondary data were collected from different government and non-government sources.

EMPIRICAL FINDINGS AND ANALYSES

The findings that were obtained in the empirical situation have been analyzed here through two different steps. In the first step, the major poverty situations of the members of the sample WSHGs have been identified. The second step discusses the nature and extent of changes these women are experiencing due to the effect of collective awareness and practice of their rights.

Poverty that Disempowers the Rural Woman

Financial crisis or factor is not the one and only factor that contributes to the relegated socio-economic conditions and status of these rural women of Balangir district. Besides, there are many more factors, mainly socio-cultural by nature and content, which push these women into a complex poverty-stricken atmosphere. This is how the multi-faceted poverty situation have been identified and depicted below, from the holistic angle of anthropology:

Financial Poverty

Financial problem may not be the sole cause of the human poverty condition in totality, but it is certainly the most obvious symptom. Table 2 enumerates the BPL status of the members of the sample WSHGs, which shows that subdued economic status is undoubtedly the prime factor for disempowered position of these women. Table 3 shows per centages of women engaged in wage labour, in different ethnic groups. In fact, the principal reason for their subjugated economic status is their less or no accessibility to resources and family property-hardly differs from the overall rural Indian scenario. Despite of the fact that they are the major participants in land based production and have the legal right to jointly own lands with their husbands, but in practice, are denied the ownership. The patriarchal system clearly defies and ignores the implementation of the resolutions taken by the International Commission for Human Rights (ICHR) in the years 2000 and 2001, that is: (rural) women should have the right of equal ownership of, access to and control over land[2].

Above all, they undergo the greatest economic deprivation in the form of the insensitive denial to acknowledge their huge contributions towards household responsibilities, which have never been evaluated fiscally. In a nutshell, they seriously suffer from the poverty of right to livelihood.

The Poverty of Literacy and Technology Socialization

This a crucial social poverty condition for these rural women of the study groups, with average literacy rate of 31.53 per cent only (Table 2). This is lower than the corresponding rate of 35.77 per cent at the district level and much lower than that of 46.66 per cent at the state level (Government of Orissa, 2005: 8-9). High rate of illiteracy not only delimits their access to the existing vocational training programmes, but also stagnates exposure to various information and knowledge on modern technologies that would upgrade their skills for their own socio-economic sustainability.

Downgraded by 'Doxa'- Poverty of Self-Dignity

The age old practice of male dominance and subjugation has lead to accept these women simply as 'taken for granted' (Bourdieu, 2001; Lewin, 2006; Deshmukh-Ranadive, 2005), which has explicitly disempowered them and exacerbated their low-esteem state. As a result of such imbalanced gender and power relations they hardly have right to decision–making, either at the public or the domestic domain. In a rural area with such a low economic and literacy statuses, the dignity position of these women can be well understood. Such relegated status debars them to utilize their potentials and positive opportunities, and practice due rights in their lives.

Information Poverty

This is the age when need-based, multi-dimensional inventions and structural reforms are occurring at a faster pace. And it has become essential to keep track of these transformations to assimilate them in the development process. Thus, knowledge and information have become powerful assets today. But unfortunately, there is a dearth of basic information amongst the members of these WSHGs, as has been observed. Most of the supporting agencies do not take any special care to disseminate the basic ideas about the development programmes and schemes, though all these are meant for them. Moreover, they also get misguided by some wrong information that misleads their self-help activities, often at the cost of financial losses.

Poverty of Awareness about Rights

This may be viewed as an accumulative result of the other poverty situations already discussed. Possession of knowledge and skills is an essential prerequisite for utilization of the due rights. With the handicaps of insufficient financial capability, poor literacy and technology socialization, lack of exposure to opportunities due to dominant patriarchy, and inaccessibility to necessary information-all keep them in the dark, ignorant of their own potentials and of most of the rights they are entitled to. It is mention worthy here that, with inaccess to the right to information they are thus denied the most fundamental human right.

From Disempowerment to Empowerment

The WSHGs in the study block are found to be supported by both the governmental and non-governmental Project Implementing Agencies (PIAs). The latter, however, includes very few organizations of the international level like UNDP, DANIDA, NR International UK, etc. The most remarkable government project is the 'Mission Shakti' that has been launched under Women and Child Development (WCD) Department, as a women specific initiative to empower women through self-help movement. Besides, there are also several local and state level NGOs working in this area.

In this study, 65 per cent of the sample WSHGs are supported by the State Government and the rest 35 per cent are supported by non-governmental agencies (Table 2). This shows the predominance of the governmental coverage. But the government's objectives and efforts for promotion, capacity building, awareness generation and enhancing marketing opportunities- all have been found to be more in pen-and-paper than in reality. Whereas the non-governmental endeavours, especially those working jointly with the international agencies have been found to be more efficient in generating improvements for economic as well as social empowerment of these rural women. But these few international agencies working here cover very selectively only a small part of the whole region. Still then, their ingenious action plans and strategies obviously surpass the local strategies. This undoubtedly opens a window to look for the positive role of the global trend with more optimism and less pessimism, for the sake of the rural women's development.

In spite of the 'Universal Declaration of Human Rights, 1948' (Kaushik, *ibid*), the awareness of the essential rights symbolizing dignity have not reached women sufficiently, in comparison to men. This situation is always more depressing for rural women who are often denied the basic economic and social rights, both at the public domain and the domestic or private domain. The same condition has been reflected in the study situation, rather in a more impoverished state.

Before practising any right the most important pre-condition is that, there should be sufficient awareness of the nature and content of the right. The rights would become null-and-void if women are not made aware of their due rights and are not properly sensitized about the utility of the same. And this job of awareness generation or sensitization is possible through the process of empowerment, as empowerment is basically about the aware and well-informed state of mind. Therefore, an attempt has been made here to explore the awareness levels of these sample WSHG members of different ethnic categories, of the general economic, social, legal and political rights as well as the rights formulated for women.

The schematic presentations (Figure 1 and 2) show the broad criteriaor indicators that have been taken here to assess the awareness levels categorized into public and domestic divides. The indicators taken here for assessing the economic empowerment are: transaction with the financial institutions (FIs), economic skill development, awareness of the gender egalitarian right to employment, awareness of the right to family property (including land), decision-making capabilities on WSHG related economic activities while at home (Figure 1). In the public domain, social empowerment levels have been assessed on the basis of awareness of common social, legal and political rights and issues (Figure 2). These are: right to free primary education, to free legal aid, to political rights (to vote and to get elected to one-thirds of seats reserved for women at the local governance), and awareness of the major women welfare programmes. The social empowerment in the domestic domain has been assessed through the awareness of family health care provisions like awareness of: minimum marriageable age for girls, family planning methods (contraception, birth spacing, limiting number of children per family, etc.), the knowledge of the basic vaccinations for children and equal health attention to girls.

While analyzing the economic performances and social awareness of these groups, it has been found that more

Figure 1

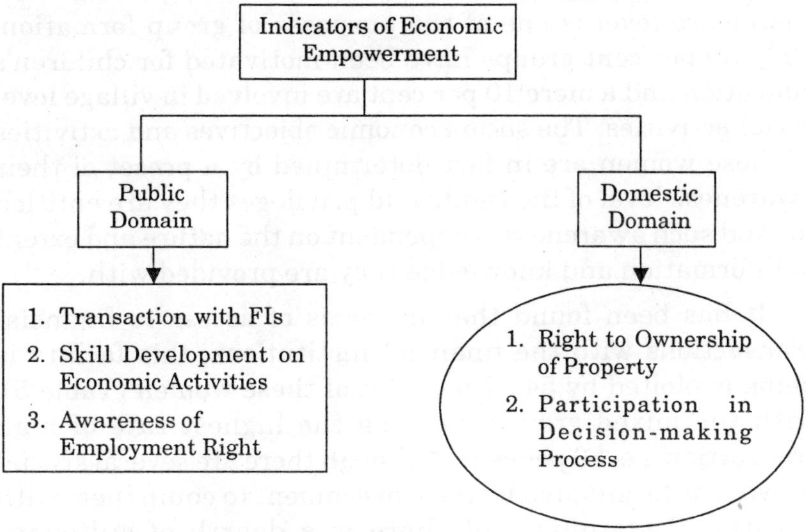

Figure 2

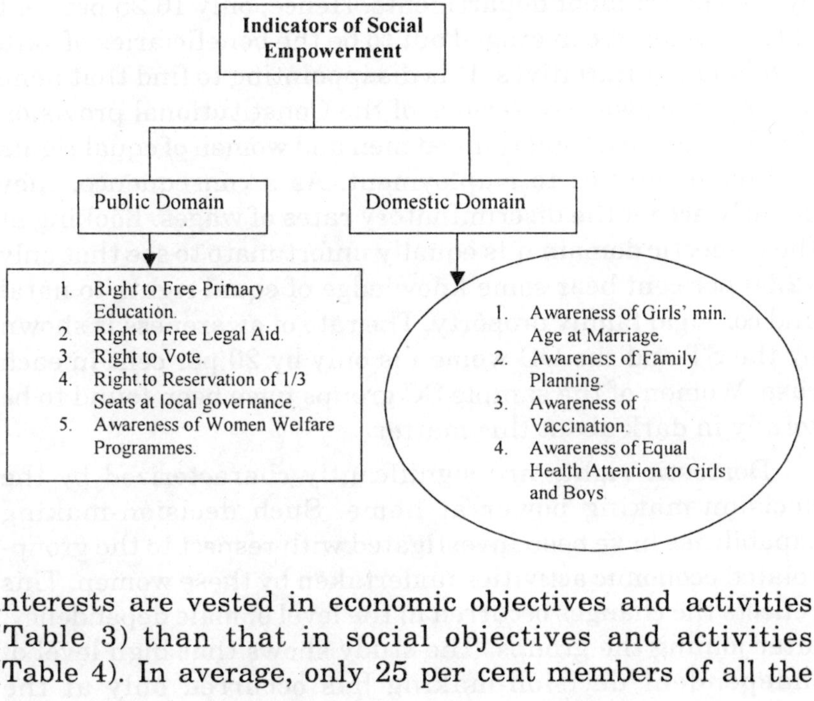

interests are vested in economic objectives and activities (Table 3) than that in social objectives and activities (Table 4). In average, only 25 per cent members of all the sample WSHGs believe that building and upgrading their confidence level is one of the purposes of group formation. Only 30 per cent groups have been motivated for children's education and a mere 10 per cent are involved in village level social activities. The socio-economic objectives and activities of these women are in fact determined by a preset of their awareness level of the rights and privileges they are entitled to. And such awareness is dependent on the nature and extent of information and knowledge they are provided with.

It has been found that in terms of access to financial transactions with the financial institutions, this facility is being exploited by 54.37 per cent of these women (Table 5), with the mixed groups showing the highest rate of high transaction, i.e. 80 per cent. Although there are several special provisions formulated by the Government to equip them with vocational training, but there is a dearth of sufficient arrangement and management supposed to be undertaken by the Government departments. Hence, only 16.25 per cent of the women are averaged out to be the beneficiaries of skill development initiatives. It is disappointing to find that none of them are aware or serious of the Constitutional provision that has long back guaranteed men and women of equal rights and opportunities to employment. As a consequence, they silently accept the discriminatory rates of wages. Looking at the domestic domain it is equally unfortunate to see that only 12.50 per cent bear some knowledge of equal rights to natal and conjugal family property. The rate of awareness is shown by the ST and the OC women is only by 20 per cent in each case. Women of the sample SC groups have been found to be totally in dark about this matter.

Domestic rights are significantly characterized by the decision-making power at home. Such decision-making capabilities have been investigated with respect to the group-related economic activities undertaken by these women. This reflects the changes occurred in the level of male dependency, after joining the groups. The study shows that high level of independent decision-making has occurred only at the

Table 3
Economic Objectives and Activities of the Study Groups

Ethnic Category	*Economic Objectives followed* *Income security (%)*	*Saving (%)*	*Economic Activities performed* *Members involved in Wage Labour (%)*	*Members involved in IGAs (%)*
SC Groups	100.00	100.00	96.60	48.25
ST Groups	100.00	100.00	100.00	75.38
OC Groups	100.00	100.00	82.14	58.33
Mixed Groups	100.00	100.00	96.00	100.00
Average	100.00	100.00	93.68	70.49

Source: Fieldwork 2005-'06
Note: SC = Scheduled Caste; ST = Scheduled Tribe; OC = Other Caste; Mixed Group = A group comprised of members of all or any two of the first three ethnic categories; IGAs = Income generation activities.

Table 4
Social Objectives and Activities of the Study Groups

Ethnic Category	*Social Objectives followed* *Fulfill Basic Needs (%)*	*Build Confidence (%)*	*Afford Children's Education (%)*	*Groups involved in Social Activities (%)*
SC Groups	100.00	20.00	20.00	20.00
ST Groups	100.00	0.00	20.00	0.00
OC Groups	100.00	20.00	20.00	0.00
Mixed Groups	100.00	60.00	60.00	20.00
Average	100.00	25.00	30.00	10.00

Source: Fieldwork 2005-'06.
Note: SC = Scheduled Caste; ST = Scheduled Tribe; OC = Other Caste; Mixed Group = A group comprised of members of all or any two of the first three ethnic categories.

average of 18.12 per cent (Table 5); whereas, most of them (81.87 per cent) have become independent at a medium level. This indicates that they still prefer to seek the views of the males (mainly husbands) without underestimating their own decisions though. It is definitely a positive sign that none of them are totally depending on men now. It is also to be specially noted here that, the ST women show an inadequate

Table 5
Awareness and Practice of Economic Rights (through WSHGs): Public and Domestic Domains

Ethnic	*Transaction with Financial Institutions (%)*			*Economic Skill Development (%)*	*Awareness: Equal Right to Employment (%)*	*Awareness: Property Rights (%)*	*Participation in Economic Decision-making at home (%)*		
Category	*H*	*M*	*L*				*H*	*M*	*L*
SC Groups	37.50	62.50	0.00	25.00	0.00	0.00	12.50	87.50	0.00
ST Groups	40.00	0.00	60.00	0.00	0.00	20.00	20.00	80.00	0.00
OC Groups	60.00	0.00	40.00	0.00	0.00	20.00	0.00	100.00	0.00
Mixed Groups	80.00	0.00	20.00	40.00	0.00	10.00	40.00	60.00	0.00
Average	54.37	15.62	30.00	16.25	0.00	12.50	18.12	81.87	0.00

Source: Fieldwork 2005-'06.

Note: H = High, M = Medium, L = Low; SC = Scheduled Caste; ST = Scheduled Tribe; OC = Other Caste; Mixed Group = A group comprised of members of all or any two of the first three ethnic categories.

rate of independent decision-making that is unlikely as per their traditional gender egalitarian values and who are more actively involved in economic performances (Table 3). This has some attribution to their significantly low rate of literacy (Table 2) and of course, the impact of the non-tribal culture.

While coming to the point of social awareness or social empowerment of the study WSHG members, one would encounter a shocking experience. Journey towards political empowerment and legal consciousness is absolutely difficult without awareness for social concerns—a ground reality neither being realized by these rural women nor by the government staff who interact with them. A meager per centage of them have little idea even about a common right like right to free primary education (Table 6). Surprisingly, none of these respondents have any information about the legal provisions for women or the free legal aid conferred to them. So far as the political rights are concerned, they practice the franchise just as a habit and mostly due to the persuasion of the male members of the family. They do not realize it to be their fundamental right— the right that empowers them to select the government of their own choice. None of them even have any information that one-thirds of total seats of the Panchayat are reserved for women.

They, however, have shown considerable awareness regarding family related health matters (Table 7). A significant average of 85.62 per cent have agreed on giving equal health attention to their daughters along with their sons; and the ST women have expressed the highest rate of inclination (90 per cent) in this matter.

SUGGESTION AND CONCLUSION

Each and every women development programme and scheme have the positive potentials to secure the rights of women. The following suggestions may be opted as a stepping stone for their pragmatic implementation, as have been prompted by the findings from the study context:

Table 6
Awareness of Social/Legal/Political Rights and Issues: Public Domain

Ethnic Category	*Right to Free Primary Education (%)*	*Right to Free Legal Aid (%)*	*Political Rights (%)*	*of Women Welfare Programmes (%)*		
				Highest	*Medium*	*Lowest*
SC Groups	36.36	0.00	0.00	0.00	100.00	0.00
ST Groups	0.00	0.00	0.00	15.00	85.00	0.00
OC Groups	15.00	0.00	0.00	0.00	100.00	0.00
Mixed Groups	10.00	0.00	0.00	0.00	100.00	0.00
Average	15.34	0.00	0.00	3.75	96.25	0.00

Source: Fieldwork 2005-'06.

Note: SC = Scheduled Caste; ST = Scheduled Tribe; OC = Other Caste; Mixed Group = A group comprised of members of all or any two of the first three ethnic categories.

Table 7
Awareness of Family Health Care

Ethnic Category	*Girls' min Age at Marriage (%)*	*Family Planning (%) High*	*Medium*	*Low*	*Children's Vaccination Programmes (%)*	*Equal Care to Girl Child (%)*
SC Groups	87.50	25.00	37.50	37.50	100.00	87.50
STGroups	20.00	60.00	40.00	0.00	100.00	90.00
OC Groups	60.00	40.00	40.00	20.00	100.00	80.00
MixedGroups	80.00	0.00	80.00	20.00	100.00	85.00
Average	61.87	31.25	49.37	19.37	100.00	85.62

Source: Fieldwork 2005-'06.
Note: SC = Scheduled Caste; ST = Scheduled Tribe; OC = Other Caste; Mixed Group = A group comprised of members of all or any two of the first three ethnic categories.

National issues cannot be incorporated without addressing the local perspectives and this is especially true for Indian rural women whose lives are interwoven with multifarious traditional elements. Therefore, to get the best out of modern approach care should be taken of the contextuality aspect in order to smoothen the path of modernization moulded in accordance with the local reasons, needs and emotions.

Nowadays NGOs are emerging as dynamic actors of the civil society to complement the governmental efforts for development; and have also become a major means for spreading the global messages on the development front. Therefore, the possibility of more accountability, transparency and mutual co-ordination is apprehended if these organizations are consulted in the pro-poor women policies and thus, enable them to give their best services in the local context. The women development scenario of the area could be more mobilized with greater interventions of global organizations.

Establishing an efficient network of gender oriented communication and information should take precedence over all training and awareness generation programmes for rural women. This definitely ensures better participation rights of these women in the development process, by facilitating community based problem articulation and providing enhanced exposure to the socio-economic changes that are taking place world wide through the human rights instruments.

In a caste-oriented multi-ethnic social matrix, especially when the perspective is rural a generalized process of framing gender policies and programmes would yield very less effect. Therefore separate care and positive discrimination is required for socio-economically backward sections like SCs and STs, before mainstreaming them into the broader development front.

No empowerment is complete with economic progress only. Hence rural women, along with their stronger economic position need also to be aware of and practise their socio-political rights as well. In this respect, to follow the global agencies that are adopting well-structured decentralization policies in the decision-making processes, would be certainly fruitful for these women to reshape their status within the household and the community as well.

NOTES

1. Source: www.unchr.ch
2. Source: www.fao.org

REFERENCES

Banerji, Anita and Raj Kumar Sen (eds) (2000), *Women and Economic Development*. New Delhi: Deep & Deep Publications Pvt. Ltd.

Bourdieu, Pierre and Richard Nice (2001), *Masculine Domination*. USA: Stanford University Press.

Deshmukh-Ranadive, Joy (2005), "Gender, Power and Empowerment: An Analysis of Household Dynamics," in Deepa Narayan (ed.) *Measuring Empowerment: Cross Disciplinary Perspectives*. Washington DC: The World Bank.

Government of Orissa (2005), *Statistical Abstract of Orissa 2005*. Bhubaneswar (India): Directorate of Economics and Statistics, Orissa.

Jha, Uma Shankar and Premlata Pujari (eds) (1998), *Indian Women Today: Tradition, Modernity and Challenge*. Vol. 1, New Delhi: Kanishka Publishers.

Kapur, Ratna (1996), *Feminist Terrains in Legal Domains: Interdisciplinary Essays on Women and law in India*. New Delhi: Kali for Women.

Kaushik, Vijay (1997), *Women's Movements and Human Rights*. Jaipur (Rajasthan): Pointer Publishers.

Kuriakose, Tina (2005), "Women's Rights Movement- International Dimensions and National Experiences," *Women's Link,* 11 (2): 10-15.

Lewellen, Ted C. (2002), *The Anthropology of Globalization: Cultural Anthropology Enters the 21st Century*. USA: Bergin & Garvey (Greenswood Publishing Group).

Lewin, Ellen (2006), *Feminist Anthropology: A Reader*. USA: Blackwell Publishing, Inc.

Madhubala (1992), "Women's Issues: From the Periphery to the Centre," *Journal of Rural Development,* 11 (5): 515.

Medhi, Kunja (1996), *Status of Women and Social Change*. Guahati: Women's Studies Research Centre.

Mohanty, Aliva (2004), "Women in Management of Micro-enterprises: Problems and Prospects," *Journal of Social Sciences*, 6(1): 53-57.

National Institute of Public Cooperation and Child Development (NIPCCD) (2005), *Factsheet on Women in India 2005*. New Delhi: NIPCCD.

Registrar General and Census Commissioner, India (2004), *Census of India 2001, Primary Census Abstract: Total Population* (pp. 1-18). New Delhi: Government of India.

Schuurman, Frans J. (ed) (2001), *Globalization and Development Studies: Challenges for the 21st Century*. New Delhi: Vistaar Publications.

United Nations Development Programme (UNDP) (1995), *Human Development Report*. Delhi: Oxford University Press.

Xavier Institute of Management (XIM) /CENDERET/ Western Orissa Resource Centre (2002), *A Report on Women Empowerment Through Self-Help: from April 2000 to October 2002*. Bhubaneswar: XIM.

IS WOMEN'S ROLE IN SERICULTURE MATTERS FOR THE COMMUNITY DEVELOPMENT: A STUDY FROM SOUTH INDIAN VILLAGE

*Eswarappa Kasi**

INTRODUCTION

In this paper an attempt has been made to explain the role of women in the success of SHG movement in Andhra Pradesh, which is related to other activities to sustain their livelihoods. The paper also discusses about the role of women in sericulture. This includes the concept of work, division of labour, segregation of occupations, dimension of labour and household activities, and role of DWCRA in relation to sericulture, etc. This paper also discusses perception of women towards silkworm, feeding, etc., and the role of children in sericultural activities.

WOMEN'S ROLE IN SELF HELP GROUPS:

The Government of Andhra Pradesh has taken up the theme of women's empowerment as one of the strategies to tackle the socio–economic poverty. Self Help movement through savings has been taken up as a mass movement by women– a path chosen by them to shape their destiny for better. Development Agenda of the State in the last few years placing

* ICSSR Senior Doctoral Fellow, Department of Anthropology, University of Hyderabad, Central University (P.O), Hyderabad- 500046, Andhra Pradesh, India, *e-mail: kasieswar@yahoo.com*

the people, especially women in the fore –front has enabled formation of a large number of Self Help Groups (SHGs) throughout the State and majority of women are saving one rupee a day. The State government is consciously making an effort to assist SHGs by providing Revolving Fund/Matching grant under various programmes.

SHGS MOVEMENT IN ANDHRA PRADESH

There are about 4.65 lakhs women SHGs in Andhra Pradesh covering nearly 61.70 lakhs poor women. Andhra Pradesh alone has about half of SHGs organized in the Country. The SHGs are also popularly called DWCRA Groups, and this name after the DWCRA programme (Development of Women and Children in Rural Areas) through which women's groups were assisted initially. The SHGs are not only resorting to thrift but also are taking small loans out of the corpus available with the group. The group corpus consists of savings, government assistance and also bank loan. Members use the loan out of group corpus for their personal needs initially. However, in the long run such loans are utilised for income generation activities. Since inception an amount of Rs.1556.90 crores is mobilized as corpus by these groups.

MICRO CREDIT TO SHGS

Micro credit summit conducted in 1997 in Washington resolved to reach 100 million poor women by 2005 all over the world. In Andhra Pradesh alone, 61.70 lakh women were covered under micro credit with a saving of one rupee per day and the financial institutions extending loans upto 4 times to the amount of group savings. From the year 1997 to January 2003, Banks extended a loan of Rs.1345 crores to SHG and the recovery of loans is more than 95%. Recently commercial banks have reduced interest rate on the loans extended to SHGs from 12% to 9%.

BUILDING INSTITUTIONS FOR SHGS

Women's savings movement started in 1993 as an off shoot of total literacy campaigns successfully conducted by the pro-active government initiatives in the southern part of Andhra Pradesh, poor women agitated against sale of arrack, organized themselves into 'Thrift and Credit groups' with one rupee saving in a day had now turned into a mass movement in which 61.70 lakh members saved more than Rs.887.47 crores which is rotated internally and lent amongst the members twice in a year as per the interest rates fixed by the groups. Such amounts are used for their daily consumption needs and also for production of goods for sales to earn incomes.

GEOGRAPHICAL SPREAD

All the villages in the state have at least one SHG and 75% of the villages have 15- 20 groups in each. Government felt the necessity of building institutions for SHG at the village and mandal level ('Mandal' is an administrative unit equivalent to 1/3 size of a block). Village organisations and mandal federations are formed and the latter are registered under the mutually aided Co-operative Societies Act 1995. Such federations take up functions like pensions to old people, insurance services to members, procurement of raw materials and marketing of finished products, accessing community infrastructure facilities, providing market information and other services to the members.

ECONOMIC EMPOWERMENT OF SHGs

60% of the women take up economic activities related to agriculture and allied activities. Land lease for growing agricultural crop is a common practice in the 9 Telangana districts. Vegetable and flower cultivation, food crops and pulses, oil seeds cultivation are taken up on leased lands. Similarly, rearing of calves, ram lamb, chicks, piggery and duckery, dairy, value addition to milk and milk products are preferred by women agricultural labourers. Illiterate and unskilled women engage in small business activities. Nearly 20% of the SHG members are artisans and engaged in making handicrafts and handloom products.

Public private partnership method is adopted in promoting economic opportunities to SHG members by appointing them as dealers for the sale of prodcts manufactured by companies like Hindustan Levers Limited, TVS, TTK-Prestige, Colgate-Palmolive, Philips etc. Companies in return train SHGs in finance management, enterprise development, packaging, branding and pricing of products. This partnership is a win- win model. Andhra Pradesh is now engaged in intense pursuit of development programmes utilizing information technology (IT) and to strategize as to how the benefits of IT could be taken to rural areas.

SHGs are encouraged to get PCs and software for accessing information and developing their business. Their products are photographed, scanned and displayed on websites. These are put on the portals of e-commerce companies. Handicrafts, herbal medicines and cosmetics, hand woven and embroidered curtains, toys, paintings etc., are thus finding national and international markets. This would not have been possible, but for the internet. The members are enabled to take a mobile telephone and use it not only for the sales but as a public telephone.

IMPACT OF SHGs MOVEMENT:

Various organisations evaluated SHGs. NGOs, universities, National Bank for Agricultural & Rural Development (NABARD) and ORG-Marg. Some of the salient features are:

- 98% of the members make savings regularly as the norms prescribed by the groups.
- All the groups meet at least once in a month to discuss various social issues related to their day to day life.
- 98% of eligible members adopt small family norms.

- 100% children of SHG members are able to access immunization services against the 6 diseases.
- 30% of the members have access to safe cooking fuels (LPG) under the Government promoted scheme popularly known as "DEEPAM".
- 80% of the total SHGs have accessed financial assistance from banks and repayment is 98%.
- 10,000 SHG members were elected to the local bodies (3 term Panchayat Raj Institutions) in 1997 November elections.
- Members are engaged in 450 varieties of income generating activities.
- Additional family incomes to member range from Rs.1000-3000 per annum depending on the income generating activities.
- Increase in self confidence and self esteem
- Increase in awareness levels about the society and community. Voluntary participation in community activities like laying roads, planting trees conserving environment, construction of water harvesting structures, donations to the victims of natural calamities, helping to reduce crime against girls & women, campaign against eradication of social evils like dowry, child marriages, untouchability, AIDS, rescue and rehabilitation of orphaned children, counseling adolescent girls, support to widows and destitutes are a few to mention.

SHG members learning from the past experiences are walking through the present are marching ahead for a bright future. Government of Andhra Pradesh has rightly realized that the involvement of the rural poor women in development will speed up attainment of Swarnandhra Pradesh and realising the Vision indeed!

In the Third World countries much of the work on gender has been influenced by socialist and liberal feminists who are dominant in the 1970s. Sarker (2006) further quotes Waylen's (1996) idea that the Socialist feminist believes that societies are fundamentally structured around patriarchy and profound inequalities in gender relations. Besides the economic class structure, they attack all forms of male oppression. Liberal feminism is the most diverse strand. Liberal feminists are less concerned with finding structural explanation for women's subordination than socialist feminists. Instead, they find the socialization of men and women into different roles reinforced by discrimination, prejudice and irrationality as responsible for women's unequal position in society. The solutions to inequality are changes which will give women a better deal in the existing system, such as, legal changes and the promotion of equal opportunities allowing women access to things on the same terms as men. Liberal feminism has been criticized for its overtly individualistic approach and its lack of a coherent analysis of women's oppression (Sarker 2006:63-4).

Boserup (1970) has observed that new technology in farming actually lowered women's status by reducing their access to productive work. As each crop production and wage jobs were only made available to men, women were increasingly relegated to the subsistence economy during and after the colonial period.

Development planners ignored women's productive activities, partly because their national accounting systems ignored much of women's work within the household and subsistence economy, assuming women to be only housewives (Rogers 1980).

METHODOLOGY

This paper is based on the data collected from Kotha Indlu village of Chittoor district in Andhra Pradesh during the year 1999-2000. This study is a qualitative micro-level study of a sericulture village. The primary data was collected through a structured household schedule, informal interviews using detailed checklists, key informant interviews, case studies and observation from all respondents in the village. Quantitative information with regard to the technological development, land holding, demographic aspects, cropping patterns, irrigation systems were collected by using household schedules and District statistical hand book. Secondary data and information are collected from the annual reports of the Department of Sericulture, Andhra Pradesh, the studies and reports brought out by the Central Silk Board, Bangalore, Institute of Social and Economic Change (ISEC), Bangalore, National Institute of Rural Development, Hyderabad, and Central Sericulture Research and Training Institute, Mysore.

VILLAGE PROFILE

Kotha Indlu is situated in the Kotha Indlu Panchayat of Kuppam Mandal in Chittoor district, about 15 kilometres from Kuppam, the mandal head quarters. It is a multi caste village inhabited by Balija, Vanniar, Scheduled Castes and washer men castes. The Balija, are the dominant castes in this village. They are dominant politically, economically, educationally and also numerically. While the Balija occupy the highest position in the local caste hierarchy, Vanniar, Chakali and the SCs occupy the subsequent positions in that order. Vanniar, who are a backward caste, competing with the Balija Caste economically and educationally, though they are weak numerically and politically. Next to Balija, the Scheduled Castes are numerically higher than Vanniar and Chakali. The total population is 274 formed by 50 families. On the basis of land holdings, the residents of Kotha Indlu are classified into marginal, small, medium and large farmers, and the landless. In Kotha Indlu the number of small farmers forms the majority. The next bigger group is the medium farmers. The numbers of large and marginal farmers are quite few, while the landless are almost insignificant. The crops cultivated are Paddy and Ragi, which are the staple crops and they constitute the staple diet of all communities. Commercial crops like flowers and groundnuts are also grown in the village. Floriculture is specially found among the Balija farmers, while all the castes raise groundnut crop in their lands. Though sericulture occupies the second position after agriculture, it is the major source of income for the farmers in the village. Cattle, goat, sheep, buffaloes and donkeys are the major livestock in the area. Several varieties of grass along with stocked paddy straw; maize stalk, groundnut and bhoosa are used as fodder. Poultry is widely prevalent in the village and only the SCs practise piggery. The village is very well connected by road and it has good transport facilities. Except Scheduled Caste sericulturists, the remaining sericulture farmers of the village use the tillers, tractors and bullock carts to transport their produce to the towns. The village has telephone as well as postal facilities. The village has an upper primary school and a high school. It also has a ration shop under the public distribution system to supply the necessary commodities to the people who comes under below poverty line (BPL) at concessional rates. In Kotha Indlu village people give more importance to rituals. Rituals are associated with all their activities. The president of the Gram Panchayat is from the Scheduled caste community. In fact, this (Panchayat) seat was reserved for the Scheduled Castes in the last elections held for the local bodies on rotatory basis. There is a farmers' club in the village, which takes care of their problems both in the society and outside.

ARE WOMEN'S ROLE MATTERS FOR DEVELOPMENT?

Sericulture is an extremely labour intensive industry and occupies an enviable position for providing employment and additional income to weaker sections. In this context, the transformation of sericulture industry from subsistence type of operation to a modern scientific system requires the attention of the policy makers, administrators and personnel working in the industry. Here the word personnel, mainly refers to women labourers who are the full time workers and who look after silkworm raring and management and whose contribution is more than that of men in rearing silkworms. It is reported that women contribute about 50 and 60 per cent of labour to mulberry cultivation and silkworm rearing, respectively (Ranganayaka and Sidderamaiah, 1995: 25).

It is rightly observed by Inbanathan and Vijayalakshmi that, "Economic development has been one of the main objectives of many governments of countries around the world. And, improving the socio-economic condition of women has also been an important aim in their development programs. In this context, and in India, sericulture has been found to be very helpful in meeting the development objectives of the Government. This is because it is labour intensive, and provides employment and income to many people, both in rural and urban areas. As such, it is of particular significance in anti-poverty programs. Sericulture is not one occupation but includes several activities, from planting and growing mulberry plants, rearing of silkworms to reeling of silk yarn from cocoons. In much of these activities, the labour contribution of women is significant" (1997: 37-8).

From time immemorial, women are involved in different sectors of silk industry. A legend says that the discovery of the silkworm and cocoon is by a woman, a beautiful Chinese Princess. But for her foresight and imagination, perhaps, the silk industry would not have been what it is today. The industry is well established in the traditional countries like Japan, China and Korea. The progress is equally rapid in the developed and under developed countries. In India sericulture is practiced as an agro-husbandry based subsidiary occupation. From the household, women are employed in sericulture operations. As mentioned earlier, about 51 per cent of women are assisting men in this lucrative industry to produce the queen of textiles (Kannan, 1987).

Women are mostly favored because of their delicate nature, patience and hard work. They are employed in a mulberry garden or silkworm rearing or in a grainage or in weaving or in a garment-making factory, etc. By and large, sericulture offers a vast scope to augment the family income. Women are actively engaged in the mulberry fields for the removal of weeds and in leaf plucking. The leaf plucking is a skilled and delicate operation. They must have full knowledge about which leaves should be plucked that suit different ages of silkworms. Women go to the fields in the morning for plucking the mulberry leaves and return to the rearing house before noon.

In the rearing house it is not uncommon to find women folk assisting men in feeding the silkworms. Feeding is an art very aptly done by the fair sex, though men do chopping of leaves. Women assist in bed changing and they do this with utmost tenderness so as not to hurt the delicate worms. Women have become experts in Chawki rearing, which is a highly delicate operation and will have to be done with care and patience. Good harvests depend on good Chawki rearing. When the silkworm matures and is ready for spinning the cocoons, it is again women who are employed for picking the ripe worms and putting them on the chandrikas (bamboo mountages on which silkworms are placed when they are just about to spin their cocoons). Any over crowding will lead to an increase in the spinning of double cocoons, which are unfit for the production of high-grade raw silk. When the cocoons are ready for harvesting, it is mostly women who sort out the flimsy, stained, double and deformed cocoons from the chandrikas.

Coming to the post cocoon technology, the involvement of women is greater, commencing from silk reeling, weaving and garment manufacturing industry. Whether it be a charkha, cottage basin, steam filature or automatic or semi-automatic reeling, women are preferred due to the dexterity of their fingers in getting the fine filaments from the cocoons, casting of the ends and they possess the patience to work in hot water and seam for long hours. It is really a pitiable sight to see women sitting near the boiling water all day long, reeling the crude charkha silk. Women's greater involvement in reeling industry is seen not only in India but also in all silk producing countries. In the post reeling, the ultimate success depends much on good winding, that is, yarn without breaks. There should be continuity in the yarn, otherwise there will be too many knots which hinder good weaving, be it on a handloom or a power loom.

However, their work has not always been recognized or rewarded. Cultural factors have complicated the proper evaluation of the quantum and quality of women's contribution. It includes elements such as the structure of work in each society, segregation of women and men in specific occupations, and the division of labour.

WORK AND DIVISION OF LABOUR

Inbanathan and Vijayalakshmi rightly stated that, "Work is regarded in many ways in different societies, and, the conception of work has also varied from time to time. The transition from simple hunting and gathering communities to agrarian technology entailed a major shift in gender relations... The primary responsibility of women was considered as attending to the needs of children and their husbands, and in the patriarchal culture this was seen to follow naturally from their role in biological reproduction.... The sociology of gender and to some extent sociology of work has attempted to explain the work of women by relating it to two realms prevalent in society. The "separate spheres" for men and women have been variously referred to as "inside/outside" or "private/public" and have been extensively used by anthropologists to explain the cross-cultural phenomenon of women's lower status vis-à-vis men. It has been argued that women's involvement with child rearing and domestic work was responsible for their exclusion from the public sphere" (ibid: 38-9).

Further, Inbanathan and Vijayalakshmi continue that, "Certain occupations were reserved exclusively for men and certain occupations were considered as women's work. Though much of the conceptualizing of these separate spheres is based on biological reductionism, empirical evidence shows that the dichotomy is related more to the social than to the economic sphere. However, it was the intellectual potential of women, which was portrayed as their weak point, and provided a doubtful rationale to confine them to work which did not involve substantial mental ability. There is no scientific support for such an impression, but the answers lie within culture rather than in biological factors. For instance, people assume or even believe that certain activities associated with silkworm rearing such as *Chawki rearing* (involving very young silkworms) require extremely high skill which only men can provide. As we saw during our field visits, when the situation demanded, women could and did carry out such work, with no noticeable harm to silkworms or to sericulture productivity" (ibid.: 39).

It is amply demonstrated that though women participated in both spheres of work, they are still confined to 'home base' jobs than 'outside home' jobs or tasks. Even in cases where they do both jobs, these are to be done under the guidance or supervision of men. These home base jobs are not even considered as productive work and in the same vein all home base jobs done by women, including silkworm rearing, are relegated to lower status and are virtually considered insignificant and unskilled. This also has a bearing on their decision-making power vis-à-vis men (Inbanathan and Vijayalakshmi, 1997).

DIVISION OF LABOUR

The division of labour in Kotha Indlu shows a typical gender divide in various activities that the women and girls do as compared to men and boys. All the household chores, tending children, looking after the needs of their husbands and other members of the family are all women's tasks.

Besides, workings on agricultural lands as well as looking after sericultural tasks, which are usually branded as 'feminine' tasks, are not recognized as productive jobs. They include a wide variety of tasks like domestic chores, agricultural and sericultural tasks like sowing, weeding, cutting or plucking leaves, etc., are as a matter of fact more arduous and back-breaking. The above two tables amply demonstrate this (Table 1 and 2).

Table 1
Division of Household Activities (in %)

Activities	*Men*	*Women*	*Others**
Washing/cleaning utensils, clothes	—	98	2
Taking care of children	—	84	16
Supervision of children	—	67	33
Collecting drinking water	—	54	46
Bringing Firewood	18	63	19
Bringing grass	23	67	10
Rearing Cows / goats	34	64	2
Milking the cows	14	86	—
Washing the cattle	21	71	8

*Mostly women, either hired or related to the family

Table 2
Division of Labour in Establishing Mulberry Gardens (in %)

S. No.	*Activities*	*Family*		*Hired*	
		Male	*Female*	*Male*	*Female*
1	Ploughing	94	—	6	—
2	Levelling	92	—	8	—
3	Harrowing	92	—	8	—
4	Irrigation	64	36	—	—
5	FYM application	49	51	—	—
6	Fertilizer application	72	28	—	—
7	Weeding	—	86	—	14
8	Planting	46	54	—	—

People in Kotha Indlu believe that men are considered more skilled and knowledgeable in the application of fertilizers and wherever women are involved they work under the supervision of men. A division of labour is also seen in the activities pertaining to maintenance of mulberry gardens. Both men and women participate in FYM application and irrigation. Thus, men are mainly held responsible for activities like pruning, ploughing and fertilizer application, and women for weeding. Maintenance and upkeep of mulberry garden is the male realm and any 'skilled work', be it in raising and maintenance of mulberry garden or silkworm rearing and marketing of cocoons, is a male domain and if women are involved in these tasks they have to 'consult' and work under the 'guidance' of men. Men do not engage themselves in 'less skilled'; 'unskilled' or 'no skilled' jobs (Table 3).

Table 3
Division of Labour in Mulberry Garden Maintenance (in %)

S. No.	*Activities*	*Family*		*Hired*	
		Male	*Female*	*Male*	*Female*
1	Pruning	91	—	9	—
2	Ploughing	94	—	6	—
3	FYM application	46	54	—	—
4	Fertilizer application	79	21	—	—
5	Weeding	—	84	—	16
6	Irrigation	54	32	14	—

Even in silkworm rearing, the sharing of tasks follows the same logic of 'skilled' and 'unskilled' jobs in mulberry cultivation. Thus, except for chawki rearing and harvesting of cocoons, which are 'skilled' jobs and hence are done mostly by men, women in Kotha Indlu perform all the other tasks. Bed cleaning and disinfecting the trays are considered a "women's Job" and 92.5 per cent of Women are involved in it. However, both men and women perform disinfecting of the rearing house (Table 4). Hiring of labour is not a practice commonly found in Kotha Indlu. Still there is the prevalence of exchange labour, which stresses on the traditional linkages.

Table 4
Division of labour in silkworm rearing (In %)

Activities	*Male*	*Female*
Brushing	74	26
Harvesting leaves	11	89
Chopping the leaves	17	83
Feeding	12	88
Bed cleaning	7	93
Molt setting	53	47
Mounting	39	61
Disinfecting	8	92

When the workload is more and when more hands are required they take the help of their kinsmen and friends.

Marketing of cocoons is considered a predominantly male activity. Similarly purchasing of disinfectants, trays and nets was considered a male domain. Women are more involved in renting of the chandrikas because a majority of the households rent chandrikas from the DWCRA groups in Kotha Indlu or from the neighbouring villages. In the study village there are 7 DWCRA groups, each group consisting of 10-15 members, and each group has its own (different) name. In every group there is a first leader and second leader, who convene and coordinates the meetings. For all the groups, there is one accountant, called cluster associate, who looks after the money transactions and accounts.

Udayalaxmi, aged 28, whose husband practices floriculture, has three children and all of them are put in school (convent and Montessori) in Kuppam. Her husband studied up to 5th class, while she studied up to 9th class. After joining as a member in the DWCRA group, "Bhagylakshmi", she became a little bold. Slowly she became a leader and now she is cluster associate to 15 DWCRA groups, which are functioning in the Kotha Indlu Gram Panchayat. Out of these 15 DWCRA groups, 9 are in Kotha Indlu only. She is also an accountant to all these nine groups. Without Udaylakshmi, they cannot conduct meetings. She is a cluster associate in "DAN" Foundation, which is an N.G.O., whose headquarter is at Madhurai in Tamil Nadu.

"DAN" society has been conducting training classes to women in Andhra Pradesh, especially in Chittoor district, where number of Dwcra groups and Thrift groups are located in Tirupati and Chittoor regions. According to 'DAN' estimates, there are 350 Dwcra groups in Kuppam mandal only. They are conducting women awareness camps, 10 days in Tirupati and 3 days in Kuppam. They are also participating in the Akshara Tapashman programmes, vaccination programmes Janmabhoomi, V.S.S., Shramadanam and other awareness kind of programmes which are voluntary in nature.

Udaylakshmi says that before joining the group she was very short tempered and was getting very angry even for small incidents. But after joining the group she became more tempered, patient and bold, and confidence in her has improved. Now she does not think about caste distinction, but more concerned about one's effective participation in DWCRA. She said that earlier she had lot of caste bias, some kind of bias against lower caste women / men. She is now very much interested in educating woman.

She gave one example of a problem, which was sorted out through her intervention in the village. There is a problem of stomachache to one woman. Her husband is a drunkard and does not take care of his wife. Because of her pressure, the Project Director wrote a letter to the Government General Hospital for checking and scanning. They found that she has *kanithi* (*gadda*). For operating they asked Rs. 10,000/-. Because of Udaylakshmi's pressure, Government gave her money for operation. Now she is all right. This is just small example of her role in the village is a member of DAN foundation in general, cluster associate in DWCRA in particular. This amply demonstrates the emergence of some leadership among women.

ACTIVITIES OF DWCRA IN RELATION TO SERICULTURE:

DWCRA arranges meetings with sericulture officials to learn about new methods of technology / crops / seeds. It coordinates the members training programmes. It conducts awareness programmes (about the) in relation to the cleanliness of the rearing house and trays and chandrikas and acts as a mediator between sericulturists and Department of Sericulture. It enquires and advises the members on issues related to their personal health. DWCRA provides chandrikas to the rearers on rent and it also constructs the shed to keep chandrikas and trays. It provides loan to members to buy silkworm seed (Matti).

Whenever women were associated in marketing, it was always with the help of a male member of the household since it is considered a "male activity" and a relatively difficult task to perform. This is mainly because it involved going out of the village, interacting with strangers, and money transactions. The dominant culture of the village does not encourage women to undertake activities where they have to travel away from home. In this situation, marketing is a male preserve, and is likely to remain so in the foreseeable future. However, this principle was not always strictly followed, and according to the class/caste, and economic circumstances, women may need to take up marketing and also wage labour, and their families would condone this act through force of necessity. Marketing under these circumstances i.e., whenever women had to travel relatively long distances away from the village, is usually in the company of male escorts.

In the households, which are engaged in both agriculture and sericulture, women are usually more active in sericulture, which involved staying back at home. However, they are more often restricted to 'less skilled' occupations, as perceived by the sericulturists. While agriculture has a relatively clear-cut division of labour, sericulture in Kotha Indlu also has divisions based on gender. Agriculture is still the major activity for the people of Kotha Indlu. The approximate contribution of men and women in certain agricultural activities showed that women are engaged also in agricultural work, apart from sericulture and other activities.

WOMEN AND SILKWORM REARING:

Women in Kotha Indlu village feel that worms are very sensitive in nature. For them tending the worms is like tending the children. While feeding worms, women take utmost care. Sometimes they feel that, they do not take that much care of their children also. Women consider bed cleaning and litter cleaning as a natural thing that they do in case of children, and it requires utmost patience. Here girls are mostly involved in all of these activities. Most of the sericulture households in Kotha Indlu, girls' participation in sericulture activity is higher than boys. There is couple of exceptions to this general rule. This is evident in the case of Tulasibabu.

Tulasibabu, aged 15, is studying 10th class, and is the eldest son of the family. He can do all work relating to sericulture. Even though he is in the 10th standard he can concentrate sericulture as well. The officials, right from Assistant Director to lower staff, came to the village and gave guidance to him. He is the third man to grow Swarnandhra in this village.

He is very intelligent and hard working, according to the Convenor of Farmers Club. He had learnt about sericulture from his father and other persons in the village through observation and experiences. He says that because of sericulture their life style has changed and their living conditions improved very much. They have modern gadgets like T.V. and Tape Recorder, etc. He said that though he is still a 'child', he should be bit careful about his future too. After joining the 10th class, he has spent around Rs.1, 000/- for books and other materials.

He is studying 10th class, but somebody will be there to see all the works in the house. If he gets the chance to study, he will go for college and enjoy the college life. He has great desire to pursue higher studies and after that he wants to become 'Chief Minister' of Andhra Pradesh.

Regarding health he does not have any complaints. Very rarely he may get cold and fever, which is not because of sericulture. There is no complaint about any disease with this crop.

He did not feel sorry for doing sericulture along with his education. Though his father is there, he is very busy with politics and other meetings of the Telugu Desam Party and that to he is he president of Education (Vidya) volunteers committee and electricity committee. His teachers and friends have been encouraging him to do both works. Most of the teachers know him doing both works reasonably well.

POLLUTION AND PURITY

They are practicing pollution and purity very sincerely. During pollution time, they do not allow the polluted people into rearing house. Purity was very much important to get good yield. Everyday, they apply the bleaching powder to surroundings to control the other smells and to maintain the purity. They also apply "*samrani*" with the belief that after offering samrani worms eat more leaves.

During the Chawki period, they will have a puja and put Lord Ganesh's photo and observe it for one-day with coconut and distribute the sweets, and when they get good yield. Officials gave them small training like in the beginning, because this crop was a bivoltine (Swarnandhra). They also offer potato and coconut to officers after getting good yield.

Old people play an important role in sericulturists' households. Their role can be seen from third molt stage onwards, where labour requirement is more and at the same time they look after their grandchildren. To look after the worms in chandrikas, children's role is unforgettable.

Generally, in most areas where sericulture is practiced, women have a relatively poorer access to productive resources such as land, credit and extension (government provided support of technical services and sericulture materials). While the quality of extension services may vary from place to place, it is almost uniformly found that land is not a resource that is within the reach of women. In most cases, land was in the name of male member of the family. Only in very rare cases could one find that women have land in their names. This has directly affected the credit opportunities for women, when banks consider them as less than credit worthy since they do not fulfil collateral requirements for taking loans. In rural areas, land provides the most visible and tangible collateral for loans.

CONCLUSION

To sum up, women play a significant role in sericulture activity of Kotha Indlu. In some spheres her role may be limited, but women do majority of sericultural work. This indicates her role in the development of community and also able to manage their house in her husbands absence. Here, I quote Kabeer (1996) to conclude my argument in favour of rights and social justice perspective. She says, Women's issues of development theory came to be criticized from different quarters. Since the early 1960s, UN has marked each official 'decade of development' with a declaration summarizing the lessons learnt from past experience and its priorities for the coming ten years.

Between 1960s and 1970s, the feminist movement gained momentum, and the research done by women scholars pointed out that the so-called modernisation theory of development promoted by the development agencies had not benefited women and, in some cases, had adverse effect on women in the Third World. Women had not been given access to new productive opportunities; technology had not liberated them from domestic drudgery; gender-neutral outcomes had not been led by market forces; and, in spite of the forces of modernisation, prejudice and preconceptions about women persisted in society. But, it is true that UN declaration of women's century and international meetings on women issues are paved the way for the recognition of their rights, acts and activities in the families which are not recognised or noticed prominently earlier. It is in this context that this paper addressed the women's role in the community development. This can be probed further to achieve the millennium development goals under gender equality and rights based perspectives on women.

REFERENCES

Boserup, E. (1970), Women's role in Economic Development, New York: St Martin's Press.

Eswarappa Kasi, (2000), Development and Change due to Sericulture- A Study in Chittoor District (An unpublished M. Phil Dissertation submitted to the University of Hyderabad for the Award of M. Phil Degree).

Eswarappa Kasi, (2005), *'Socio-Cultural Dimensions of Sericulture: A Village Study from Andhra Pradesh'*, Theme papers of 'Rural India and Grassroots Development-Volume 1, Bhoovigyan Vikas Foundation, pp. 196-207, New Delhi.

Eswarappa Kasi, (2005), "Sericulture and Community Development in the context of Globalisation: Empirical Evidence of a Village" in the *web Journal of View Point*, No (6) January-July 2005, in HU Sociology group of University of Hyderabad.

Eswarappa Kasi, (2006), *'Sericulture as a Case of Development in the context of Globalisation': A Village Study from Andhra Pradesh*, in *"Trends in Sociology: Education, Development, and Diaspora"*, by Ajay Kumar Sahoo, Sadanand Sahoo and G. Nagaraju, New Delhi: Abhijeet Publisher, pp. 113-139.

Eswarappa Kasi, (2007), *'Role of Sericulturists in the Development of a Village: An Anthropological Study from South India in the Post Green Revolution'* Sucha Singh Gill Stefan Lindberg (Eds) Post Green Revolution Scenarios in South Asia: Ecology and Peasant Life under Globalisation, New Delhi: Sage/Manohar Publications (Forthcoming).

Eswarappa Kasi and R. Siva Prasad titled *"Sericulture and Community Development in the Context of Globalisation: An Empirical Evidence of a Village"* in Bhabani Shankar Nayak (ed) Nationalizing Crisis: The Political Economy of Public Policy in Contemporary India, New Delhi: Atlantic Publishers & Distributors (p) Ltd, Chapter 5, pp. 101-125.

Inbanathan, Anand (1993), Scheduled Caste Women in Reeling Industry, Indian Silk, Vol.32, No.7, pp.13-21.

Inbanathan and Vijayalakshmi, (1997), Women, Sericulture and Development: A Case in South India, in The Journal of Third World Studies, Vol. XIV, No.1.

Kabeer, N. (1996), Reversed realities: Gender hierarchies in development thought. London: Verso.

Kannan, V. A. (1987), Women in Silk Industry, in Indian Silk, May.

Rogers, B. (1980), The Domestication of Women Discrimination in Developing Societies. London: Kogan Page.

Sarker, Debnarayan (2006) Development Theory and Gendered Approach to Development: A Review in the Third World Perspective, *Sociological Bulletin*, 55 (1): 45-66.

Vijayalakshmi *et al.* (1991), 'Employment Generation through Sericulture in Andhra Pradesh', Indian Silk, Vol. XIX;, No. 10, February.

Vijayalakshmi, G. S. (1991), 'Sericulture the Queen of Rural Industry', *Yojana*, Vol. XXIII, No. 21.

EMPOWERING WOMEN BY IMPARTING LEGAL EDUCATION

Rameshwari Pandya[*]

INTRODUCTION

Women have been idolized in India and yet they have also been exploited and denied social justice. This is seen in the increasing incidents of violence on women. In recent years, violence against women has become increasingly visible and an important social issue. Police officials, lawyers, social workers, policy makers and educationists are of the opinion that only a small number of incidents, especially those involving severe injury or death, get newspaper and media coverage. There are social, cultural and economic factors which combine to compel Indian women to play the role of silent victims of violence. All Indian laws get their sanction from the Indian Constitution which guarantees justice, liberty and equality to all citizens of India. The preamble speaks of equality of status and of opportunity for all citizens. Article 14 of the Indian Constitution states that "The State shall not deny to any person equality before the law or the equal protection of the laws within the territory of India".

The Constitution, however, is a document at a high level of abstraction. It is the guiding document of the State. The Indian Constitution is remarkable for its clear-cut emphasis

* Department of Home Science Extension and Communication, M.S. University of Baroda, Gujrat.

towards justice and equality for all. Women in particular, are recognized by the Constitution as weak and vulnerable, therefore are to be given special protection. The Constitution has guaranteed equality to women not only before the law, but also in education, in providing equal opportunities and in public appointments. Women have been made an integral part of the Constitution so that the goals of justice-social, economic and political equality of opportunity for all, can be achieved. Furthermore the Constitution makes special provisions for women to help them improve their social status in society. In the Planning process, under the trickle down theory, it was expected that women will equally benefit along with men. This has been belied by actual developments. The Sixth Plan Document recognizes that "in spite of the Constitutional legal equality given to women, they have lagged behind in almost all sectors". In the past decade, there have been various forces and pressures which have pushed women in to a low and inferior place. These forces have been more dominant than those which should have tried to bring up women towards growth and development.

LAWS: IGNORED; UNKNOWN: UNIMPLEMENTED

Whether legislation exists or does not exist, the benefits are virtually zero. For many women the laws are non-existent or, if existing, insignificant, ill-conceived, delayed or simply not implemented for the women. Though several ameliorative legal provisions have been passed for the welfare of women, they continue to suffer. There is a big gap in the enactment of legal provisions and the benefits reaching the women. Lack of awareness of the rights and lack of knowledge of law is the reason why women continue to be mute victims of an unjust and irrational society.

In short, despite the amendments in laws over a period of time, the advantages of laws have not been used to its fullest which can be attributed to the lack of proper understanding of the law by the women. That is the reason crime rate is on an increase. It is indeed sad that whatever changes and amendments have been made, for the improvement of the legal status of women, have not reached them. The benefits have not reached due to lack of awareness of the beneficiaries as stated in several studies. To a lay person a law is very strange - something distant and incomprehensible. If the law says so, it is irrevocably right and just, even though apparently it may not be so. In the case of women, basically there is injustice built into the system, or justice which has not been brought out forcefully, nor often enough. It is not enough to pass a law. There should be continuous education of the people, for the real purpose behind the various laws so that they themselves can become the epitomes of law and justice.

ROLE OF MEDIA IN SPREADING LEGAL AWARENESS

The laws are seen to remain a dead letter until there is pressure for its implementation. There are many examples all over the country where progressive laws exist but have had no impact because they remain unimplemented. The findings of the various studies and the observations made by the Joshi Committee on software, confirm the invisibility of women. T.V., the medium which is supposed to educate and inform, has very little information about the actual condition of women. (Sharmskati 1987, p. 189). Women are provided beauty tips, but no advice is given to women who are unhappy in their marital home, on how they should take help from the law. Advice is given on how to be a good wife and a good mother by making adjustments within the family situation. Doordarshan repeatedly portrays women as house bound engaged in homemaking entirely dependent for their existence and fulfillment on their husbands and children. The struggle that women are facing for economic and political autonomy, legal rights and identify is almost completely ignored.

> Laws relating to women are rarely covered in the media and issues related to women are let out. It rarely receive the

> necessary exposure, so that at least through word-of-mouth, information may trickle down from one literate, informed women to another. Women's plight, hardly seen newsworthy matters. Even when media attention is given they are usually sensationalized with headlines such as 'Minor raped in K.E.M. Hopital'.
>
> Sharmskati 1987, p. 179

There is an attempt in print media to maintain the status quo, and counteract good articles on women with negative ideas and images. For example, an article on harassment of women may be subsequently trivialized by a light-hearted account on 'eve teasing' highlighted by a cartoon. However, lately radio, television and other mass communication media have exposed the women to information and knowledge about legal provisions. However, such exposure has not yet resulted in creating consciousness to the desired extent among women, nor have they succeeded in loosening the hold of tradition-oriented thinking of the masses. Over the last two decades, due to the constant campaigns of women's groups and the overall impact of the women's decade, which was declared by U.N.O., there has been a steady increase in the serious coverage on women's issues. This is also because women themselves are becoming articulate, bold and expressive. Issues such as violence, dowry and sexual harassment, which were at one time dismissed as the problems of an individual woman, are being seen within socio-political structural context. The result is that, there is an awareness in the print media with women wishing to discuss problems such as gender subordination, social and sexual exploitation, legal disabilities and wage discrimination. Committed individuals and groups are leaving no stone unturned to get the message to the concerned persons.

> By and large, women have been ignored or treated as sex objects. Attempts have been made by free lanse, journalists, activists, academicians and concerned staff to counteract these features.
>
> Sharmskati 1987, p. 202

Some research organizations also produce journals and newsletters wherein information about women in the organized sector is disseminated and for the first time, attention has been drawn to the oppressive conditions of women in India.

> The Commission strongly recommends a special drive for imparting legal literacy to women so as to enable them to be aware of the existing legislations and the methodologies through which they can take benefit under the legislation.
>
> Sharmskati 1987, p. 293

The struggle for legal equality has been one of the major concerns of women movement all over the world. Whether in the internal situation of her position in the parental or matrilineal home or in the external situation of acquiring education, skills, profession, employment, all these involve law. Even best of the intentions to generate an atmosphere of equality can not easily overcome the thousands of years of social distance perpetrated by caste, class, community and gender differences. Women themselves need to develop a self identity so that they can lead a life of security and dignity. This can be achieved by making them aware of their legal rights and potentials. A number of social enactments have been put on the status books for removing various constraints which hinder women's progress. Inspite of these measures, women have been lagged behind by men in different spheres. Home science, today is inadequate without inclusion of legal knowledge in its curricula. The University Grants Commission has also emphatically recommended guidelines for restructuring and reviewing courses so that new ideas, concepts, content and structure can be incorporated. It has suggested that the courses at college should have more application-oriented components. The National Policy of Education (1986) had also laid special emphasis on the education of women and suggested reviewing and reorganizing the educational activities to ensure that it makes a substantial contribution towards women's equality. Therefore, by introducing a course on women and law, which will make students aware of their legal rights. The investigator reviewed the literature in the form of reports of Government of India, Seminar and workshop reports, research reports, books, journals and newspaper articles. All these confirm the fact that there are various laws for the benefit of women but because of lack of their awareness, women are victimized.

LEGAL EDUCATION: THE NEED OF THE HOUR

Today's girls are going to be future women and they may have to face the world where the crime rates are progressively increasing. It, therefore, becomes very important to educate these young girls about their legal rights. This would also help to create awareness, understanding and sensitivity among them. Moreover, the home scientists must use their foresight to prepare women for the time of crises. The general observation and practical experiences of the investigator is that the legal knowledge and awareness among Home Science students is very poor. The results of the feasibility study conducted by the investigator with a sample of first year Home Science students in March 1990, revealed that students have a positive opinion towards legal education as a course in Home Science. More than 90 per cent respondents agreed that legal education is desirable for Home Science students. Further, the findings showed that, there were only about 40 per cent girls who had correct awareness of the different laws concerning women. The remaining 60 per cent either did not have any awareness or had incorrect awareness. The feasibility study also supports the need for legal education to be given to Home Science students, because only 10 per cent of the respondents never had a course on legal education in school or outside the school by any other agency. This highlights the need for a formal education system to impart legal education to the girls so that it could be of some help at the time of distress.

Generally one avoids reading about the laws as it is assumed that legal jargon is too difficult to understand and that laws are not pertinent to our lives. Therefore, an introductory course could be planned in simple and understandable language, highlighting the issues relevant to women. Women in India suffer from a variety of social and economic disabilities which prevent them from exercising their human rights and freedom in society. During the last few decades, a number of legislations have been passed with a view to ensuring equality of status and opportunities for women. In practice, however, it seems it has eluded women. Therefore, it is important to educate the women about the radical changes in the law. Reviews of the studies conducted established that awareness of women regarding laws is very poor. It was further revealed that a change was creeping slowly and steadily in policies of government, women's organizations and need to spread legal education is felt.

A sizeable theoretical literature was available on effectiveness of T.V. or Video but very limited literature was found on teaching college students through video.

There is a need to develop systematic video film on "Women and Law". The amount of investigation, research on video film is limited which necessitated further exploration in this area. It is established that the law related course are strongly recommended for women. Although need to educate women about law is felt, a systematic beginning has not been done. Therefore, undertaking a study to develop the content of "Women and Law" to teach Home Science students assumes significance. Thus, it is obvious that course "Women and Law" can play a catalytic role in bringing about social change which is also one of the ultimate aims of Home Science education.

Legal education in Home Science should be considered more seriously than anything else because in recent years crime against women has assumed giant shape. Even facts related to figures on crime serve as an eye opener for Home Scientists whose activities are geared towards betterment of family, community and nation, keeping the women as their focus. Undertaking a study to develop the content of course "Women and Law" in relation to the curriculum of Home Science assumed significance and should be given appropriate priority. Keeping the above justifications in mind, a study on

"Developing a course and video instructional package on "Women and Law" and measuring the effectiveness of package with the students of Faculty of Home Science, Baroda", was undertaken.

The very nature of investigation necessitated undertaking multidimensional study revolving around those aspects of "Women and Law", which were not investigated in the past. The study was carried out using content analysis, experimentation and survey methods. Developing course, producing video films, experimentation with the video films on "Women and Law" formed the nucleus of the study.

MAJOR OBJECTIVES

1. To develop an effective introductory course on "Women and Law".
2. To develop video instructional package on "Women and Law".
3. To study the effectiveness of video package to teach "Women and Law" to the first year Home Science students in terms of performance of students of knowledge test.

FEASIBILITY STUDY

The investigator conducted a feasibility study in March 1990 in the Faculty of Home Science, M. S. University, Baroda. Sixty First Year students were selected in such a way that there were twenty students, each representing Art, Commerce, Science streams. Such a selection permitted a comparison between the awareness of students regarding laws pertaining to women and enabled the investigator to know whether the type of school education and characteristics of the students affected the awareness and opinions of the students. The purpose of the feasibility study was to find out the data and background information of the students, source of legal information, their opinion about legal education being given to the girls and the correct knowledge about laws related to women like age for marriage, divorce, dowry, rape, eve teasing, inheritance, maintenance, etc. It was intended that the findings of the feasibility study will help the investigator to crystallize her problem, to determine the feasibility of the doctoral study, to draw a meaningful sample and to select the relevant variables. The data were collected with the help of questionnaire.

IMPLICATION OF THE FINDINGS AND FEASIBILITY STUDY FOR THE PRESENT STUDY

The feasibility study showed that there is a lack of awareness among Home Science students regarding laws related to women. Findings showed that there were only 30 per cent girls who had correct awareness of the different laws concerning women. The remaining 70 per cent did not have any awareness or had incorrect awareness. This implies that corrective measures need to be taken and education on this aspect need to be provided. The feasibility study also supported the need for legal education to be given to Home Science students because only 10 per cent of the respondents have had formal legal education, and rest had never been offered a course on legal education in either school or college. An encouraging observation of the feasibility study was that the girls had very favourable opinions about the need for imparting legal education. Thus, if a course on "Women and Law", is initiated it would be well received. The variability of different characteristics of Home Science students confirmed certain assumptions and helped the investigator to formulate hypotheses like relationship between personal and demographic variables with awareness regarding laws and opinions about legal education to be give to Home Science students.

POPULATION OF THE STUDY

The population of the present experimental study consisted of 306 First Year students of the Faculty of Home Science, M. S. University of Baroda, in the year 1992-93. However, in reality only 279 students were attending the classes and the others dropped out. In other words, the population consisted of 279 students.

SAMPLE

The following summary shows the number of student viewers and absentees for each video film.

Summary of Number of Viewers and Absentees for Seven Video Films

Video Film	*Class Strength*	*Viewers*		*Absentees*	
	(N)	*f*	*%*	*f*	*%*
Introduction	279	207	74.2	72	25.8
Eve Teasing	279	225	90.6	54	19.4
Inheritance	279	184	65.9	95	34.1
Marriage	279	217	77.8	62	22.2
Dowry	279	237	84.9	42	15.1
Divorce	279	233	83.5	46	16.5
Rape	279	215	77.1	64	22.9

It was decided to let the whole class of the Ist year view all the seven video films. But as the whole population did not remain present to view the video films, selective sample were only available for each video film instead of the population. Upon checking the attendance at the viewing of each film it was found that some students were absent at each viewing. Therefore, the numbers of viewers and absentees is presented in the summary. 306 students paid the fees in the Faculty office, but only 279 students attended the classes. From the total number of 279, different number of students were absent at the viewing of the video films. Thus, the selective samples for each video film had different number, as shown in the summary.

TOOLS FOR DATA COLLECTION

A battery of tools was prepared by the researcher to collect the required information. The data collection tool for each purpose was as follows.

Purpose	*Tool*
1. Background Information	Questionnaire cum Checklist with structured items.
2. English language competence	Examination office records
3. Academic Achievement	Office records
4. Socio-economic status	Standardized Socio-Economic Scale prepared by Desai (1987).
5. Modernity	Scale to measure level of modernity adapted and standardized by Mehta et al (1974) from the original 'OM' Scale of Modernity for Indian conditions
6. Personality	The personality inventory by A. Hafeez and V. S. Shantamani (1974)
7. Gain in Knowledge	Seven tests on "Women and Law" having recall and recognition items, True and False, Fill in the blanks, multiple choice.

SCORING AND CATEGORIZATION

For scoring and categorization of data, different procedures were used. The weightage was given to all the items of the questionnaire. The total number of respondents which might fall in each category was divided by the scores which they received. The scores of the respondents were considered for deciding the range of each category.

The first part of the questionnaire contained questions regarding background information of the respondents of the study. No scoring had to be done for this part and the variables were categorized directly according to the questions.

Variable	*Categories*	*Range of Score*
1. Stream in Higher Secondary	Arts, Science, Commerce, Any other	-
2. Medium of instruction	English, Gujarati, Any Other	-
3. Place of residence	City, Town, Village	

4. Choosing Major	Related to Science, Related to Social Science	1, 2
5. Legal education in family	LL.B., LL.M.	0-1, 0-1
6. Family's social work background		0-1
7. Involvement in Legal cases		0-1
8. Mother's occupation		0-
9. Exposure to television and video		

Scores were given to the students for this variable. The possible scores ranged from least (0) to maximum (37). The respondents were divided into two categories under this variable as follows.

Criterion	*Range of Score*	*Category*
Below mean	0-18	Less exposure
Mean and above	19 and above	More exposure

Second part of the questionnaire had items to measure socio-economic status of the respondents. The scoring was done according to Desai scoring pattern, 1987. The categorization was done as follows:

Variables	*Category*	*Range of Score*
Socio-economic status	High	26-35
	Middle	21-25
	Low	0-20

Third part of the questionnaire had items to measure level of overall modernity. The scoring was done according to the Alex Inkele's scoring pattern, 1974. The categorization was done as follows:

Criterion	Range of Score	Category
Overall	Modern	8-13
Modernity	Conservative	4-7

The fourth part of the questionnaire had items to measure personality of the respondents. The scoring was done accordingly of the respondents. The scoring was done accordingly to A. Hafeez and V. S. Shanthamani scoring pattern, 1974. The categorization was done as follows.

Range of Score	Personality traits
8-10	High extroversion
5-10	High introversion
below 8 in extroversion below 5in introversion	Ambiversion

For the variable Academic achievement, the office record was used by the researcher by obtaining the percentage of the marks secured by the First Year B.Sc. (Home) students in the Board examinations of twelfth standard. The categorization was done as follows.

Variable	Categories	Scores
Academic achievement	High	60-75 Ist division
	Low	45-59 IInd division

For the variable of competence in English, the student's previous semester's grade in English subject was taken as an indicator of their competence in English. The grades for the English course were collected from Faculty examination office. The respondents were divided into two categories according to the grades secured by them in English subject in first semester in the seven point scale.

They were as follows:

English grade	*Category of competence*
B and above	Good
C and below	Poor

Knowledge Tests: As discussed before, the knowledge tests were completely objective in nature. Each correct answer was given a score of one and the incorrect answer was given zero score. The maximum obtainable score for one knowledge test was 20. A key was prepared for scoring the tests. Thus, seven tests were made to check the knowledge gian from seven video films.

METHOD OF PROCEDURE

Developing Outline for the Course "Women and Law"

In order to develop the outline of the present course, content analysis of the course outline of the related courses was done. An outline was drawn in light of broad objectives of the course "Women and Law". The developed outline was validated by the experts and ws revised according to their suggestions.

Planning for Experimental Teaching

The units for the experimental teaching were selected and five libraries were consulted for collecting subject matter for teaching. The subject matter obtained for the course "Women and Law" was then organized. Unit plans for teaching the experimental units were developed and were validated by the experts.

Preparation of The Video Films

For preparation of the video films full length of scripts with a complete list of visual illustration and accompanying sound was made.

Mode of Presentation

The mode of presentation of the content was as follows:

Topic of the Unit	*Title of the Film*	*Format*	*Type of the Film*
Introduction	Introduction to Law	Documentary, Interview	Informative
Eve Teasing	Are you Eve teased?	Documentary, Interview	Informative
Inheritance	Law of Inheritance	Interview, Illustrative talk	Informative
Dowry	Is Dowry legal?	Dramatization, Illustrative talk	Persuasive Information
Marriage	Marriage made easy with law	Dramatization, Illustrative talk	Persuasive Information
Divorce	Law of Divorce	Interview, Lecture	Informative
Rape	Trauma of Rape !	Lecture, Illustrative talk	Informative

Mode of presentation of video films was decided mainly in such a way that it achieves the objectives and yet presentation is done in interesting and practical manner. Since the films were made to impart information about various laws related to women mainly informative approach was used in writing the scripts.

Experimental Teaching

Experimental teaching with the video film was done after conducting the pretest for all seven video films.

Administering The Post-test

The post-test was administered immediately after the video teaching. The researcher personally with the help of two assistants took the classes of First Year for experimentation. One theory class of 55 minutes was taken for one session of pretest, experimental teaching and post-test. Thus, each group had seven classes of teaching of the selected units of "Women and Law" through seven video films.

THE EXPERIMENTAL TEACHING AND DATA COLLECTION

The questionnaires were printed in different colours, one for each law. The experiment was conducted with 279 First Year Home Science students in the month of March and April 1993. For data collection, the groups formed by the Faculty office were used. The experiment was conducted by administering pre-test, experimental teaching and post-test on the students. Personality, Modernity and Socio-economic scale were also administered. Data thus gathered, were scored using the predetermined keys for the respective research tools.

ANALYSIS OF DATA

The analysis of data was done in IBM-PC/AT 386 compatible computer system. The various statistical procedure were used for the analysis of data. Keeping in view the objectives of the study, the following statistical methods were used for analyzing the data.

1. Frequency and percentage distribution
2. Mean Scores
3. Paired 't' test
4. Analysis of covariance

MAJOR FINDINGS

1. Majority of the students were from general stream having urban background with social science inclination and majority did not possess legal and social work background.
2. Majority of the respondents were modern and extroverts although their mothers were housewives.
3. Nearly equal percentages of respondents were having high as well as low exposure to TV and video.

4. Majority of students were form high socio-economic status and nearly 60 per cent had high English competence, but low academic achievement.
5. All the seven video films were effective as there was considerable increase in the mean scores of the students achievement on post-test for all the seven video films.
6. Overall, the film "Trauma of Rape!" was found to be most effective and film on "Introduction of Law" was least effective.
7. The Science stream respondents gained significantly higher than the general stream respondents for all the seven video films.
8. There was significant difference in gain in knowledge of students from English medium school as they learnt more in comparison to the students form vernacular schools.
9. Respondents who had science inclination learnt significantly higher than the respondents having social science inclination.
10. The presence and absence of legal exposure had nothing to do with the knowledge gain. However, in some ıses, the previous legal exposure of student's family raised this awareness.
11. The respondents from city learnt significantly higher from the film 'Are you eve-teased ?' For rest of the films variable place of residence did not play any.
12. The film 'Marriage made easy with law' was found most effective by the respondents whose mothers were housewives.
13. The effect of variable 'English competence' was found to be significant for all the seven video films.
14. The respondents form high socio-economic status gained significantly higher from the video films in comparison to students from middle and low socio economic groups.

15. There was no significant difference in learning, in relation to Social work background, TV and video exposure, Modernity, Academic achievement and Personality.

CONCLUSIONS AND IMPLICATIONS BASED ON FINDINGS

In order to use video films in teaching a course "Women and Law", certain conclusions can be drawn on the basis of the findings of the present study. It is difficult to conclude with maximum certainty on the basis of this study, because it is the first study of its kind, and has built-in limitations of the sample and the nature of the experiment. It can be said from this first multidimensional study, that the developed outline of the course "Women and Law" is learnable and acceptable by students and yet there is a wide scope for its expansion. The course outline was developed logically as a 'Model' was adopted to develop the course and precautions were taken to assure that no psychological gaps in learning occurs. As this was the first attempt, the content was deliberately simplified and the evaluation of learning was also simple. May be later on some advanced course can be planned.

However, it can be concluded from the present findings that the detailed outline of a course "Women and Law", was feasible for learning as there was apparent gain knowledge of the students after viewing the video films based on such a course outline. The trends of findings of quasi-experiment further supported learning theories which postulate that the increased reinforcement, recapitulation, cumulative sequence, and psychological arrangement of the topics enhance learning, as a significant gain in knowledge was found for all the seven video films on "Women and Law". Therefore, it can be concluded that well balanced and systematically organized films can be produced by teachers. The teachers should be encouraged to use such video films for teaching instead of lectures alone.

As the films tried to include most of the required teaching resources which are not always possible in the class room situation, they added to the clarity and understanding regarding the topic. For example, the 'Drama' shown in the video film may not be brought to the classroom in the live situation. Thus, video films tried to overcome the limitations of a lecture method and thereby helping the students to gain more knowledge. It is said, 'seeing is believing' and these videos have visuals with the commentary on the subject matter, to illustrate this principle. Illustration and motion in the video films held the attention of the learners and helped to score high in the knowledge test.

Considering the wider, and modern concept of the Home Science Education, the course on law becomes very much a part of its content. Therefore, teaching laws through video films will prove very useful in Home Science colleges. The delivery of content through the video films was direct, simple, open, down to earth, which facilitated learning of law. The entire positive findings can be attributed to ease, simplicity and directness of the video films. Along with this finding, the investigator took great care of making everybody comfortably seated while viewing. The whole class was divided into small groups, close to the video which helped the students in internalizing the content.

The laws which were selected were for young women regardless of their characteristics. The teaching of laws through seven video films concretely showed that women need to know these laws related to women. However, significant differences were found in the gain in knowledge regarding "Women and Law", in relation to stream of study, medium of instruction, social science inclination, and English competence. Thus, these variables were found to be very relevant. Although some other variables were relevant from a social point of view, very small portions of the sample were having variables namely, Legal Exposure, Social work background and place of residence. The effect of these variables could not be found because of sample size was very small. It is also possible to describe and operationally define these variables in a totally different manner in a future study, and to discover about their relation to learning of laws.

On the other hand, there may bc some other variables which could help in learning of law. The Home Science students perceive the need to learn laws related to women. Perhaps today's college students face situations of crimes against women like disregard of property rights, marriage and divorce problem. Therefore, their sensitivity to learn laws could have developed. The present students thus, can be considered more motivated to learn laws. It is the prime time for them to be taught laws. The need to become more independent, more self protective and more knowledgeable, seems to have developed in college students. Therefore, it is justified to teach laws.

In the video films the laws were described in a straight forward informative manner and the content on law was simplified for the undergraduate level. There were not many analytical situations regarding the use or knowledge of laws. The test was simple and it lacked the use of analytical power. It was a direct test having only recall and recognition items, and, therefore, much discrimination among the students was not possible. This was deliberately done as there was no precedence for teaching of laws. Moreover, there is a general feeling that teaching of law is dry and boring. So to overcome these difficulties, investigator purposely made such video films and tests. No special method to teach and evaluate learning of laws was found by the investigator in her literature search. Hence, teaching and testing of knowledge both were rather simple. In future it could be tougher than this.

A more clear picture may be derived when a tight experiment is employed by exercising control on the variables and randomizing the sample. The methods of teaching and evaluating the learning can be more specific in a future study.

RECOMMENDATIONS

The investigator on the basis of her experience during experimentation and findings of the study recommends that:

1. A similar type of study can be conducted including control group and retention test.
2. A similar type of study can be conducted with other variables related to media utilization.
3. Production and validation of the video films on more laws related to women other than included in the present study can be tried out.
4. A comparative study of the effectiveness of the present video package in teaching formal and non-formal group of women can be conducted.
5. A similar type of study can be conducted with other samples like, students form different levels and specializations.
6. A study can be taken up with other instructional strategies on the same topic.
7. The strategies having both software and hardware components can be developed and tried out.

REFERENCES

Agarwal, B. C. and Chandiram J. Towards Equality : Women in Indian T.V. Media Asea 1982.

Anderson, H. R. Selecting and Developing Media for Instruction. Van Nostrand Reinhold Co. Inc. 1976.

Barbro, O. H. Violence Against Women. Women and Health 13 (3-4) Studies on Women Abstracts, Vol. 7, No. 3, 1989.

Bhagat, R. Impact of Mass Media on Farm Women, A Study *Kurukshetra* August 1988.

Bhoite, A. Sex Ratio and the Status of Women in India. *Ahfad Journal* 5(7) 1988.

Chandra, A. Introduction to Home science, New Delhi, Metropolitan Book Company Pvt. Ltd., 1978.

Chatterji, S. A. The Indian Women's Search for an Identity, Delhi, Vikas Publishing House.

Decade for Women-world Conference Nairobi Kenya, July 1985. Report by Centre for Women's Development Studies, New Delhi, 1986.

Dosi, J. K. Television for Development, *Journal of the Council for Social Development,* 13(4), 1983.

Dowry Deaths. *Hindustan Times* (Delhi) 12 Aug. 1989.

Dua M. R. Themes in Indian Communication. Metropolitan Book Co. (P) Ltd. New Delhi, 1980.

Gore, M. S. Education for Women's Equality, New Delhi. Centre of Women's Development Studies, 1988.

Women's Religion and Family Law" Asian Women's Conference Report. Bombay, Dec. 16-20, 1987.

Haksar, N. and Singh N. Demystification of Law for Women, New Delhi, Lancer Press, 1986.

India Ministry of Human Resource Development. National Policy on Education. New Delhi, May 1986.

Joshi, V. Menon, G. Research on Women's Education in India. A Review, Perspectives in Education, 1986, Vol. 2, No. 2.

Majority of Women Unaware of Rights. (Hindustan Times, Patna, 7 Dec. 1987) in *Legal News and Views* 1987, Vol. XII (12).

Mittal L. N. Women's Studies in Curriculum Development. *University News* April 20, 1992.

Sharmaskati : Report on the National Commission on Self-employed Women and Women in the Informal Sector, 1988.

ISSUE OF UNIFORM CIVIL CODE IN INDIA AND THE OPINION OF THE KOLKATA MUSLIMS

*Ujjwal Bhui**

PLAN OF WORK

I. Executive Summary.

II. Supreme Court's Recommendations for Uniform Civil Code (UCC).

III. Origin and Development of the idea of UCC in India.

IV. Post Independence Debate (Recent General Tendency).

V. Indian Government's Policy or Attitude towards UCC.

VI. Conclusion and Suggestion.

VII. Survey work (conducted to know Kolkata Muslims opinion about UCC related issues).

EXECUTIVE SUMMARY

The existing/growing inconsistencies within the personal laws of different religious communities have all along been a subject of academic debate having serious practical implications. The social unrest turned out after pronouncement of the judgment in the Shah Bano case, the non-proper functioning of the Hindu Code Bill of 1955, the Indian Census Report of 1961 which made known that the

---

* Lecturer, Centre for Himalayan Studies, North Bengal University, West Bengal.

percentage of Hindus having more than one wife was more than many of the other religious communities specially of the Muslims, the recent judgment of the Darul Qaza (Shariat court) on Imrana case which is considered as in conflict with or parallel to the Indian judicial system[1] - all these happenings continuously remind us of the Uniform Civil Code, whether it is necessary or not in India.

This paper desires to discuss theoretically- the development of the issue of uniform civil code in India and also the knowledge- practically gained in the Kolkata Muslim society to make out its opinion related to the above mentioned issue in addition to the existing Muslim personal law in India.

SUPREME COURTS RECOMMENDATIONS FOR UNIFORM CIVIL CODE (UCC)

The issue of uniform civil code in India is an aspect which is always surrounded by controversy. It took a high momentum in 1995 which had arisen not due to the agenda of any political party or any community demand, but because of the Supreme Court judgment in the Sarla Mudgal vs. Government of India Case. Justice Kuldeep Singh and Justice R. Sahay, the two Judges of the Division Bench for that case, raised the question of necessity of the Uniform Civil Code on the ground that the absence of such a code resulted in some Hindus adopting or converting themselves to Islam so that they could marry one/ more women regardless of the fact that their wives were alive and had not been divorced, for the reason that the Muslim Personal Law permitted a Muslim man to marry four women or can keep four wives at a time. The Division Bench of this case made the following pronouncement: "We, therefore, request the Government of India through the Prime Minister of the country to have a fresh look at Article 44 of the Constitution and endeavour to secure for the citizens a uniform civil code throughout the territory of India".[2]

The other Judge of that Division Bench, Justice Sahay remarked, "but religious practices, violative of human rights and dignity and sacerdotal suffocation of essentially civil and material freedoms are not autonomy but oppression. Therefore, a unified code is imperative both for protection of the oppressed and promotion of national unity and solidarity".[3]

The Supreme Court had also given instructions to the Indian government to carryout the principles as enshrined in the Constitution under Article 44. This article under Directive Principles of State Policy directs the government to ensure uniform civil code through all parts of the country. Based on this article, the court opined that the second marriage of a Hindu male after conversion to Islam should lawfully make him prosecute for bigamy – the criminal offence of marrying one person which still legally married to another. This type of marriage would be treated as non-existent and a void marriage in terms of Section 494 of the Indian Penal Code which deals with bigamy. In such a case, even though the husband has adopted Islam, the marriage would be treated under the Hindu marriage act.

Earlier, in April 1985, the Supreme Court of India gave an exceptional judicial decision- the grant of maintenance right to Shah Bano, a divorced Muslim woman. The judgment had a considerable contemporary social significance. It formulated and issued a decree that Shah Bano, divorced by her husband after 43 years of marriage, was entitled or has a legal claim to maintenance from her husband. Addressing itself to this maintenance issue whether the Muslim personal law laying an obligation up to the husband, the court further ruled that a Muslim woman, unable to maintain herself, was entitled to apply under section 125 of the Criminal Procedure Code which applied to all communities irrespective of their separate personal laws. In case of clash between some provisions of the criminal procedure code and the Muslim personal law the former would prevail. The Supreme Court also questioned what steps the government was taking for adopting a uniform civil code as stipulated in Article 44 of the Indian constitution.

In a recent judgment[4], the Supreme Court has instructed the Indian government for a uniform civil code in India as enshrined in Indian constitution under Article 44. This judgment was given in a case related to discrepancies in the Christian Inheritance Act. Section 118 of Indian Inheritance Act restricts a Christian from donating his/her property for charitable or religious purposes. Chief Justice Khare, Justice S.B Sinha and Justice A.R.Laxman - the three Judges of the Division Bench for that case cancelled the Section 118 as according to them this section is 'unconstitutional'and 'discriminating to the Christians'. They reminded that this section does not protect the assurance of 'Equality of Law' (Article 14) of Indian Constitution.

ORIGIN AND DEVELOPMENT OF THE IDEA OF UCC IN INDIA

The National Planning committee which was constituted by the National Congress introduced the notion of uniform civil code in the political arena of the forties of twentieth century when it made a demand for the code. At that time, when the Constituent Assembly Debates were going on, Minoo Masani, Rajkumari Amrit Kaur, Hansa Mehta voted in favour of a clause on a uniform civil code, but many of the members of the sub-committee voted against it on the reason that it was outside the scope of fundamental rights.

Here it is necessary to discuss the earlier developments regarding the unified civil laws of India. During the days of struggle for independence, some sections of Muslim society were very much anxious about their personal laws' constitutional status in the forthcoming independence era. They organized themselves to bring efforts to get constitutional protection of the Muslim personal law. But the Government of India Act, 1935 did not consider either the ultimate ambitions of the Muslim organizations or the concessions granted upon by the National Congress[5] in respect of Muslim personal law. In opposition to what was expected, the Act authorized the federal as well as the Provincial legislatures to formulate laws relating to "marriages and divorce; infants and minors; adoption and wills."[6] The

Government of India Act, 1935 made those Muslims unhappy who had been contending for long to secure constitutional protection of their personal law. The Muslim personal law (Shariat)Application Act and the Dissolution of Muslim Marriages Act were enacted in between 1937 and 1939 which made the Muslims more anxious as some provisions of these Acts were against the proposals of the Muslim organizations.[7] Hence, the leaders of these organizations became more vociferous about a constitutional protection for Muslim personal law. For this purpose, Pocker Saheb in his speech on the report on minority rights in August 1947, demanded separate electorates for the Muslims to elect candidates of their choices in the Central and Provincial legislatures[8] but his demand was ruled out by the Constituent Assembly.[9]

In November, 1948, Dr.Ambedkar presented the draft constitution to the Constituent Assembly for discussion. At the time of discussion, he observed that the Draft Constitution has adopted to secure "uniformity in fundamental laws, civil and criminal"[10], which are essential "to maintain the unity of the country".[11] Accordingly, Article 35(The present Article 44) of the Draft Constitution provided that "The State shall endeavour to secure for citizens a uniform civil code throughout the territory of India". The objective of the article is to eliminate the conflicting practices of various communities in the field of civil laws comprising marriage, divorce, inheritance and succession etc. with the enactment of such a code.

There was a heated discussion when Article 35 was debated in the Constituent Assembly. Some members wanted amendments to that article so as to exclude the personal laws from the domain of the common civil code. Mohammad Ismail, Naziruddin Ahmed, Mahboob Ali Baig, Pocker Bahadur Saheb and Hussain Imam were in favour of such amendments. On the other hand, Alladi Krishnaswamy Ayyar, K.M.Munshi, Dr.Ambedkar opposed such desired amendments and emphasized on the adoption of Article 35 by the Assembly without any exemption of personal laws from the domain of the potential civil code.

K.M. Munshi, one of the members of the Constituent Assembly commented on the importance of this subject in the Assembly, "We are going go consolidate and unify our personal laws in such away that the way of the whole country may, in course of time, be unified and secular."[12] In this respect Alladi Krishnaswamy Ayyar also observed–"The idea is that differential systems of inheritance and other matters are some of the factors which contribute to differences among the different peoples of India. What it aims at is to try to arrive at a measure of agreement in regard to these matters"[13]

However there was a contrary opinion also as some of the Muslim members of the Constituent Assembly tried to exempt the Muslim personal law from any type of state control.

Mohammad Ismail stated that a secular state should not interfere with the personal laws of a people. The right of every community to follow its personal law is apart of the fundamental right to religious freedom. He also opined that to secure 'harmony through unity', it is not necessary to 'regiment' the civil law of the people."[14]

Whereas Hussain Imam[15] wondered whether there could be uniformity of civil laws in a multiform country like India. He questioned the possibility and desirability of having uniformity on subjects like marriage, divorce, succession, inheritance, etc. which are based on the necessities of different communities. He also mentioned that for bringing uniformity in civil law, we should wait till the time when people became advanced; their economic conditions improved and mass illiteracy should be removed.

Naziruddin Ahmed wished for a security that the personal law of any community would not be altered without the "previous approval of that community". He also said that the provision of Article 35 failed to agree with the fundamental right to religious freedom, which had already been adopted by the Assembly; it would permit the state to violate that guarantee as the laws related to the validity of marriages and divorces were regulated by religion. He also mentioned that time was not 'ripe for effecting uniformity in civil laws; the power given to the state to make the civil code uniform was in advance of time'. The enactment of that Code should be done gradually and with the consent of the people concerned.[16]

At the same time, Pocker Sahib Bahadur put forward some objections in the constituent assembly against the making of uniform civil code throughout India: firstly, it would violate the fundamental right of freedom of religion as mentioned in Article 25 and secondly, it would be a tyranny to minority.[17]

But Munshi and Alladi dismissed the rationale and substance of these objections.[18] The first objection was dismissed as the Directive included in Article 35 (present Article 44) in no way violates the freedom of religion guaranteed by Article 25 Clause (2) of Article 25 specifically saves the secular activities associated with religious practices from the guarantee of religious freedom included in clause (1).

The second disagreement was also invalidated by K.M. Munshi by remarking that when the Shariat Act, 1937 was passed; the Khojas and Cutchi Memons were highly dissatisfied as that time they followed certain Hindu customs for generations since they became converts and so they did not want to conform to the Shariat. Then certain Muslim members who felt that the Shariat law should be enforced upon the whole community carried their point. The Khojas and Cutchi Memons most unwillingly had to submit to it. Where the rights of minorities then....It were is not, therefore, correct to say that such an act is tyranny of the majority."

According to the framers of the constitution, the proposed formation on of uniform civil code would be more tyrannous to the majority than the minority. K. M. Munshi while reaching to this point remarked in the Constituent Assembly –"I know there are many among Hindus who don't like a uniform civil code.... they felt that the personal law of inheritance, succession etc., is really a part of their religion. If that were so, you can never give, for instance, equality to women. But you have already passed a fundamental right to that effect and you have an article which lies down that there should be no discrimination against sex. Look at Hindu law, you get any amount of discrimination against women; and if that is part of Hindu religion or Hindu religious practice, you cannot pass a single law which would elevate the position of Hindu women to that of men. Therefore, apart from matters which strictly belong to religion, the rest of life must be regulated, unified and modified."[19]

Dr. B.R.Ambedkar emphasized that in a secular state, religion should not be allowed to govern all human activities and that personal laws should be divorced from religion. He rejected the proposals for amendments to article 35 and said that if India could have uniform laws of crimes, contract, property, trade and commerce it could have uniform laws of marriage and succession as well. He also gave an assurance that the future parliament might enact uniform civil code but would apply it only to those who voluntarily submit to its provisions.[20]

Finally the Constituent Assembly refused all the amendments[21] and adopted Article 35 (present Article 44). In spite of that (rejection of the amendments), the Assembly agreed to include the stipulation within the Directive Principles to relieve Muslim anxiety or fear. The Directive Principles of State Policy aimed, as laid down in the Constitution under Article 44 (the Constitution was adopted on 26 January 1950), to have a uniform civil code for all the Indians. The Article states: "The State endeavours to secure for the citizens a uniform civil code throughout the territory of India". As Article 44 is a part of Directive Principles of State Policy (Part IV), it shall not be enforceable by any court. It shall be the duty of the State to apply these principles in making laws.

POST INDEPENDENCE DEBATE (RECENT GENERAL TENDENCY)

After India's independence and adoption of a new constitution, the Indian government continued with the systematization and improvement of the Hindu personal law. When the opponents of this reform reminded the government of the constitutional directive to enact a uniform civil code, the government said in a session of the Lok Shabha that the reform in the Hindu Code was the first step towards the enactment of a uniform civil code in India.

However after the enactment of the Hindu reform laws in 1956, there had been no notable movement on the part of the government to introduce the process of formulating a uniform civil code up to the time of the Shah Bano dispute. In these days, when uniform civil code is endeavoured to be formulated, there are resistances. The resistance has come from woman groups also. The erudite persons of constitutional subjects are also in a different mood towards the formulation of the proposed common civil code.

Prof. Paras Dewan[22] remarked: "It is simply a question of equal facility of law to all sections of our people. The question is simply this that all people of India, in all matters- except the matters coming under protective discrimination- should be governed by the same set of laws". Regarding the anomalies in the different personal laws of different communities, he states: "Should a male or female belonging to one community have more than one spouse? Does it lay in our mouth to say that guardianship or custody of a child should be differently determined just because the child belongs to one or the other religion?[23]

Prof. Mahendra Pal Singh, Dean, Faculty of Law, Delhi University mentions that this social situation is not perfect for 'imposing'uniform civil code all over India. According to him, there 'can' be different laws for different people. No community would like to be governed by other community's laws- the community may be Hindu or Muslim or other any.

A Hindu would not like to be governed by a law of Shariat. The same case would happen to a Muslim who would not like to be governed by a Hindu law. He also supports Mr. H.L.A. Hart's opinion on this issue. According to Hart, any law must have the quality that any individual feels an obligation to obey it. But a UCC which is forced upon another or others would not serve the goal. Prof. Singh says that gradual achievement of UCC must come from the demands of the very sections who are opposing it.[24]

Eminent constitutional scholar H.M. Seervai attacked the very 'request' of the Supreme Court to the Indian government to implement the provision of article 44. According to him it is the executive not judiciary, which can consider what law should be submitted to the Parliament. And the parliament alone can decide whether or not to enact the proposed law. He argued- "Those who have studied Hindu law and Mohammedan law will realize that a UCC for Hindus and Muslims alike is an impossibility."[25]

It can be said that the Hindu law is not applicable to all Hindus. In the cases of succession and partition, the customs of different groups are preserved. The devolution of property may be done different under Hindu law in Kerala, Uttar Predesh, and some other states in India. In the Hindu Marriage Act, there can be two types of marriages-religious or civil marriages.

Some again cite the case of the Muslims who are divided into two sects and many sub-sects. The sects are Shia and Sunnis. Sunnis are divided into four sub-sects- Hanafis, Malivis, Shafies and Hanbalis (Mullah's Mohammedan law). Thus the Muslim law does not apply uniformly to all the Muslims.

Eminent social worker Salauddin Tyabji found a reason behind the demand for uniform civil code as "the imperative heed to break as under the unifying force of the Islamic brotherhood which is bound together by the Sharia."[26]

But, on the other hand, a number of scholars and intellectuals from among the Muslim community itself have pleaded for the reform of their personal law.

Dr. Tahir Mohmood [27] has made a powerful plea for framing a uniform civil code for all citizens of India. He says: "In pursuance of the goal of secularism, the state should stop administering religion-based personal laws".

The author has gone to the extent to make an appeal to the Muslim community that instead of wasting their energies in exerting theological and political pressure in order to secure an "immunity" for their traditional personal laws from the state's legislative jurisdiction, the Muslims will do well to begin exploring and demonstrating how the true Islamic laws, purged of their time-worn and anachronistic interpretation, can enrich the common civil code of India.

A.G.Noorani, a famous journalist remarks-"The Muslim law, as in force India, cries for reform."[28]

Dr. Mohammad Iman[29] tells that a great deal of Muslim law as in force in India may reformed by devising procedural or regulatory measures to check or control like exercise of rights and power there under arbitrarily, injuriously or oppressively.

The opinion of Prof. Tahir Mohmood may also be mentioned here as he says-"Existing personal laws of the various religious communities may not be altogether scrapped; through each of them, and more particularly the Muslim personal law, must be purged of all unsatisfactory elements, in a way ensuring the maximum possible social equality"[30]

Mr. M.C.Chagla, a distinguished Judge, viewed that "Indian Muslims (should) adapt themselves to the conditions of secular India where they enjoyed the same rights as their Hindu fellow citizens".[31]

Along with these viewpoints women from various corners of Indian society have also expressed their opinion for drafting of a common or uniform civil code. The demand of the women's movement is that a woman would have equal rights as a man. They also make a demand that cultural heritage, religious traditions shouldn't give protection to the communities to refuse to grant their present-day demands.

Indira Jaising, the distinguished lawyer, has opined in 'The Lawyers',- "the demand for reform (in personal laws in favour of a common civil code) must be a demand for sexual equality. It would be better to reformulate the demand so as to focus on the sex discrimination which is written into all personal laws. This will have the merit of not only emphasizing the secular nature of the demand but also its rational, namely, the urgent need to make equality for women a reality under a constitution that guarantees equality between sexes."[32]

Ansuya Dutt, an eminent lawyer mentioned that there must be a common civil code as it will bring a significant influence on the social status of all Indian women who are prejudiced in several spheres by the present existing laws. According to her, it is due to the different personal laws that the Indian women are divided and thus exploited. She also feels that the Indian women should unite themselves on a common platform and then it would be easy for them to fight for more effectively for changes in their present day position.[33]

Ms. Dutt also opined that some provisions of the existing personal laws could be included for drawing up a common civil code which are useful to women. Such provisions are- divorce by mutual consent as available in the Hindu Marriage Act or the Special Marriage Act, the Mehr system of the Muslim personal law should be generalized for all communities in addition to a guarantee of maintenance.

It was not her position that the advancing elements of the present personal laws way just be put together so as to form a new one to meet the present needs. On the other hand, she proposed to include some new provisions such as dissolution of marriage when it is beyond repair as a ground for divorce, right of a divorced woman on her husband's assets not merely as a demand for maintenance, and that both the father and the mother should to be treated as joint natural guardians of children.

Ashgar Ali Engineer the famous Muslim reformist and scholar says that if complete equality between the sexes is the basic implication of a uniformity in all personal laws, then it does not in any way violate the spirit or the normative feature of the Quran. He says that common civil code or no common civil code, what is fundamental is women's rights and status. Their rights should be as inviolable as those of men. The Quran accepts this position.[34]

INDIAN GOVERNMENT'S POLICY OR ATTITUDE TOWARDS UCC

The Indian Government's policy during all these years has been to respect the opinion of the Muslim community in India. In this regard, Dr.B.R.Ambedkar, the chief architect of Indian Constitution, says "in our country.....the profession of a particular religion carries with it the personal law of the person. You cannot get away from that position.[35]

During the period of Jawaharlal Nehru's premiership, the Central Government consistently followed the path of non-interference in regard to Muslim personal law. There were no effects to bring change in the traditional family law of the Muslims. It is also a fact that the Hindu personal law has been systematized in 1955 and 1956 by giving effect to the Hindu Marriage Bill, the Hindu Succession Bill, the Hindu Adoptions and Maintenance Bill. But the Muslim personal law has remained unchanged or untouched. At that time, when the Hindu personal laws were being systematized, some sections of people demanded for reform in the Muslim personal law but this demand was rejected by Jawaharlal Nehru.

So it can be said that the Indian Muslims have been left to themselves to determine the nature, scope and extent to reforms that should take place in their personal law. In this regard, D.E.Smith observes: "the task of codifying Hindu personal law has been completed; but yet the Muslim Shariat has remained untouched by the Indian parliament."[36]

It means that the assurance which was given by Dr. Ambedkar to the Muslims in the Constituent Assembly regarding the unilateral change of their personal law still holds good. Regarding the significance of Article 44, he mentioned: "There is no obligation upon the state to do away with personal laws. It is only giving a power. Therefore, no one need be apprehensive of the fact that if state has the power, the state will immediately proceed to execute or enforce that power in a manner that may be found to be objectionable by the Muslims or by the Christians or by any other community in India."[37]

These assurances which have been given by the framers of the constitution are keeping the government from taking initiation in this direction. At the same time the constitution specifically authorizes the state to make any such legislation or law. Under Article 25, Clause2: "Nothing in this article shall affect the operation of any existing law or prevent the state from making any law regulating or restricting any economic, political or other secular activity which may be associated with religious practices."

When the Hindu code bill was being codified, the then law minister commented in the parliament: "The State has retained all along in Article 25, the right to interfere in the personal law of any community in this country. There can be no argument against that.... This parliament is absolutely supreme and we deal with any community so far as their personal law is concerned apart from their religion. Let no community be in a state of mind that they are immune from the sovereign authority of this parliament."[38]

So, it is clear that the state has absolute authority to interfere in the affairs of the personal law of any community. But the Indian Government, despite the fact, has not done so. It has shown regard and respect to the feelings of minority communities, particularly of the Muslims by putting all the reservations and considerations of the Muslims of India. The government has so far maintained the Nehru's policy of perseverance (non-interference) in regard to Muslim personal law. However in 1972, late Prime Minister Indira Gandhi advised Indian Muslims "to start a process considering change in their personal law with an open mind."[39]

When late Rajib Gandhi was prime minister of India in 1986, the Indian government showed similar attitude in the Shah Bano Case. In the judgment of that case, the Supreme Court again asked the government to formulate a uniform civil code as per Article 44 of the Indian Constitution but the central government submitted an affidavit to the Supreme Court regarding its inability to enact a uniform civil code in the country at that time. Then the government enacted the Muslim women's Right and Divorce Act, 1986 which was the result of the pressure coming from the Muslim fundamentalists upon the then central government. This law makes the Muslim women divorcee's position insecure.

CONCLUSION AND SUGGESTION

From the above discussion, it can be concluded that uniform civil code always has remained a controversial issue in India and it may also remain the same in the near future. The protagonists (mostly Hindus particularly Hindu communalists, feminists etc.) emphasize that the UCC should be enacted. The antagonists among whom Muslims (fundamentalists and communalist Muslims, common Muslims) who are too much sensitive to their minority identity are most vocal. They are of the opinion that the democratic arrangement of India ensured to them the independence and privilege to follow closely their personal laws and so are in opposition to the enactment of UCC. The position of the secularists in this issue is indefinite and is situated on two poles as one group (mostly Muslims) is against of it and the other group (mostly Hindus) is a position to support the enactment of UCC or at least they want some reformation in the Muslim personal law.

The antagonists- majority of them are Muslims regard Islamic laws of marriage, divorce and successions as a part of their religion. They consider that their personal law has originated from the Quran and Sunna and so it is immutable. At the same time, a common Muslim has faith in the belief that it will be a great sin to follow the principles of marriage, divorce and succession other than those dictated in the Quran and Sunna. They also consider their personal law as a symbol of their cultural identity in India. At the same time, they are also facing the majoritarian communalism in the fields of education (teaching of Hindu mythology in schools and colleges), in social and cultural ceremonies (governmental or public inauguration ceremonies). These incidents have made them too much precautious in maintaining their cultural identity and so they refuse to give up any of their distinguishing cultural traits. The Indian Muslims also think that to follow the UCC means may be to follow the Hindu jurisprudence which will be unIslamic for them. So they are reluctant to go against the UCC as they think it will create a situation which will go against Islam in India.

The enactment of a UCC is faced with a number of other problems also. Even though there is a constitutional directive, there is little lucidity regarding the shape of UCC and consequently it is not clear as to which subject matters will be included in it. It is noteworthy that the legal diversities existing in this country are so broad and varied that the enactment of a UCC will brings bitterness and conflict among the different communities including many tribal communities such as the Nagas, Mizos, Santhal, Munda etc.

Women in India in general have demanded a uniform civil code through movement from the days of pre-independence. The primary aim of their movement has been to bring equality between the two sexes. This movement is essentially secular and the main principle in this struggle is to realize equality by taking away the barriers erected to the name of religion. caste, creed, custom or tradition. They cannot be parted from the concepts of 'democracy', 'equality', 'secularism', and 'modernity' and all these concepts must be entertained to them along with the males of this country.

So it can be said from the above discussion that the concept of uniform civil code has two angles: uniformity among communities (Hindus, Muslims, Sikhs, Christians, and Buddhists etc. all being governed by one law) as well as uniformity within communities (between men and women). Uniform civil code must include gender-just code from each angle otherwise it would be a code for the uniformity of male privilege. At present, supporters of uniform civil code are claiming that since the Hindu laws have been coded and reformed, there is already uniformity and equality within the community. So their target of a uniform civil code is with the personal laws of minority communities. But it cannot be denied that till today, Hindu women are worst victims of unequal laws regarding marriage, inheritance, guardianship and adoption (regarding guardianship of child, now the mother also will be the natural guardian as the father of the child according to the judgment of the Supreme Court on 17 February 1999).[40]

Now the supporters of the common code have proposed that UCC will be based on the "best of all laws" of the different communities' personal laws. Such a type of code, it is argued will bring uniformity between communities. But actually, it will not bring uniformity within communities. As far as women's issues and rights are concerned, the argument is misleading as the existing laws are not the "best laws". Some laws may be relatively better but these are not also free from being unjust to women or are unacceptable from the standpoint of equality between men and women. And so they cannot form the genuine base for the enactment of uniform civil code.

Muslim women have better privileges related to the laws of inheritance in comparison to Hindu women but when they are compared to Muslim men, they are still far behind. Bigamy is illegal but the present law has so many loopholes that in spite of an increase in the cases of bigamous marriages, it is very difficult to prove men guilty of such a practice. The issues of maintenance and custody of children which are related to the divorce cases are extremely weak. Adultery is a ground of divorce for men although it is not for women. Thus every law has made the women's positions weak. Then the 'best' laws of all existing laws will be a ghastly law for women irrespective of their different communal or religious identities.

Again there are tensions between certain provisions of the personal laws of the different communities and the laws of the constitution. In this regard, the argument of the antagonists of common code is that within a secular democratic framework communities must have the right to follow their personal laws without any type of restrictions or interference. But such standards of democratic principles should not be allowed to degenerate into a license to deny to one section of their members the rights guaranteed by the constitution. From another standpoint, it can be argued that the democratic principle that communities should enjoy the benefit of having their personal laws but these should not be used by them to exercise dominance over the weaker groups or sections within the communities. A member of any community who feels oppressed or exploited would be free to make complain in the court that her/his fundamental right is being violated and it cannot be allowed merely because the community has got an autonomous space as an assurance to practice its personal laws.

In the face of such great difficulties which are faced in the enactment of a common civil code in India, the communities themselves should take the appropriate path to rationalize their personal laws. Those aspects of their personal laws which have a conflicting tendency with the constitutional laws should be reformed through entirely internal initiative. The initiative for rationalization and reform in the laws as well as the formation of suitable institutional structures for developing a majority view over such rationalization or reform have to come within the different cultural / religious communities. Such initiative and the development of a majority view (consensus) may vary among the different communities as these communities are at varying stages of social development. Irrespective of this varying stages or degrees of social and economic development, a beginning has to make by concerned sections in the different communities. Among these communities, the Muslims of India must think about their personal law. It is a common belief of the Muslims that the Muslim personal law is based on the Shariat. And as the Shariat is divine and immutable so MPL is also divine and immutable. No human authority can change the injunctions and divine commands of the Shariat (MPL).

In this respect, it can be mentioned here that the MPL which is prevailed in India are made up of four sources-(a) Shariat or fiqh; (b) laws made by legislatures; (c) previous judgments; and (d) customs.[41]So it is partly divine in as much as it is based on the Holy Quran and partly human in as much as it is based on human opinion.

It also can be mentioned here that the Corpus Juris of Islam is made up of four recognized sources (1) the Holy Quran (2) Sunna (the Prophet's sayings and practices) (3) Qiyas (analogy) and (4) Ijma (consensus). The first two sources are divine and so these may sacrosanct, the last two sources are human, so these are mutable. The last two sources made the existence of may schools of jurisprudence among the Muslims such as Hanafi, Hanabali, Maliki, Shafi (among Sunnis); and Ithna Ashari, Fatimi etc. (among Shia).[42]

So it can be concluded than human made laws of MPL can be changed or reformed according to the present day's necessities. The reform should be taken on a priority basis in those aspects of the personal law which are in a position of contradiction with the constitutional law and which also go against the democratic principles of gender-based equality and justice.

In this respect Muslim jurists, advocates, ulema, social scientists and also some distinguished figures of Muslim society can play an important role to find out the rationalized versions of the existing laws. It is needful to mention here that two Judges of the Dacca High Court have delivered a Judgment on January 9, 1995 which allowed maintenance for life to a Muslim divorcee by interpretating the Quranic verse 2:241.[43] In this way, if such a codification is achieved, the foundation for codification of the Muslim personal law will also be set.

The Indian Muslims must also think about their contemporary social situation which is not at all free from social problems. All the spheres of social life of the Muslims are influenced by religious practices, beliefs. But when these practices become contrary to the religious norms (due to some members ignorance, misbelieve, illiteracy etc.), these practices create many social problems. Some of such problems are relative e.g. lack of emancipation of women, comparatively higher rates of birth in the poorer section of the community which cause malnutrition , illiteracy, deviant behavior among the children and it is resulted due to their lack of knowledge about Quranic injunctions of family planning. Islam does not forbid family planning.[44] Islam prohibits abortions and sterilizations but these are also permitted on health grounds. Unilateral divorces (triple talaq) create problems for the divorcee (women) and her children (if any). These incidents caused many associated problems and evils in the larger society. Drawing away attention from these problematic situations will not help the Indian Muslims to develop their society in accordance with the modern era. In this respect, the Muslim Shariat should be given more contemporary expression in accordance with its own sprit than law books which were compiled in an entirely different environment. This would not mean to turn away from the path of the Shariat. Rather, it would be an authentic return to the Shariat, which has been the ultimate desire of the Muslims. It is too difficult to make prediction about the Indian Muslims' return to Shariat. But one should remember the Quranic Verse: "God does not change the condition of a people unless they change it themselves."

SURVEY WORK

The present survey work intends to study the attitude of the Kolkata Muslims regarding the enactment of UCC in India. This study also aims to find out their opinion about Muslim women's position in the Muslim personal law in comparison to Muslim men and in this regard their opinion about the reformation in the Muslim personal law prevailed in India.

SOME FACTS ABOUT KOLKATA MUSLIMS

Kolkata Muslim population reflects all India or at least predominantly the north Indian character as Muslims of different regions of India with different occupational, cultural and even historical background are found in this metropolitan city. Linguistically, Urdu speaking Muslims constitute 70 percent of the entire Muslim population of the city. The next is of Bengali Muslims followed by Rajasthani, Gujarati and Malayali.[45]The two sects of Islam–the Sunni and Shiites are found in different parts of the city but Shiites are minority and their proportion in total Muslim population is too small. Mostly of them are Gujarati and Uttar Pradeshi and their concentration is around Metiaburuz, Barabazar and some particular areas of Khidirpur. The other sect-Sunnis are found in Barabazar, Mechauabazaar, and Rajabazar in north Kolkata, Park circus, Narkeldanga and Ultadanga in the east and in the port area of Khidirpur, Gardenreach and Metiaburuz. Most of them are bustee dwellers and economically not sound as majority of them are engaged in unorganized types of employment and even today in a metropolitan urban situation (culture) they represent various traditional occupational groups.

Above discussion has contended the Muslim community of this city has a relatively complex structure. Besides the linguistic and sectarian divisions, they are further sub-divided into several sub-segments of the basis of caste and occupation.[46]

UNIVERSE OF THE STUDY

The present survey for the study was done in two Muslim localities–Khidirpur and Rajabazar (including Narkeldanga). Rajabazar is one of the oldest Muslim localities situated in north-east Kolkata where they have been living before independence and majority of them are bustee dwellers. Where as Khidirpur is a port area located in south Kolkata and here Muslims are provided with various types of economic pursuits. Many of them have migrated from different regions of India and presently they are permanent inhabitants of this locality. One can find Muslims of different classes residing in Khidirpur.

SAMPLING AND COLLECTION OF DATA

Different areas of these two localities and total 289 respondents were selected from these areas on the basis of random sampling of which the number of male and female respondents were 244 and 45 respectively. Interview schedule has been used for the collection of needed information from the respondents. The age of the sampled respondents' was 25+ years and their marital status was married or/ divorcee/ widower/ widow. Among these respondents the number of Urdu, Bengali and other language speaking Muslims was 220, 65 and 04 respectively.

The researcher asked three questions to the respondents:-

(i) Do you want the enactment of UCC in India?

(ii) Do you think that the Muslim personal law gives equal status to Muslim female in comparison to Muslim male?

(iii) Do you think that MPL should be reformed or it should be retained the same?

The respondents' opinions related to the above mentioned questions have shown in the following tables:-

Table 1
Opinion of the respondents for enactment of UCC:

Enactment of UCC	*General (%)*	*Female (%)*	*Male (%)*
Yes	23.9	46.7	19.7
No	74.0	51.1	78.3
No comment	2.1	2.2	2.0
Total (%)	100.0	100.0	100.0

Graphical Representation of the above Statistical Data

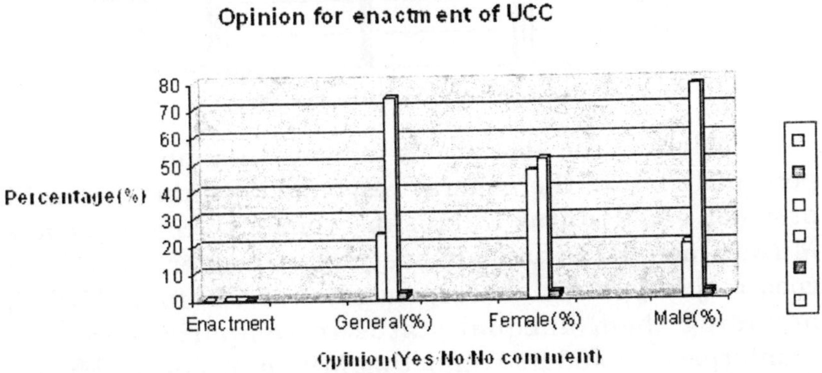

The data in the above table are showing that majority of the Muslims (74%) does not want the enactment of the uniform civil code in India. It is also showing that Muslim men (78.3%) are most vocal against the formation of the UCC whereas it is quite surprising that near about fifty percent (46.7%) of the female respondents want its enactment.

Table 2
Muslim Women's Status in Comparison to Muslim Men in Muslim Personal Law (MPL)

Status of Muslim women in (%) MPL	*General*	*Female (%)*	*Male (%)*
Equal	53.6	33.3	56.2
Unequal	44.3	64.5	41.8
No comment	2.1	2.2	2.0
Total (%)	100.0	100.0	100.0

Graphical Representation of the above Mentioned Statistical Data

Status of Muslim women in MPL in comparision to Muslim men

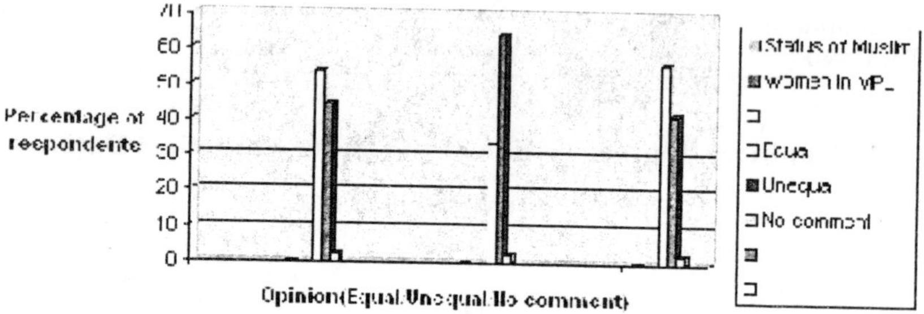

The data in the above table indicate that more than fifty percent (53.6) of the general respondents think that MPL provides equal status to Muslim women in comparison to Muslim men. If the data are analyzed on gender basis then a good majority of female respondents (64.5%) finds MPL as providing them unequal status in comparison to their counterpart who(56.2%) think that MPL provides the Muslim females an equal status as to them.

More than fifty percent (57.8) general Muslims are in a mood to retain the existing form of the MPL but if it is discussed in a gender line then it is clear that majority of the male respondents (61.5%) are in favour of the retention/ preservation of the existing MPL while it is quite interesting to mention here that about same percentage of the female respondents (62.2%) want reformation in the MPL. The data in the below mentioned table 3 and it's graphical representation show all these happenings.

Table 3
Opinion Related to Muslim Personal Law's reformation

MPL's reformation	*General (%)*	*Female (%)*	*Male (%)*
Retained	57.8	37.8	61.5
Reformed	40.1	62.2	36.1
No comment	2.1	—	2.4
Total (%)	100.0	100.0	100.0

Graphical Representation of the Above Mentioned Statistical Data

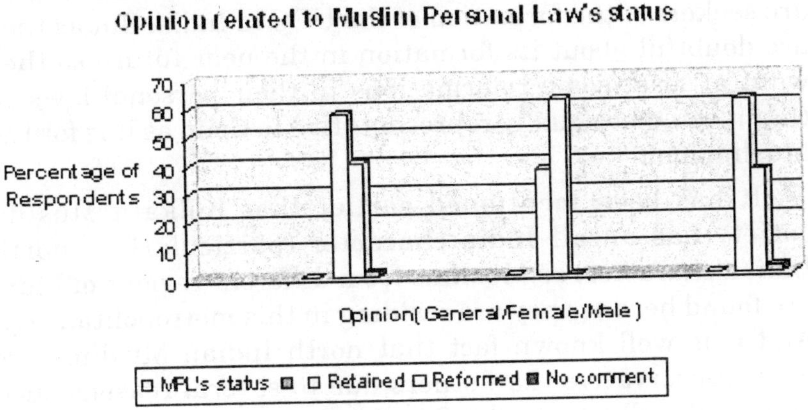

CONCLUSION OF THE SURVEY WORK

It is well known fact that Indian Muslims are excessively rigid in practicing their Islamic traditions and long established customs and any effort to bring alteration in these traditions and customs is strongly resist by them as they think that these are the fundamental part of their religious conviction or their religion inquires them to follow these traditions.

While the present survey has found out some changes in this respect in the attitude of Muslims of Kolkata but till today majority of them does not want the enactment of the UCC in India. Although in the present Kolkata Muslim community there is awareness about social upliftment and equality of rights in both sexes and presently a group in the society is emerging who are trying to interpret the Islamic ideas more correctly and opposing the irrational old traditions and customs prevalent in the society but there are still some members both from males and females who consider that MPL is not representative on gender basis but do not want reformation in it as it(MPL) is divinely ordained. But it is also noteworthy that now there is a consciousness among Muslim women to raise their voice about the equal rights as majority of them find MPL unfavourable to them against the Muslim males especially in the cases of polygamy and divorce as this study shows that a good portion of Muslim women are seekers of the formation of the UCC in India. But as they are doubtful about its formation in the near future so they want at least some reformations in their personal laws so that it could be equally representative to them as it is for the Muslim men.

It has been mentioned earlier that Kolkata Muslim society has an all India character (particularly a north Indian character) as Muslims from different regions of India are found here as they are residing in this metropolitan city. And it is well known fact that north Indian Muslims are more conservative than others due to several reasons such as poverty, illiteracy etc. So when a good portion of them want reformation in the existing MPL then it can be consider as the opinion of the rest of the Muslims of this country as favouring the reformation to some extent in the MPL. So in this respect it can be concluded that the human made laws of MPL can be changed or reformed according to the present day's necessities. And regarding the reform in their personal law it should be taken on a priority basis in those aspects of the personal law which are in a position of contradiction with the constitutional law and which also go against the democratic principles of gender-based equality and justice.

In this respect Muslim jurists, ulema, Muslim social reformers and also some distinguished personalities of Muslim society can play an important role to find out the rationalized versions of the existing unreasonable laws. It is needful to mention here that common Indian Muslims have a strong faith in the doings and sayings of their religious leaders in religious matters and so if the religious leaders consider some reformations in the personal law according to the present day necessities, then the common Muslims may accept the changes without any hesitation.

NOTES

1. The Supreme Court admitted a PIL challenging the validity of Shariat courts. For more details see The Telegraph, Calcutta, p. 4, 6 April, 2007.
2. Supreme Court Cases (1995), Vol. 3, p. 638 (Eastern Book Company, Lucknow).
3. *Ibid.*
4. Ananda Bazar Patrika, Kolkata, 24 July 2003.
5. B. Pattabhi Sitaramayya, History of the Indian National Congress–Vol. I, (S. Chand & Co., New Delhi, 1969). p. 480.
6. Govt.of India Act 1935, Schedule VII, Concurrent List, Entries 6-7.
7. Quoted by Tahir Mahmood in Muslim Personal Law (Note 22), All India Reporter Ltd., Nagpur 1983, p. 79.
8. Constituent Assembly Debates, Vol. V, p. 213 (1947).
9. *Ibid*, p. 225.
10. CAD, Vol. VII, p. 111(1949).
11. *Ibid.*
12. CAD, Vol. VII, p. 547 (1948).
13. *Ibid*, p. 549.
14. *Ibid*, pp. 540-541.
15. *Ibid*, p. 546.
16. CAD, Vol. VII, pp. 541-43.
17. *Ibid*, pp. 544-546.
18. *Ibid*, pp. 543, 547-48.
19. CAD, Vol. VII, p. 548.
20. *Ibid*, pp. 550-552.
21. CAD, Vol-VII, p. 552.
22. P. Dewan: 'The Uniform Civil Code' in Mohammed Imam(Ed)-Minorities and the law, (Bombay: N.M. Tripathy Pvt. Ltd., 1972), p. 420.
23. *Ibid*, p. 423.
24. Civil Services Chronicle, October 1995.
25. Civil Services Chronicle, October, 1995.

26. Salauddin Tyabji–"Uniform Civil Code–A Challengeable Proposition", (The Islamic Publications Society of Hyderabad 1966), p.17
27. Tahir Mohammed (ed)–Muslim Personal Law, 1977, New Delhi, Vikas, pp. 200-202.
28. The Indian Express, New Delhi, 14 May 1972.
29. Mohammed Imam(ed)– Minorities and the Law, (N.M. Tripathy Pvt. Ltd., Bombay, 1972) p. 116.
30. Tahir Mahmood: *'Common Civil Code, Personal Laws and Religious Minorities'*, in Mohammed Imam (ed)– Minorities and the Law, p. 476.
31. Quoted in Moin Shakir's Muslims in Free India, (New Delhi, Kalamkar Prakashan,1972) pp. 125-6.
32. Javed Anand, The Sunday Observer, 23 February, 1986.
33. Javed Anand, The Sunday Observer, 23 February, 1986
34. Ashgar Ali Engineer (ed), Problems of Muslim Women in India- An Introduction, (Orient Longman, 1995). p. XIX.
35. PD, Vol. VIII (1951), 2949, Quoted by V.P. Luthera, the Concept of the Secular State and India, (Calcutta OUP, 1964). p. 96.
36. D.E. Smith, *op.cit* p. 420.
37. Constituent Assembly Debates, Vol. VII, pp. 781-82 (1948).
38. PD, Vol.VIII (1951), 2950, Quoted by V. P. Luthera, *op. cit*, p. 102.
39. Hindustan Times, New Delhi, 10 October, 1972.
40. Ananda Bazaar Patrika, 13 November, 1999, p. 2.
41. Prof. Asaf Fyzee, Muslim Personal Law (Urdu), (Delhi, n.d.), p. 11 [Also mentioned in A.A. Engineer (ed) Shah Bano Controversy, (Hyderabad, Orient Longman, 1987). Introduction, p. 3.
42. Ashgar Ali Engineer(ed), *op.cit* p. 3.
43. For more details, See Ashgar Ali Engineer's– "Muslim Women and Maintenance", EPW June 12, 1999, pp. 1488-89.
44. M.E. Khan–Family planning among Muslims in India, (Manohar, New Delhi, 1979), pp. 184-192.
45. M. K. A. Siddiqui: Muslims of Calcutta– A Study of Their Social Organization, ASI, 1974, pp. 25.
46. *Ibid.*

REFERENCES

S.P. Sathe (1995), "Union Civil Code–Implications of Supreme Court Intervention", *Economic and Political Weekly,* September 2.

Brinda Karat (1995), "Union Civil Code–Uniformity vs. Equality", *Indian Express,* Bangalore, September 30.

Imtiaz Ahmed (1995), "Personal Laws: Promoting Reform from within", *Economic and Political Weekly,* November 11.

VIOLATION OF HUMAN RIGHTS OF DALIT WOMEN: ISSUES, FACTORS AND CONCERNS

*Prabha Tirmare**

INTRODUCTION

All human beings have the right to live as human beings. Human rights are not conferred or given. They already exist in society. The concept human rights aims at protection of rights like right to life, liberty and property. These rights have to be available to all the human beings irrespective of class, caste, gender, colour and religion. The Universal Declaration of Human Rights was unanimously adopted by the UN General Assembly on December 10th, 1948. The preamble of Indian constitution adequately empowers the central and state government to eliminate violation of human rights in the country (Pal and Bhargav, 1999).

Inspite of these international and national declarations and resolutions, human rights are voutinely violated in different countries all over the world. In Indian society, due to the social barriers such as casteism, untouchability, patriarchy, disparity, superstition, religious exploitation and class variations, specific groups are becoming weaker and marginalised. These groups are facing the problems of identity crisis, deprivation, discrimination and atrocities. These marginalised groups are also identified and recognised as

* College of Social Work, Mumbai.

dalits, SC (scheduled castes) ST (scheduled tribes), OBC (other backward castes) NT (nomadic tribes) DT (denotified tribes) religious and linguistic minorities (Michael, 1999).

Violence on human beings in any form result in violation of human rights. Human rights of dalits and women in general are normally violated by high castes and powerful communities to practice and exhibit patriarchy and castetism. But human rights of dalit women are not only violated extremely but are violated in peculiar form. Dalit women are in worst position than dalits in general, in terms of sex ratio, wages, employment, occupation, assets, education, health, social mobility and political participation (Bandhu cited in Rao, 2003). Hence, it is important to discuss the status of dalit women and various problems facing them even after 60 years of independence.

This article makes an attempt to discuss basic facts, issues and concerns related to dalit women and suggest some alternatives to combat violation of their rights for social justice and equality. Explanation of relevant terms such as 'dalit', 'dalitism', and 'dalit women', is given below to broaden the understanding about the issue. Further, the vulnerable situation of dalit women is also discussed in detail.

DALIT

Dalit ('oppressed' or 'broken') is not a new word. This term is known to have been used in the year 1930 as a Hindi and Marathi translation of 'depressed classes'. The British used this term for what are now called the scheduled caste. Dr. Ambedkar chose the term 'broken men', as English translation of 'Dalit', to refer to the original ancestors of the untouchables. Dalit Panthers, the youth activists from dalit community, revived the term and in their 1973 manifesto expanded its reference to include the scheduled tribes, neo Buddhists, the working people, the landless and poor peasants, women and also those who are being exploited politically, economically in the name of religion (Omvedt cited in Webster, J, 1999).

DALITISM

Dalitism essentially implies conditions of subjugation; economic, political, social and cultural. Dalitism also embodies different degrees of marginalisation. It includes not only marginalized status in the economic sphere but also in cultural, political, religious and social domains. That means Dalitism symbolizes marginalisation. It is a well known fact that marginalisation denies basic human rights and social justice (Punalekar, cited in Jogdand 1995)

DALIT WOMEN

Dalit women are one of the most marginalized segments in the society. The condition of dalit women is more vulnerable than non-dalit women. Dalit women are suffering from multi-disadvantages:

(a) of being dalit i.e socio-economically and culturally marginalized section,

(b) being women and sharing the gender based inequalities and subordination (Jogdand, 1995)

To explore these and other crucial issues concerning dalit women there is a need to discuss some basic facts concerning the vulnerable situation of dalit women.

VULNERABLE STATUS OF DALIT WOMEN

It is easy for the historically dominating caste and gender to violate human rights of dalit women who are at the lowest rung of the hierarchical ladder. The type of violence inflicted on dalits is in the form of severest violation of human rights. Dalit and tribal women are raped as part of an effort by upper caste leaders, land lords and police to suppress movements to demand payment of minimum wages, to settle share cropping disputes or to reclaim lost lands. (Human Watch Report, 1998).

The recent incident of Khairlanji Massacare is not something new. A dalit family had refused to let upper caste villagers built a road through their fields. Hence on September, 29th, 2006, Bhaiyalal Bhotmange's family–wife Surekha, daughter Prinyanka and two sons were killed by the villagers of Khairlangi in Bhandara district of Maharashtra. They were first attacked with huge iron chains and than abused by the other caste women of the village. Surekha and Priyanka were paraded naked and raped, and later, their bodies were mutilated and thrown into a pond. (Hindustan Times, 14th November, 2006).

This shows that dalit women are easy targets for any perpetrator Upper caste considers them to be sexually available. Hence, they are largely unprotected by the state machinery. Further, there is prevalence of violence, making dalit women eat human excreta, parading them naked, gang-rape, murder, dacoity, robbery and burning of their huts or communities. These are the types of crime, which violate their human rights (Human Watch Report, 1998). According to SC/ ST commission report between 1981 and 1986 about 4000 dalit women became victim of rape. In 1993 –94 this figure rose to 798 and 992 respectively. This means annually about 700 dalit women fall prey to sexual assault by high caste people. (Pal and Bhargav, 1999)

The main complaints of the poorer dalit women are that they have no good houses. In urban areas most of them stay in unhygienic slums and in rural areas their houses are away from main stream society (Pillai, cited in Michael 1999). Under conditions of grinding poverty and severe exploitation at work place, dalit women also suffer caste specific ban on water access from upper castes and may be beaten up in their own houses as well. A poem by a dalit poetess Teressama, a teacher from Guntur, puts the situation in the following words:

> We go to work for we are poor
> But the same silken beds mock us,
> While we are ravished in broad daylight.
> Ill-starred our horoscopes are
> Even our tottering husbands
> Lying on the cots in the corner

Hiss and shout for revenge
If we cannot stand their touch

(Dietrich in Rao 2003)

At the outset, prevailing caste and secondary status of women in the society is largely responsible for violation of human rights of dalit women. To understand the root cause of the situation it is essential to examine basic factors responsible for their vulnerability.

SOCIO-CULTURAL AND RELIGIOUS FACTORS

First and foremost dalit women are victims of social, religious and cultural practices like Devdasis and Jogins. In the name of these practices, village girls are married to God by their helpless parents. These girls are then sexually exploited by the upper caste landlords and rich men and directed in to trafficking and prostitution. In his autobiography, Kale (1994) has described a ritual called 'chira'. The literal meaning of the word 'chira', is to cut or break. In this ritual when a girl from the lower caste community reaches the age of puberty, an elderly prestigious man from the higher caste breaks the hymen of the girl child by sexual act. This ritual is performed in a way to make the girl accept this fact as a routine practice.

The 28th report of SC/ST commission reported that in February 1986 there were about ten thousand Jogins belonging to SC in Nizamabad district of Andhra Pradesh. The survey submitted by the district collector to Schedule Caste Finance Corporation revealed prevalence of 15,850 cases. Eighty percent of these Jogins belonged to SC (Pal and Bhargav,1999). This data is just an example of one district of the country. Practices such as Chira, Jogins, Devdasi which are prevalent even today are harmful and threaten the dignity of dalit women and violate their human rights (P. Sainath, not dated).

EDUCATIONAL STATUS

Low level of education is a problem in itself and in turn gives rise to many other problems. (Thorat and Umakant, 2004).

In 1991, literacy among the dalit women was indeed quite low. In rural areas only 19.46 percentage women were literate. A report published by Ministry of Welfare, Government of India in 1998 showed that there is much difference in the literacy rate of dalits and non-dalits in general, and in terms of gender. Literacy rate of non-dalits is 64.13% and literacy rate of women is 39.29%, where as dalit women's literacy rate is only 23.76% (Paswan and Jaidev, 2002). There is a large disparity in the literacy rate due to wide spread prejudice based on casteism and patriarchy against dalits and women in general and dalit women in particular.

ECONOMIC DEPRIVATION AND UNEMPLOYMENT

A careful look at the economic situation of dalit women reveals that their work force structure is such that they rarely own any land. A large majority of them are agricultural labourers. The rate of unemployment among them is also quite high. About 90% of women working in unorganized sector are mainly from lower castes (Jogdand 1999). In 1991, about 71% of dalit women workers in rural area were agricultural labourers. Only 19% of them owned land (Pal and Bhargav, 1999).

A prominent researcher and sociologist while sharing her experience from a research on gender and land issue, informed that, when she enquired with dalit women about land owned by them in their names, they wondered about permissibility of owning land in their name. This indicates that neither they own any land nor they are aware of their rights on land. When enquiries were made with Stri-mukti sanghatana and Prerana, Mumbai based organizations working on the issue of rag picking and prostitution respectively, to ascertain the proportion of dalit women in these occupations, it was learnt that NGOs usually do not keep record of caste (Tirmare, 2004). However, Human Rights Watch Report (1998) mentioned that a large number of dalit women are engaged in unclean, inferior occupation such as sweeping, scavenging and working in dumping grounds, rag picking and also in prostitution.

These women have to face steep discrimination in the matters of social relation and employment due to their engagement in these occupations.

HEALTH AND NUTRITION STATUS

Dalit women's daily diet is the leftover of family meals, inadequate in quantity and quality. Health services are either not available in case of illness or are unaffordable if available. In addition to that, due to early marriage and too many pregnancies their health is always at risk. If birth control is practiced at all, 91% cases of tubectomy are performed on the women who have to carry the burden of family planning. In an overall situation where dalits are prone to ailments in general, women suffer from more serious and more varied kind of sickness. More than 80% of women in reproductive age group (15 to 45) are anemic. Poor health status of dalit women pushes them into more vulnerable situation (Bandhu cited in Rao 2003).

POLITICAL STATUS

Women constitute half of total population, but are unable to get equal share in active politics. Their socio-economic status directly depends on their participation in politics. Political parties in India speak much about equality of women but have totally ignored the dalit women (Jogdand, 1999).

Traditionally, leadership in the village was confined to 'rural elites', who were aged and belonging to higher castes. In the year 1993, 73rd amendment in the constitution granted reservation to dalits, tribals and women in local government. This amendment made it compulsory that one third of the seats reserved for dalits be filled by dalit women. In some states, there has been little or no acceptance of reservation for the lower castes and dalit women by the upper castes. This has resulted in atrocities against panchayat members including women. Dalits who stood for election were beaten, and dalit women were raped and ill-treated. The members of the higher castes, who are not prepared to relinquish power to the lower castes, grabbed their land. An easier method to retain power is to put-up proxy candidates but keep the control in the hands of the dominant castes, always men (Kumar and Raj, 2006).

The incapacity of women, particularly dalit women, to assert their rights is at the root of the problem. The reservation for dalits, particularly for women, is accepted in form but seldom in substance. Any change in the status quo is resisted. Dalit women's sitting on chairs is seen as a threat to social hierarchy. So, the upper castes in the village vetoed chairs in the panchayat office (P. Sainath in Rao 2003).

Dalit women also faced many problems in performing their duties due to illiteracy, lack of information and dependency on the male members of their families. An important obstacle is the no-confidence motion against dalit women as pradhan by the dominant sections. Rural elites are unable to accept the power, which has been given into the hands of the poorer and disadvantaged women (Manipal, 1998). Despite recognition and legal sanction for political rights, rigid caste system and patriarchy directly and indirectly has been suppressing dalit women and violating their political rights.

This proves that human rights of dalit women are violated right from her family to the society at large by one and all. All these factors are largely responsible for the precarious position of dalit women as far as their social, cultural, religious, economic, health and political status in the society is concerned. These factors force them to mutely allow violation of their civic and human rights. Thus they become victims of universal violence.

EFFORTS TO PROTECT HUMAN RIGHTS OF DALIT WOMEN

With the realization that violence is one of the potent threats to the peaceful existence of human beings, whole hearted and all round efforts are made at international, national and local level to protect the Human Rights. The preamble to the Universal Declaration of Human Rights (UDHR) serves as a foundation and philosophy of Human rights. There are a host of international conventions including those for prevention and punishment of genocide and elimination of all forms of racial and gender based discrimination (Chitnis, 2005).

The World Conference Against Racism (WCAR) related to racial discrimination, xenophobia and intolerance held in Durban, South Africa in 2001, brought the issue of caste and untouchability based discrimination on the agenda of UN Conference. Among the several organisations, the National Campaign on Dalit Human Rights (NCDHR) – a group of dalit NGOs, other NGOs, academicians', activists and large number of supporters spearheaded the national campaign in India for inclusion of the issue of caste and untouchability based discrimination in the Durban Conference (Thorat and Umakant, 2004).

The preamble of Indian constitution adequately empowers the central and state government to eliminate human right violation in the country (Pal and Bhargav, 1999) Article 17 of the constitution provides for removal of untouchability. Based on this article Protection of Civil Rights Act' (PCR), was passed in 1955. However since there was no provision conviction/ in this Act Thirty-four years after the introduction of PCR Act, the Scheduled Caste and Schedule Tribes (Prevention of Atrocities) Act 1989 was enacted to bring various forms of atrocities to an end. In this Act the complainant is given more weightage. There are stringent provisions against the police for negligence. (Pandit, 1995).

EMERGING IDENTITY OF DALIT WOMEN AND FORMATION OF DALIT WOMEN'S ORGANISATIONS

The focus on education of low caste women is one of the important factors responsible for the emerging identity of Dalit women. Reformist intervention by Savitribai and Mahatma Phule of opening school for untouchable girls way back in 1848 was a turning point for changing status of dalit women. (Chakrvarti in Rao 2003). Dr. Ambedkar's thought and action made important differences in the lives of dalit women. His movement and espccially his organisations encouraged many dalit women to become educated, to be active in public life and to gain leadership. Self respect in the contemporary period encouraged women to participate in organisation for dalit women at regional, state and national level. [Zelliot in Rao 2003).

After independence, in 1960's and 70's, the dalit movement and women's movement emerged to demand their rights against caste and gender respectively. However, specific problems of dalit women were not acknowledged by these movements. Hence in 1990's there were several special, independent and autonomous assertions of dalit women's identity; a case in point is the formation of National Federation for Dalit Women (NFDW) and All India Dalit Women's Forum (AIDWF) at the state level. The Maharashtra Dalit Mahila Sanghatana (MDMS) was formed in 1995. A year earlier, the women's wing of Bhartiya Republican Party (BRP) and the Bahujan Mahila Sangha (BMS) was set up the Bahujan Mahila Parishad. In December 1996, at Chandrapur, a Vikas Vanchit Dalit Mahila Parishad (VVDMP) was organised and a proposal to commemorate 25th December (the day on which Ambedkar had set Manu smriti on fire) as Bhartiya Smriti Divas was advanced. The Christi Mahila Sanghatana, an organisation of Dalit Christian Women was established in 1997. These organisations have come together on several issues such as celebration of Bhartiya Stree Mukti Divas and on the issue of reservation for OBC women in parliament bodies. Indian Association of Women Studies (IAWS) network with dalit feminist across different regions had brought special issues on problems and identity of dalit women (Rege in Rao 2003).

Several efforts have been made since independence to secure human rights of women in general and dalit women in particular. Despite this, human rights of dalit women are seen to be violated in different forms. Such infringement of human rights echoes the need of evolving suitable mechanism to empower dalit women to assert for equal rights and justice in order to live a dignified life.

MECHANISM TO STRENGTHEN THE CAPACITY OF DALIT WOMEN

To be human is to respond to human sufferings and pain with compassion and concern. It is not enough to sympathise with the dalit women in their pain. There is a need for effective action. Otherwise it would be just sentimentalism, says Sequeira in his article 'Human Response to Dalit Women (Jogdand 1999). The needs and the problems of dalit women differ with city, village, area and caste. It is essential to keep in mind that dalit women are not mere individuals but belong to a sociological and dialectical system. Therefore in order to recognise the problem and to prohibit violation, proper perspectives about these issues have to be developed among all by considering following suggestions.

AWARENESS FOR ASSERTION

Extensive reading of available literature can be done by young generation to understand the profile and problems of dalit women. Factual incidents & success stories of dalit women namely, 'We made History Too' by Meenakshi Moon & Urmila Pawar can be included in the educational texts.

ACCESS & EXPOSURE VISITS

Special exposure visits to dalit localities can be organised for school and college students to assess basic amenities accessible to dalit women namely, water, electricity, health and hygiene. Similarly dalit women's visit to urban structured colonies can be arranged to impress upon them the importance of standard of living. Such purposeful visits will broaden their horizons and result in improved living of marginalised sections.

ACADEMIC ACTIVITIES

Academic institutions need to be encouraged to undertake studies to assess the problems of violence and atrocities against dalit women, the reasons therefor and the ways to overcome them. Thought provoking sessions on harmful social and religious practices namely, Chira, Devdasi, Jogin etc. need to be held for developing basic understanding and to work out effective interventional strategies.

CAMPAIGNS AND SESSIONS

Campaigns for equal and rational distribution of natural resources among weaker sections can be organised to secure them their rightful means of livelihood. Proper rehabilitation and shelter can be provided to those communities, which are out of the social periphery (NT/DT). This will also protect them from the risk of sexual abuse.

INCLUSION OF DALIT WOMEN IN VARIOUS SYSTEM

More dalit women in proportion to their population (16.5% SC, 7.5% ST) should be given chance to enter in the systems like police, judiciary, education, health and politics.

Sessions can be organised for dalit activist and women activists to sensitize them about the magnitude of torture and oppression faced by the dalit women. Legal education dealing with protection of human rights of dalits and Prevention of Atrocities Act (1989) can be organised to prevent the problems of castism.

CONCLUSION

At the threshold of 21st century it is absolutely necessary that common people are sensitized about the prevailing atrocities against Dalit women. There is a growing need to capture violation of human rights of dalit women, so that talent and potential of Dalit Women can be used for development of the nation.

According to Vippal (Jogdand, cited in 1995) a nation does not prosper only on fertile soil, dense forests and everflowing rivers. It is the healthy people who make a nation. A society is made up of both men and women from all states. If women from whichever state is weak and exploited, it is not a healthy society. And when a society is healthy, then the nation will march ahead. To fulfill these dreams women in general and particularly from weaker section need to be empowered for development of the nation.

REFERENCES

Ahuja, R. (1998), *Violence Against Women*, Rawat Publication, New Delhi.

Bandhu, P. (2003), *Dalit Women's cry for Liberation: My Rights Are Rising like the Sun, will you deny this sunrise"?* Edited in Rao (2003) *Caste and Gender*, Kali For Women, New Delhi.

Chakravati, V. (2003), *Reconceptualising Gender; Phule, Brahmanisam and Brahminial Patriarchy,* edited in Rao (2003) *Caste and Gender*, Kali for women, New Delhi.

Chitnis, V. (2005), *Human Rights of the vulnerable groups*, Futuristic Digital, Pune.

Dietrich, G. (2003), *Dalit Movement and Women's Movement*, Edited in Rao (2003) *Caste and Gender*, Kali for women, New Delhi.

Jogdand, P. (1995), *Dalit Women, Issues and Perspectives*, Gyan Publication, New Delhi.

Kale, R. (1994), *Kolhatyachre por*, Granthali, Publication, Mumbai.

Kumar, N. (2004), *Dalit Policies, Politics and Parliament, Shipra* Publication, New Delhi.

Kumar, N. and Raj, M. (2006), *Dalit Leadership in Panchayats*, Institute of Dalit Studies, Rawat, New Delhi.

Michael, S. (1999), *Dalits in Modern India, Vision and Values*, Vistar Publication, New Delhi.

Omvedt, G. (1995), *Dalit Women and Communalism,* edited in Jogdand (1995) *Dalit Women, Issues and Perspectives,* Gyan Publication, New Delhi.

Pal, R. and Bhargav, G. (1999), *Human Rights of Dalits: Societal violation*, Gyan, Publication, New Delhi.

Paswan, S. and Jaidev (2002), *Encyclopedia of Dalits in India* (Vol. No. 10 education), Kalpaz Publication, New Delhi.

Pandit, V. (1995), Handbook on Prevention of Atrocities (SC/ST) Vidnayak Sansod Prakashan, Ujgaon, Maharashtra.

Punalekar, S. (1995), *On Dalitism and Gender,* edited in Jogadand (1995) *Dalit Women's Issues and Perspectives*, Gyan Prakashan, New Delhi.

Pillai, T. (1999), *Ambedkar's Daughters: A Study of Mahar Women in Ahmednagar District of Maharashtra* edited in Michaels (1999) *Dalits in Modern India, Vision and Values*, Vistar Publication, New Delhi.

Rao, A. (2003), *Gender and caste*, Kali for women, New Delhi.

Rege, U. (2003), 'A Dalit Feminist Stand point' edited in Rao, A. Coste and Gender, *Kali for Women*, New Delhi.

Sainath, P. (2003), *Unmusical chairs* edited in Rao (2003) *Gender and Caste*, Kali for women, New Delhi

Sequeira, L. (1995), *Human Response to Dalit Women Today*, edited in Jogdand (1995) *Dalit Women Issues and Prespectives*, Gyan Publication, New Delhi.

Thorat, S and Umakant (2004), *Caste, Role and Discrimination, Discourses in International Context*, Rawat Publication, New Delhi.

Zelliot, E. (2003), *Dr. Ambedkar and the Empowerment of Women*, edited in Rao (2003) *Caste and Gender*, Kali for women, New Delhi.

Webstar, J (1999), *Who is Dalit?* edited in Michael (1999) *Dalit's in Modern India, Vision and Values,* Vistar Publication, New Delhi.

Reports

Human watch Report (1998), Broken people, New York, Press.

Dalit Human Rights (2000), Report of the proceedings of International conference on Dalit Human Rights, Voice of Dalit International, London (UK)

Published Papers

Jogdand, P. (Sept-Dec., 2000), *Indian Social Reality and Inequality in to the Human Right Violence of Dalit,* Perspectives, College of Social Work, Mumbai.

Mahipal, (1998), *Women in Panchayats, Experience of Training Camp*, Economic and Political Weekly, Vol XXIII, No-4, Jan (24-30).

Unpublished papers

Mary, G. (2004), *The Struggle of Dalit Women, Resource Sheet Paper Presented In Dalit Theology Seminar, Barmingham.*

Sainath, P. (2003), Dalit's and Human Rights: The Battles Ahead

Tirmare, P. (2004), Violation of Human Rights of dalit Women: Issues and Facts, paper presented in the seminar on 'Gender and Human Rights' organised by College of Social Work, Nanded, Maharashtra.

News Paper Article

Bhosale, B.V. (14th November, 2006) 'Dalits are still the Harijans of yesterday, Hindustan Times, Mumbai.

INFLUENCE OF EDUCATION AND MARITAL STATUS ON SELF-ESTEEM OF WORKING AND NON-WORKING WOMEN

Muzamil Jan & Afiya Ashraf***

INTRODUCTION

Self-esteem refers to global self-evaluations. Investigators have not always made clear distinctions between self-esteem and self-concept, sometimes using the terms interchangeably or not precisely defining them.. (John, 2007). "Self-esteem," in common usage, is defined as a high opinion of oneself and respect for oneself. (Annie Reich 1960). Self-Esteem is one of the oldest concepts in psychology, first appeared as a coinage of American psychologist and philosopher William James in 1980. It involves one's mental perception of one's qualities, not of one's physical features. Torres *et al.,* (1995) found that self-esteem was significantly correlated with mental health and safety aspects among older adolescent in Spain, which "confirms the findings of numerous previous studies that positive self-esteem has enormous influence on mental health.

* Lecturer, Extension and Communication, Institute of Home Science, University of Kashmir, Jamia Masjid, Wahab Sahab, Srinagar, Kashmir, 190002, J & K, India, *e-mail: Muzamil_research@mail.com.*

** Research Scholar, Extension and Communication, Institute of Home Science, University of Kashmir, Bohri Kadal, Srinagar 190002, J & K, India.

RELATED REVIEW

King *et al.*, (1999) indicated that students with a higher score on self-esteem were more likely to have a good relationship with their parents, to be well adjusted and successful at school and to feel happy and healthy. In turn, happy young people were said to have higher self-esteem. Overall, boys tended to be happier than girls and were less subject to other stressors.

Boyd and Hrycaiko (1997) found that self-esteem is age-dependent and impacted over time by social interaction and personal experiences. Self-esteem impacts specific factors such as physical self-efficacy, self-confidence, anxiety, and perceived control in both male and female athletes of all ages and across different sports. This Study of pre-adolescent and adolescent females revealed that the pre-adolescent low self-esteem and low physical self-concept groups derived the greatest benefit from the physical activity intervention.

Palmer (1995) conducted the study to find the effects of an eight-week walking program on self-esteem in women at Northeast Louisiana University. This study showed improvement in self-esteem following the implementation of a fitness program. The study hypothesized that walking will improve scores on depression, self-esteem, and physical fitness. The results put forth that pregnant women's increase in self-esteem could have been due to factors such as acquiring a new skill, engaging in social interaction, and having accomplished a difficult task. Additionally, significant improvements in self-esteem were more pronounced when individuals initially have very low self-esteem. Another important results was the finding that physiological improvement is not necessary for psychological improvement

Manis, (1992) found that. employed have higher self-esteem than unemployed women. Life satisfaction showed essentially the same pattern of relationships to work status.

Work status was not, however, significantly related to self-esteem or life satisfaction among women 35-44. Reasons considered for this behavior were family-state and type of job.

OBJECTIVES OF STUDY

1. To study the impact of education on self-esteem among women.
2. To evaluate self-esteem as per marital status of women.
3. To assess various dimensions of self-esteem among working and non-working women.

JUSTIFICATION AND METHODOLOGY

The focus of this study is on of self-esteem and the process of evaluating the self-negatively or positively. Studies examining self-efficacy is the level and strength of an woman's belief that she can successfully perform a given activity, have been examined given the similarity of this construct to self-esteem .This paper is an attempt of understanding and underlying structure of the self-concept which can contribute to the process of mediating change in self-esteem and improving psychological health. 100 respondents were selected for the study, which included 50 working women out of which 25 were from rural area and 25 from urban area and 50 non-working women's in which 25 were from rural area and 25 from urban area. Samples were selected. The present study was investigated through multi-stage sampling technique. The tools used to facilitate collection of data include questionnaire and "Self-Esteem Scale for Women" (SESW) constructed by Kapadia and Verma (2000). It comprised 41 items under the responses of Most Often (MO), Sometimes (S) and Rarely (R). MO was scored as 3, while S was scored as 2 and (R) was scored as 1, in case of positive items. Whereas, in case of negative items, (MO) was scored as 1, while (S) was scored as 2, and (R) was scored as 3.. The data was analyzed through statistical software namely SPSS computing percentage, chi-square value, levels of significance and degrees of freedom. The levels of significance were obtained at the p-values of < 0.01, < 0.05 and >0.05. The p-values of <0.01 was regarded as highly significant. The p-value of <0.05 was considered at significant and p-value of >0.05 was calculated as insignificant. The total score of the scale regarding 'Self-Esteem for Women" was divided into 3 categories i.e., Low, Medium and High. Low level of self-esteem comprised the scores upto 62 (50 per cent). Medium level of self-esteem comprised the scores upto 63 –87 (50-70per cent) and high level of self-esteem comprised the scores upto 80 (>70 per cent). The Scale of "Self-Esteem for Women" was divided into 5 categories i.e.,

(a) Self-Esteem in Personal Life comprised 15 items and levels of low, medium and high. Low level of self-esteem comprised the scores upto 22 (50%) medium level of self-esteem comprised the scores 23-31 (50-70%) and high level of self-esteem comprised the scores more than 31 (>70%).

(b) Self-Esteem in Family Relations comprised 7 items and levels of low, medium and high. Low level of self-esteem comprised the scores upto 10 (50%), medium level of self-esteem comprised the scores upto 11-14 (50-70%) and high level of self-esteem comprises the scores upto 15 and more than(> 70%)

(c) Self-Esteem in Social Relations comprised 11 items and levels of low, medium and high. Low level of self-esteem comprised the scores upto 16 (50%), medium level of self-esteem comprised the scores upto 17-23 (50-70%) and high level of self-esteem comprised the scores upto 24 and more (>70%).

(d) Self-Esteem in Career comprised 8 items and levels of low, medium and high. Low level of self-esteem comprised the scores upto 12 (50%), medium level of self-esteem comprised the scores upto 13-16 (50-70%)and high

Table 1
Self-Esteem among Women as per their Educational Status

(n=100)

Variables	*Education Status*										
	Illiterate		*High School*		*Graduate*		*Higher Education*		*Total*		
	N	*Per cent*	*N*	*Per cent*	*N*	*Per cent*	*N*	*Per cent*	*N*	*Per cent*	*X^2-value*
Self-Esteem in Personal Life											
Low	3	50.00	-	-	1	16.67	2	33.33	6	100.00	7.66_6^{**}
Medium	15	18.52	8	9.88	7	8.64	51	62.96	81	100.00	
High	1	7.69	1	7.69	3	23.08	8	61.54	13	100.00	
Total	19	19.00	9	9.00	11	11.00	61	61.00	100	100.00	
Self-Esteem in Family Relations											
Low	-	-	-	-	1	50.00	1	50.00	2	100.00	5.22_6^{**}
Medium	11	18.97	6	10.34	4	6.90	37	63.79	58	100.00	
High	8	20.00	3	7.50	6	15.00	23	57.50	40	100.00	
Total	19	19.00	9	9.00	11	11.00	61	61.00	100	100.00	
Self-Esteem in Social Relations											
Low	1	9.09	-	-	1	9.09	9	81.82	11	100.00	4.12_6^{**}
Medium	14	20.90	7	10.45	6	8.96	40	54.70	67	100.00	
High	4	10.18	2	9.09	4	18.18	12	54.55	22	100.00	
Total	19	19.00	9	9.00	11	11.00	61	61.00	100	100.00	

Contd....

Variables	*Education Status*										
	Illiterate		*High School*		*Graduate*		*Higher Education*		*Total*		
	N	*Per cent*	*N*	*Per cent*	*N*	*Per cent*	*N*	*Per cent*	*N*	*Per cent*	*X^2-value*
Self-Esteem in Career											
Low	4	28.57	1	7.14	-	-	9	64.29	14	100.00	5.413_6^{***}
Medium	9	21.43	2	4.76	6	14.29	25	59.52	42	100.00	
High	6	13.64	6	13.64	5	11.36	27	61.36	44	100.00	
Total	19	19.00	11	11.00	11	11.00	61	61.00	100	100.00	
Over all Self-Esteem											
Low	-	-	-	-	-	-	-	-	-	-	3.808_3^{*}
Medium	17	21.25	8	10.00	10	12.50	45	56.25	80	100.00	
High	2	10.00	1	5.00	1	5.00	16	80.00	20	100.00	
Total	19	19.00	9	9.00	11	11.00	61	61.00	100	100.00	

Row percentage

* p – value < 0.01, (highly significant)

** p – value ≤ 0.05, (significant)

*** p – value > 0.05, (insignificant)

Degree of freedom (d.f) in subscripts of χ^2 – value.

Table 2
Self-Esteem among Women as per their Marital Status

(n=100)

Variables	*Marital Status*												
	Unmarried		*Married*		*Separated*		*Divorced*		*Widow*		*Total*		
	N	*Per cent*	*N*	*Per cent*	*N*	*Per cent*	*N*	*Per cent*	*N*	*Per cent*	*N*	*Per cent*	*X^2-value*
Self-Esteem in Personal Life													
Low	2	33.33	2	33.33	1	16.67	1	16.67	-	-	6	100.00	3.38_{8}^{**}
Medium	26	32.10	37	45.68	5	6.17	11	13.58	2	2.47	81	100.00	
High	3	23.08	5	38.46	1	7.69	3	23.08	1	7.69	13	100.00	
Total	31	31.00	44	44.00	7	7.00	15	15.00	3	3.00	100	100.00	
Self-Esteem in Family Relations													
Low	1	50.00	1	50.00	-	-	-	-	-	-	2	100.00	9.381_{6}^{**}
Medium	21	36.21	25	43.10	6	10.34	5	8.62	1	1.72	58	100.00	
High	9	22.50	18	45.00	1	2.50	10	25.00	2	5.00	40	100.00	
Total	31	31.00	44	44.00	7	7.00	15	15.00	3	3.00	100	100.00	
Self-Esteem in Social Relations													
Low	4	36.36	5	45.45	-	-	2	18.18	-	-	41	100.00	5.821_{8}^{**}
Medium	18	26.87	29	43.28	7	10.45	11	16.42	2	2.99	67	100.00	

Contd....

Variables	Marital Status												
	Unmarried		Married		Separated		Divorced		Widow		Total		
	N	Per cent	N	Per cent	N	Per cent	N	Per cent	N	Per cent	N	Per cent	X^2-value
High	9	40.91	10	45.45	-	-	2	9.09	1	4.55	22	100.00	
Total	31	31.00	44	44.00	7	7.00	15	15.00	3	3.00	100	100.00	
Self-Esteem in Career													
Low	2	14.29	8	57.14	2	14.29	2	14.29	-	-	14	100.00	5.51_6^{*}
Medium	16	38.10	17	40.10	2	4.76	5	11.90	2	4.76	42	100.00	
High	13	29.55	19	43.18	3	6.82	6	18.18	1	2.27	44	100.00	
Total	31	31.00	44	44.00	7	7.00	15	15.00	3	3.00	100	100.00	
Over all Self-Esteem													
Low	-	-	-	-	-	-	-	-	-	-	-	-	6.86_4^{**}
Medium	22	27.50	38	47.50	7	8.75	10	12.50	3	3.75	80	100.00	
High	9	45.00	6	30.00	-	-	5	25.00	-	-	20	100.00	
Total	31	31.00	44	44.00	7	7.00	15	15.00	3	3.00	100	100.00	

Row percentage

* p – value < 0.01, (highly significant)

** p – value ≤ 0.05, (significant)

Degree of freedom (d.f) in subscripts of χ^2 – value.

level of self-esteem comprises the scores upto 17 and more (>70%).

Table 3
Self-Esteem among Women as per their Activity

(n=100)

Variable	*Activity*						
	Working		*Non-working*		*Total*		
	N	*Per cent*	*N*	*Per cent*	*N*	*Per cent*	*χ^2-value*
Self–Esteem in Personal Life							
Low	1	16.67	5	83.33	6	100.00	3.371_2^{*}
Medium	41	50.62	40	49.38	81	100.00	
High	8	61.54	5	38.46	13	100.00	
Total	50	50.00	50	50.00	100	100.00	
Self-Esteem in Family Relations							
Low	2	100.00	-	-	2	100.00	2.376_2^{**}
Medium	27	46.55	31	53.45	58	100.00	
High	21	52.50	19	47.50	40	100.00	
Total	50	50.00	50	50.00	100	100.00	
Self-Esteem in Social Relations							
Low	7	63.64	4	36.36	11	100.00	1.373_2^{***}
Medium	31	46.27	36	53.73	67	100.00	
High	12	54.55	10	45.45	22	100.00	
Total	50	50.00	50	50.00	100	100.00	
Self-Esteem in Career							
Low	6	42.86	8	57.14	14	100.00	0.381_2^{***}
Medium	22	52.38	20	47.62	42	100.00	
High	22	50.00	22	50.00	44	100.00	
Total	50	50.00	50	51.00	100	100.00	
Over all Self-Esteem							
Low	-	-	-	-	-	-	2.250_1^{*}
Medium	37	46.25	43	53.75	80	100.00	
High	13	65.00	7	35.00	20	100.00	
Total	50	50.00	50	50.00	100	100.00	

Row percentage

* p – value < 0.01,(highly significant)

** p – value ≤ 0.05, (significant)

*** p – value > 0.05, (insignificant)

Degree of freedom (d.f) in subscripts of χ^2–value.

Age was divided into 3 categories, i.e., low, middle and high. Low age group comprised the women respondents who were upto age of 18-20 years. Middle age comprised the women respondents who were upto age of 20-30 years. High age comprised the women respondents where were above 30years. Family income was divided into 3 categories i.e., Low, Average and High. Low Family Income means when a family earns Rs 3000 per month, Average Family Income means when a family earns Rs 3000-7000 per month, and High Family Income when comprises a family earns of Rs 7000 per month.

RESULTS AND DISCUSSIONS

Table 1 shows that majority of illiterate women i.e., 50.00 per cent have low self-esteem in personal life .The medium level of self-esteem in personal life of women is found highly among 62.96 per cent of higher educational status. The high level of self-esteem in personal life of women is found by 61.54 per cent at higher educational status. Such differences between self-esteem in personal life and educational status is found significant (p-value < 0.05) with the χ^2 value of 7.66 with the 6 degree of freedom. Fontane, (1996) found that individuals high in self-efficacy, the belief that they can be successful at an activity and in self-esteem, a perception of positive self-regard are more likely to engage and adhere to an exercise program. Equal percentage of women i.e., 50.00 per cent have low level of self-esteem in family relation at graduate and higher educational levels respectively. The medium level of self-esteem in family relations is found among majority of women i.e, 63.79 per cent at higher educational status. The high level of self-esteem in family relations of women is found by 57.50 per cent women at higher educational status. Such differences between self-esteem in family relations and educational status is found significant (p-value < 0.05) with the χ^2 value of 5.22 at the 6 degree of freedom. Illiterate women have high level of self-esteem in family relations and women at high school education have medium level of self-esteem in family relations. It is observed that women at graduate level of educational status have low level of self-esteem in family relation. The women at higher educational status have medium level of self-esteem in family relations. A number of previous studies have suggested that the perception of barriers to leisure, or constants on leisure is related to self-esteem Searie and Jackson (1985) found that increase in education and income were related to reduced perceived barriers to recreation participation. Godbey (1985) suggested that people from low or middle-low self-esteem groups may be less likely to be aware of public leisure services, thus eliminating the possibility of participation in some leisure activities.

It is also found from table 1 that majority of women i.e., 81.82 per cent have low self-esteem in social relations at higher educational status. The medium level of self-esteem in social relations of women is found by 59.70 per cent at higher educational status. The high level of self-esteem in social relations of women is found 54.55 per cent at higher educational status. Such differences between self-esteem in social relations and educational status is found significant (p-value < 0.05) with the χ^2 value of 4.12 at the 6 degree of freedom. Majority of women i.e., 64.29 per cent have low level of self-esteem in career, at higher education level .The high level of self-esteem in career of women is found highly among women i.e., 61.36 per cent at higher educational status. Such differences between self-esteem in career and educational status is found insignificant (p-value > 0.05) with the χ^2 value of 5.41 at the 6 degree of freedom. Thus, illiterate women have low level of self-esteem in career. Whileas, women at high school level of educational status have high level of self-esteem in career. It is observed that women at graduate level of educational status have medium level of self-esteem in career. Moreover, the women at higher educational status have low level of self-esteem in career.

Table also shows that majority of women i.e., 56.25 per cent have medium level of over all self-esteem at higher of educational status. The high level of over all self-esteem of women is found highly among women by 80.00 per cent. Such differences between overall self-esteem and educational status is found high significant (p-value< 0.01) with the χ^2 value of 3.80 at 3 degree of freedom.

Self-Esteem among Women as per their Marital Status

Table 2 shows that majority of married women i.e., 33.33 per cent have low self-esteem in personal life. The medium level of self-esteem in personal life of married women is found highly among 45.68 per cent. The high level of self-esteem in personal life of married women is found by 38.46 per cent .Such differences between self-esteem in personal life and marital status is found significant (p-value< 0.05) with the χ^2 value of 3.38 with the 8 degree of freedom. Un-married women have low level of self-esteem in personal life. Whileas, married women have medium level of self-esteem in personal life. It is also observed that seperated women have low level of self-esteem personal life. The medium level of self-esteem in family relations is found among majority of married women 43.10 per cent at married level of marital status. The high level of self-esteem in family relations of women is found by 45.00 per cent married women.Such differences between self-esteem in family relations and marital status is found significant (p-value < 0.05) with the χ^2 value of 9.38 at the 8 degree of freedom. Un-married women have low level of self-esteem in family relations. Separated women have medium level of self-esteem in family relations.

Table 2 also shows that majority of married women i.e. 45.45 per cent have low self-esteem in social relations. The medium level of self-esteem in social relations found among 43.28 per cent married women. The high level of self-esteem in social relations of married women is found by 45.45 per cent. Such differences between self-esteem in social relations and martial status is found significant (p-value < 0.05) with the χ^2 value of 5.82 at the 8 degree of freedom In studying the effect of fatherly affirmation on psychosexual characteristics of male University students, Naus and Theis (1994, 1995) collected evidence that fatherly affirmation had an affect on self-esteem in women but not on their fear of intimacy. The study used expanded and improved measures on a larger sample of female university students to determine the relationship between fatherly affirmation and women's self-esteem, fear of intimacy, comfort with womanhood and construction of sexuality i.e., feelings of comfort and success in sexual relationships.

It is also found from table 2 that majority of married women i.e. 57.14 per cent have low self-esteem in career. The medium level of self-esteem in career of married women is found highly among women by 40.18 per cent Such differences between self-esteem in career and martial status is found high significant (p-value < 0.05) with the χ^2 value of 5.51 at the 6 degree freedom. In line with other research, notably that of fields (1983), Foresman (1989), Owen (1983), Secunda (1992) and Sharpe (1994), it was found that the more affirmed women feel higher self-esteem. Naus and Theis (1994, 1995) obtained similar results for men.. Majority of married women i.e. 47.50 per cent have medium level of over all self-esteem. The high level of overall self-esteem is found among un-married women by 45.00. Such differences between over all self-esteem and martial status is found significant (p-value < 0.05) with the χ^2 value of 6.86 at the 4 degree of freedom. Thus,un-married women have high level of overall self-esteem, while married women have medium level of overall self-esteem. It is also observed that seperated women have medium level of overall self-esteem. This outcome fits with the conclusions of Secunda's (1992) interviews with women. This was not the case in the earlier Naus and Theis (1994) study on men.

Self-Estcem among Women as per their Status

Table 3 shows that majority of non-working women i.e. 83.33 per cent have low self-esteem in personal life .The medium level of self-esteem in personal life of working women is found by 50.62 per cent. The high level of self-esteem in personal life of women is found by 61.54 per cent working women.. Such differences between self-esteem and personal life is found high significant (p-value >0.05) with the χ^2 value of 3.37 at the 2 degree of freedom. Thus, working women have high level of self-esteem in personal life. Whileas, non-working women have low level of self-esteem in personal life. The medium level of self-esteem in family relations is found among majority of non-working women by 53.45 per cent. The high level of self-esteem in family relations of working women is found by 52.50 per cent .Such differences between self-esteem and in family relations and status is found significant (p-value < 0.05) with the χ^2 value of 2.37 at the 2 degree of freedom. Working women have low level of self-esteem in family relations, whereas, non-working women have medium level of self-esteem in family relations.

It is also found from table 3 that majority of working women i.e. 63.64 per cent have low self-esteem in social relations. The medium level of self-esteem in social relations of non-working women is found by 53.73 per cent. The high level of self-esteem in social relations is found by 54.55 per cent of working level of women. Such differences between self-esteem in social relations and status is found in significant (p-value < 0.05) with the χ^2 value of 1.37 at the 2 degree of freedom. Thus, working women have low level of self-esteem in social relations. Whileas, non-working women have medium level of self-esteem in social relations. Majority of non-working women i.e. 57.14 per cent have low self-esteem in career. The medium level of self-esteem in career is found among 52.38 per cent of working women. Such differences between self-esteem in career and their status is found in significant (p-value < 0.05) with the χ^2 value of 0.38 at the 2 degree of freedom. It is observed that working women have medium level of self-esteem in career, whereas non-working women have low level of self-esteem in career. Table 3 also shows that majority of non-working women i.e. 53.75 per cent have medium level of overall self-esteem. The high level of overall self-esteem is found among women 65.00 per cent of working women. Such differences between overall self-esteem and status is found high significant (p-value< 0.05) with the χ^2 value of 2.25 at the 1 degree of freedom.

CONCLUSION

For women with good basic self-esteem, normal "ups and down" may lead to temporary fluctuations in how they feel about themselves, but only to a limited extent. In contrast, for women with poor basic self-esteem, these "ups and downs" may make all the difference in their world. Illiterate women have medium level overall self-esteem.. Whereas, women with higher educational status have high level of overall of self-esteem. Illiterate women have low level of self-esteem in personal life. Whileas, women at high school and higher education level have medium level of self-esteem in personal life. Illiterate women have high level of self-esteem in family relation, whereas,women at high school and higher educational level of educational status have medium level of self-esteem in family relations. Whileas, women at graduate level have low level of self-esteem in family relations. Women at illiterate and women with high school level of educational status have medium level of self-esteem in social relations. Thus, women at graduate level of educational status have high level of self-esteem in social relation. Women with higher education level have low level of self-esteem in social relations. Illiterate women and women with higher education level have low level of self-esteem in career. Whileas, women at high school level of educational status have high level of self-esteem in career. Un-married women have high level of overall self-esteem. Whileas, married women have medium level of overall self-esteem. It is also observed that separated women have medium level of overall self-esteem .Un-married women and separated women have low level of self-esteem in personal life. Whileas, married women have medium level of self-esteem in personal life. Thus, seperated women also have medium level of self-esteem in social relations. Working women have high level of overall self-esteem: whereas, non-working women have medium level of overall self-Working women have low level of self-esteem in family relations, whereas, non-working women have medium level of self-esteem in family relations. Similarly, non-working women have low level of self-esteem in social relations, whereas, non-working women have medium level of self-esteem in social relations.

REFERENCES

Annie Reich. (1960), *"Pathological Forms of Self-esteem Regulation". Journal of Personality of Social Psychology*. Vol. 15, No. 21. Psychoanalytic Electronic Publishing.

Boyd, K .R and Hrycaiko. D. W. (1997), *"The Effect of a Physical Activity Interventions Package on Self-esteem of Pre-adolescent and Adolescent Females". Journal of adolescence* Vol. 32, No. 693.

Fontane, P. E. (1996), *"Exercise, Fitness, and Feeling Well"*. Journal of American Behavioural Scientist. Vol. 39, No.288.

John Santrock. W. (2007), *"Child Development"*. New Delhi Usha Publication.

Manis, Jean Denby (1992), *"Relationships among Career orientation, Employment Status self-esteem and Life Satisfaction of Women: An Analysis of Age Differences"*. Education Resources Information Centre. Vol. 3, No. 82.

Nathaniel Branden, (2007), *"A Woman's Self-esteem: Struggles and Triumphs in the Search for Identity"*. Journal of Behaviour Medicine. Vol. 2, No. 49.

Naus, P. and theis, J. (1994), *"The Significance of Fatherly Affirmation for a Man's Psychological Well-being"*. A Project updates the Canadian. *Journal of Human Sexuality*. Vol. 3, No. 338.

Palmer, L. K. (1995), *"Effects of a Walking Program on Attributional Style, Depression, and Self-esteem in Women"*. Perceptual and Motor Skills.

Secunda, V. (1992), *"Women and their Fathers. The Sexual and Romantic Import of the First Man in Your Life"*. New York: Bantam Double Day Delhi Publishing.

Shagufa Kapadia and Amita Verma, (2000), *"Self-esteem Scale for Women"* (SESW). Lucknow, Shanti Sadan, Rai Behari Lal Road Publication. Yesterday, Hindustan Times, Mumbai.

HUMAN RIGHTS OF WOMEN: INITIATIVES AND COMMITMENTS

*P. K. Vaid**

INTRODUCTION

Women are an integral part of a society. They play an important role in determining the destiny of a nation. Therefore, due recognition to them in the society and their greater involvement in socio-economic and political affairs becomes all the more important. Socially, women are a harassed and ignored a lot. They have been and still are the victims of various social taboos particularly in developing countries like India. Though they enjoy equality but this equality is more in legal terms than in reality.

Women's human rights are violated in a variety of ways. Sometimes, of course, women suffer abuses (such as political repression) in ways that are much the same as those inflicted on men. But since the dominant image of the political actor in our world is male, the problem for women is visibility. Most women's experiences of human right violations are gendered, and many forms of discrimination or abuse occur because the victim is female. Women whose rights are being violated for reasons other than gender (as political prisoners or members of persecuted ethic groups) often also experience a particular form of abuse based on gender, such as sexual assault.

* Associate Professor, Department of Public Administration (ICDEOL), H. P. University, Shimla.

Even in 21st century, there is still an enormous gap between reality and ideal with regard to the participation of women in shaping human society. Human rights do not mean merely the right to live with humanity but means the right to live with dignity. A dignified life is one that is free from social handicaps, prejudices and biases on the basis of caste, creed or sex. It requires not only the recognition of a person's civil and political rights but also the certain of such social economic, educational and cultural conditions which are essential for the full development of one's personality. Violation of human rights is a global phenomenon; the difference being only of degree. Violations are bound to be more in society where the majority of population is illiterate, uneducated and poor. India is vast country with a greater part of its masses especially women being ignorant, poor and illiterate, so they are bound to suffer more atrocities and inhuman treatments.

Human rights of women have been defined as collective rights for a woman to be seen and accepted as person with the capacity to decide or act on her own behalf and to have equal access to resources and equitable social, economic and political support to develop her full potential exercise rights as a full human being and to support the development of others.

The Muslim law treats woman with utter scorn and this is reflection by what can be termed as a contractual relations between man and woman. The *Sariat* law postulates, "Man have authority over woman because *Allah* has the one superior to other and because they spend their wealth to maintain them. Good women are obedient so for those whom you fear disobedience admonish them and send them beds and beat them." Marriage in Muslim law is based on contract theory.

In the 19th century, however, the awareness of women's need for equality with men crystallized in the movement to obtain woman suffrage rather than in any fundamental or far-reaching re-evaluation of women's social status, roles, and their place in the economy. In the later 19th century a few women began to work in the professions, and women as a whole achieved the right to vote in the first half of the 20th century, but there were still distinct limits on women's participation in the workplace, as well as a set of prevailing notions that tended to confine women to their traditional roles as wives, mothers, and homemakers.

The growth of the service sector in the Western world's economies in the decades following World War II also helped create new types of jobs that could be done as well by women as by men. All these factors made growing numbers of women aware that society's traditional notions of them had failed to change as rapidly as women's actual living conditions had. In addition, the Civil Rights Movement in the United States during the 1960s inspired women to try to obtain better conditions for themselves through similar campaigns of mass agitation and social criticism.

INTERNATIONAL INITIATIVES

Human rights for women, as for all individuals, are protected in international law. Yet women suffer the full range of human rights violations known to the modern world. Women and girl-children also face human rights violations solely or primarily because of their sex.

The United Nation's Universal Declaration of Human Rights proclaims, "All human beings are born free and equal in dignity and rights." Yet women's freedom, dignity, and equality are persistently compromised by law and by custom in ways that men's are not.

Some provisions in the 'Convention on the Elimination of All Forms of Discrimination against Women', of significance in the present context are:

Article 11

"1. States Parties shall take all appropriate measures to eliminate discrimination against women in the field of employment in order to ensure, on a basis of equality of men and women, the same rights, in particular :

(a) The right to work as an inalienable right of all human beings;

(f) The right to protection of health and to safety in working conditions, including the safeguarding of the function of reproduction.

Article 24 :

"States Parties undertake to adopt all necessary measures at the national level aimed at achieving the full realization of the rights recognised in the present Convention."

The general recommendations of CEDAW in this context in respect of Art. 11 are:

"Violence and equality in employment:

Equality in employment can be seriously impaired when women are subjected to gender specific violence, such as sexual harassment in the work place.

HUMAN RIGHTS OF WOMEN-INDIAN PERSPECTIVE

The Government of India has ratified the above resolution on June 25, 1993 with some reservations which are not material in the present context. At the Fourth World Conference on Women in Beijing, the Government of India has also made an official commitment, *inter alia*, to formulate and operationalize a national policy on women which will continuously guide and inform action at every level and in every sector; to set up a Commission for Women's to act as a public defender of women's human rights; to institutionalise a national level mechanism to monitor the implementation of the Platform for Action.

There is no reason why these international conventions and norms cannot, therefore, be used for construing the fundamental rights expressly guaranteed in the Constitution of India which embody the basic concept of gender equality in all spheres of human activity.

The women in India have to go a long way to attain the complete gender justice in political, economic, social and cultural field. The need of the hour are not welfare, but development; not charity, but entitlement; not assistance, but empowerment; not structural adjustment, but structural change; not even social security but social and gender justice, if the women is to survive and flourish in the given situation.

CONSTITUTIONAL SAFEGUARDS

The Constitution of India has ensured equal status to all, i.e. not only between men and men, women and women but also between men and women. It is clear that all the provisions of the Constitution are applicable to both the persons, i.e. men and women. But there are some of the provisions which exclusively deals with the women only.

Article 14 of the Constitution prohibits class legislation but permits reasonable classification. It is essential that classification must be based on intelligible differentia and should have a rational nexus with the object sought to be achieved by the Act or legislation. Keeping this in view such classification must have the basic object that women can be treated as a class and special laws can be made in their favour.

Article 15 (1) of the Constitution prohibits the State from making discrimination against any citizen on the ground of religion, race, caste, sex, place of birth or any of them. Article 15(2) provides that no citizen shall, on grounds only of religion, race, caste, sex, place of birth or any of them, be subject to any disability, liability, restriction or condition with regard to any access to shop, restaurants, hotels, and place of entertainment. Article 15(3), being the exceptional clause of Article 15(1) and 15(2), declares that nothing under the provision shall prevent the State from making any special provision for women and children.

Apart from this Article 16(1) provides equal opportunity in matters relating to employment or appointment to any office under the State. Article 16(2) provides specific ground on which citizen are not to be discriminated against each other in matters of opportunity and office under the State.

Article 23 of the Constitution provides for prohibition of traffic in human being and forced labour. Article 24 further prohibits employment of any child below the age of 14 years whether he or she is male or female child, to work in any factory or mine or engage in any other hazardous employment.

PROTECTION UNDER PART IV OF THE CONSTITUTION OF INDIA

Article 38 (2) lays down that "the State shall, in particular, strive to minimize the inequalities in income and endeavour to eliminate inequalities in status, facilities and opportunities, not only among individuals but also amongst groups of people residing in different areas or engaged in different vocations."

Article 39 is another manifest declaration which lays down that State shall in particular, direct its policy towards:

(a) that the citizens, men and women, equally have the right to an adequate mean of livelihood;

(b) that there is equal pay for equal work for both men and women;

(c) that the health and strength of workers, men and women and the tender age of children are not abused and that children are not forced by economic necessity to enter avocation unsuited of their age and strength.

Another Article 44 protects the interests of women, accordingly, it lays down that the State shall endavour to secure for the citizen a uniform civil code throughout the territory of India.

In Part IV-A, the Constitution deals with the Fundamental Duties. Article 51-A(e) relate to women. It lays down that it shall be the duty of every citizen of India to promote harmony and spirit of common brotherhood amongst all the people of India transcending religion, linguistic and regional or sectional diversities to renounce practices derogatory to the dignity of women.

On the basis of the spirit and great consideration, exhaustive provisions are laid down in the Constitution. On the basis of these provisions, the Government of India has enacted several legislations which deals with women. These legislations seek to protect the right of women against the oppression, unfair treatment and discrimination.

The constitutional philosophy, special legislations, innovative active role of judiciary and recently passed Domestic Violence Act provides special favour to women and direct the State to treat the women at par with males equally. But unfortunately, still in the country like India women are subject to all kinds of discrimination and humiliation. It is now right time to give proper considerations to these issues to uplift the status of women in the country like India.

REFERENCES

Encyclopedia Britannia.

The Constitution of India, 1950.

United Nations Declaration on Human Rights, 1945.

Vishakha versus State of Rajasthan, AIR 1997 SC 3011.

Human Rights are Women's Right, Amnesty International, London, 1995.

Anil Dutta Mishra, Perspectives on Human Rights, New Delhi.

Sachidananda and Sinha, Ramesh, P., Women's Right : Myth and Reality, 1984.

Yagin, A. and Anwar, B., Protection of women under the Law, 1982.

A. K. Verma, Offences against Women, Dainik Jagaran 5 Dec. 2003.

O. C. Sharma, Crime against Women, 1994.

Peter Schneider, Social Rights and Concept of Human Rights, in D. D. Raphael (ed.) *Political Theory and Rights of Man*, London, Macmillan, 1967.

Desai Neera and Patel Vibhuti, Indian Women–Changes and Challenges in the International Decade, 1975-85, (1985).

THEORIES OF DIVORCE: CONCEALED TRAPS AND LAW REFORM

S. J. Hussain & Divya Varghese***

INTRODUCTION

Traditionally speaking there are as many as three kinds of theories of divorce, the Guilt or Fault Theory, the Breakdown Theory and the Consensual Theory. The Hindu Marriage Act 1955 which incorporates all these theories has been in operation for about fifty two years. The time and context is ripe to think of reforming the divorce law in the light of the experiences that we have gained, Revision of laws in any society is indispensable. The Law Commission observed[1]

> "With the changing limes, notions of fairness and justice assume newer and wider dimensions, and customs and beliefs of the people change. These, in turn demand changes in the structure of law; every progressive society must make a rational effort to meet these demands. Between the letter of law and the prevailing customs and dictates of the current value system accepted by the community, there should not be a unduly long gap".

The Hindu law of divorce developed on similar lines as that in England. The concept of Christian Marriage is quite similar to that of Hindu concept of marriage. While the Cannon law declared that 'let no man put asunder what God hath joined together' likewise Manu, the law-giver said that

* Visiting Professor of Law, Hidayatullah National University, Raipur.
** Final year student of B.A. LL.B (Hon), Hidayatullah National Law University, Raipur.

neither by sale nor by desertion is a women released from her Lord. Under both these systems marriage was a tie which cannot be dissolved. Both under English law and the traditional Hindu Law marriage was indissoluble. Divorce could be granted only among the lower classes of Hindus. Just as slowly but surely the jurisdiction of courts from ecclesiastical courts to secular courts was transferred in 1875 under Hindu law also divorce on some specific grounds such as cruelty, adultery and desertion was allowed.

It is the purpose of this paper to put the divorce law in the correct prospective, focus the enormous interpretative difficulties, troubles disappointment and mental agony suffered by the disgruntled spouse who wants to get out of the marital tie. Added to these woes, we have the technicality of the law and its interpretative process that cause endless misery to the parties. As stated by Cheshire[2]

Divorce, since it disintegrates the family unity, is of course, a social evil in itself, but it is a necessary evil. It is better to wreck the unity of the family than to wreck the future happiness of the parties by binding them to a companionship that has become odious.

Secondly to suggest reform in our own divorce law which avoids these inherent weaknesses and overcome the concealed traps. While doing so we will deal with the law of divorce, its course of developments and the recent reforms effected in 1996 in England.

The parameters of divorce, we believe are best studied in the matrix of comparative law. Indian laws are based on common law traditions in every sphere of legal life. Divorce law, despite the difference in the social and cultural mores in England and India is a social phenomenon that cut across national boundaries.

THE GUILT OR FAULT THEORY

The matrimonial law of England was based on the concept of guilt or fault.[3] Under this theory the petitioner had to establish that the other party has committed some matrimonial wrong in order to succeed obtaining the divorce. The same thing happened in the development of Hindu law. As early as in the 1948-49 the Madras and the Bombay states enacted laws permitting divorce on cruelty, desertion and adultery. Earlier too in 1937 the state of Baroda allowed divorce on similar grounds. As early as in 1869 the Indian Divorce Act was passed to grant divorce on similar grounds. Our Hindu law, Christian law, Parsi law are also based on the concept of Guilt or Fault. Off course the Hindu Marriage Act of 1955 also envisages grounds like insanity, conversion, not being heard of for seven years etc which are not based on Guilt or Fault theory.

The guilt or fault theory in England fell into disrepute. The age old doctrine that divorce should be available only to the innocent (i.e. the petitioner who alleges matrimonial wrong against the other party) was challenged. The conventional grounds as the basis for divorce were circumvented by the parties to obtain divorce. It was realized that the ground for divorce were not the real causes for which the spouses wanted to separate. In short the guilt theory was found to be unsatisfactory. In order to find out an alternative to the divorce law in England a Law Commission was appointed to look into the unsatisfactory divorce law.[4]

In 1971 the Divorce Reform Act was passed which abolished the guilt oriented grounds and enacted irretrievable grounds of marriage as the sole ground of divorce, looking at the enormous number of cases in the law reports we realize that the same thing as has happened in England arc happening in India too. In other words the disgruntled spouses since they are finding extremely difficult to prove the grounds of adultery, desertion and cruelty are resorting to false and baseless allegations in an effort to dissolve their marriage.

A few illustrations will explain this scenario. In *S. Chatterjee v. Nilima Chatterjee*[5] where the parties were in early fifties, the husband filed a petition for divorce alleging adultery of wife with different persons on diverse occasions. Here the divorce petition was dismissed as the court observed that the husband filed the petition to take revenge upon his wife. The law requires the petitioner to prove the guilt of the respondent and when and only when he could prove 'guilt' that a court is authorised to dissolve the marriage.

The English Law abolished the basis of guilt or fault as a ground of divorce and substituted in its place irretrievable breakdown of marriage. The Law Commission of England in 1966 gave a Report "Reform of Grounds of Divorce... Field of Choice". The Royal Commission after examining the state of law stated that a good divorce law should be able to achieve two objects;[6]

(i) To buttress, rather than to undermine, the stability of marriage; and

(ii) When, regretting, a marriage has irretrievably broken down, to enable the empty shell to be destroyed with the maximum fairness, and the minimum bitterness, distress and humiliation.

Irretrievable breakdown of marriage became the sole ground of divorce. There was a great difficulty as to the question how to prove breakdown of marriage. What tests should be employed? Or how should one measure the magnitude of breakdown? What yardstick should be applied in order to conclude that a marriage has broken down irretrievably? There were five facts to prove breakdown of marriage under the Divorce Reform act of 1969. They were as follows.[7]

1. That the respondent has committed adultery and the petitioner finds it intolerable to live with the respondent.
2. That the respondent has behaved in such a manner that the petitioner cannot reasonably be expected to live with the respondent
3. That the respondent has deserted the petition for a continuous period of at least two years immediately preceding the presentation of the petition.

4. That the parties to the marriage have lived apart for a continuous period of at least two years immediately preceding the presentation of the petition and the respondent consents to decree being granted.
5. That the parties to the marriage have lived apart for a continuous period of at least five years immediately preceding the presentation of the petition.

It may be pointed out that most of the guidelines are based on the guilt theory but the courts have interpreted that these are only facts and to be taken as guidelines to prove marriage-breakdown. But as a matter of fact the ghost of guilt walks into these provision. A lot of controversy arose with regard to the interpretation of the first guideline. The question that confronted the courts revolved around the word 'and' which connects adultery with intolerability. Some courts interpreted this guideline stating that there is a nexus between adultery and intolerability.[8] In other words, the respondent must have committed adultery and as a result of adultery it has become intolerable for the petitioner to live with the respondent. Some courts[9] took the view that there is no necessary connection between adultery and intolerability. In this case the court stated that the petitioner had to prove adultery and any other conduct of the respondent which has nothing to do with adultery i.e. respondent have committed adultery and the petitioner finds it intolerable to live with the other party, not necessarily because of adultery. In this context it will be interesting to know how Lord Denning interpreted the word "and" in Bowman's case. Their lordship said "strawberries and cream" means "strawberries and cream" not "strawberries with cream".[10] It is strange that the fact of the spouses hang on the meaning give to the grammatically disjunctive word "and".

We have referred to the English Law in some detail in order to make out a case for not including the breakdown theory as advocated by some writers like Java V.S.[11] and B.D. Agarwal.[12] Adding merely breakdown of marriage along with the guilt oriented grounds may not be a good suggestion because almost in every case the petitioner will try to establish adultery, cruelty, desertion in order to prove the breakdown of marriage. The result would be virtually following the guilt theory which we want to discard.

The Law Commission in England looked into the working of the divorce laws based on the concept of breakdown theory. Later many criticisms have been made by the Law Commission relating to breakdown of marriage as a ground for divorce.[13] The Law-Commission gave the following reasons for failure of breakdown theory. It said that it was confusing and misleading. Further the real reason, it said, was that the breakdown might have nothing to do with the fact presented in the petition, the allegations becoming a peg on to which to hang the petition, regardless of their significance (or insignificance) for the parties. It was discriminatory and unjust. Moreover it distorts parties bargaining positions. And lastly it provokes unnecessary hostility and bitterness. It may be pointed out here that one of the objectives of the earlier law commission recommending breakdown of marriage as a ground for divorce was to remove hostility and bitterness to taking out the heat out of matrimonial proceedings. The Law Commission further said that the Reform Act of 1973 did nothing to save the marriage and that it did not protect the children whose parents often divorce.

In the end the Law Commission recommended further reforms by abandoning the Breakdown Theory and suggested a rational and sensible divorce law. The Law Commission[14] said that the divorce law should " ... *try to support those marriages which are capable of being saved... enable those which cannot be saved to be dissolved with minimum of avoidable distress, bitterness and hostility... encourage, so far as possible, the amicable resolution of practical issues relating to the couples' home, finances and children...*".

As we stated earlier that reforms of divorce laws are eminent and necessary and that since our divorce law has traveled on the same lines as that of common law it became inevitable to look into the reforms in English Law.

The general principles as laid down under the Family Law Act 1996[15] aims at giving support to the institution of marriage but at the same time not making it a burden Which would be rather difficult to bear. It says that parties should take practicable steps to restore the marriage, however in cases where the marriage has irretrievably broken down the divorce should be allowed in a manner which brings the least disruption to the parties and children affected, promoting a good and continuous relation between the parties. These principles arc to be borne in mind by judges and lawyers while dealing the dispute.

The procedure for divorce under the Act provides for a preliminary requirement of the party who initiates the divorce proceedings to have attended an information meeting', which intends to communicate a range of information relating to divorce, the process and its consequences and also to 'mark the seriousness of the step taken'.[16]

The divorce proceedings commence on the receipt by the courts of a statement of marital breakdown, within three months after the information meeting. The statement reflects that the parties believe the marriage is no more viable. Unlike the former law, no cross petitions are allowed by the parties once a statement has been issued by the spouse, any further statement issued will be ineffective. Statements within the period of one year after the marriage are ineffective for the purposes of any application of divorce.[17]

The irretrievable breakdown of marriage is established by the passing of due period for reflection and consideration which is a duration of nine months which maybe extended if the circumstances require such as in cases where there was delay in serving notice or statement, to allow for attempted reconciliation. Automatic extension is provided where a party seeks further time for reflection , or where a child of the family is under sixteen.

During the period for reflection and consideration the parties arc expected to undergo counseling and mediation which targets on the scope for reconciliation of the dispute between the spouses. It also intends at settling down the terms with regard to the end of the marriage and post divorce arrangements. The government policy dictates that no divorce should usually be made unless the parties' future arrangements have been finalized.

Marriage counseling may be provided to the parties at two instances first at the time of information meeting and later during the period of reflecting and consideration. Free mediation and legal aid is provided to the financially eligible. The courts having received a statement may give a direction cither on the application of either of the spouses or on its own initiative, which may require the parties to attend a meeting explaining the facilities for mediation. The court would further direct on who is to arrange and conduct the meeting requiring the person to report to the court stating the proceeds of the mediation.

Under Section 3 of the Family Law Act 1996 provision is made for application of divorce which can be made by either or both of the parties alter establishing the conditions prescribed "under the Act. Section 9 of the Act provide for three kids of arrangements between the parties.

(a) Financial Arrangements — These are provisions governing the rights and liabilities with respect of the making or securing of payments or the disposition or use of any property including such rights and liabilities with respect to the maintenance or education of any child.

(b) Religious Arrangements - The parties are required to co operate if the marriage is to be dissolved in accordance with those usages, according to which the marriage was solemnised.

(c) Arrangements for children - The arrangement for the future concerns of the children of the family is provided under this arrangement. S. 41 of the 1973 Act provides that the court has to consider the arrangement proposed for the children's future after the parents' divorce. Section 11 of the 1996 Act repeats this provision but emphasises that the court is to treat the welfare of the child as paramount when scrutinizing the proposed arrangement.[18]

CONSENSUAL THEORY

Section 13(b) of the Hindu Marriage Act 1955 provides for divorce by mutual consent. Many people think that divorce by mutual consent is an easy way out to get rid of each other in case their marriage has lost the purpose and objective and the parties do not want to live together anymore. If one looks to the interpretation put by the various courts on this section one realizes that it has so many bottlenecks and concealed traps to avoid to win a decree of divorce.[19] The law relating to mutual consent provides that both the parties must jointly petition to the court for divorce. This very liberty to obtaining divorce is dependent upon the other party agreeing to dissolve the marriage. As someone said 'It takes two people to say 'Yes' to marry, if one of them does not agree or says 'No' there is no marriage.'

Several courts took diametrically opposite view on the question whether after having submitted the petition for obtaining divorce jointly anyone party can withdraw unilaterally. The Bombay High Court in *Romesh Londhe's*[20] case has taken a view that the crucial time for consensual divorce under the relevant provision was the time when the petition was filed. If the consent was voluntary given a party by unilaterally withdrawing the petition cannot torpedo the process of obtaining a divorce decree. The court took this view relying on Order XXIII R. 1 of the Civil Procedure Code wherein it is provided that if the suit is filed jointly by one or more plaintiffs, the suit or a part of the claim cannot be abandoned or withdrawn by one of the plaintiff or one of the party to the suit. On the other hand the Kerala High Court in *Santosh Kumari v. Virendra Kumar*[21] has decided on similar lines. All these courts have held that the petition when jointly presented before the court can be withdrawn by anyone of spouses. The controversy was however (dissolved by the Supreme Court in *Suresh Devi v. Om Prakash*[22] wherein it was held that any party can unilaterally withdraw the consent at any time till the decree of divorce is passed. The very fact that the specific periods of waiting for 6 - 18 months under S. 13(b) of the Act is manifest that the party can withdraw before the lapse of this period or even after the period of 18 months, the court said.

The main criticism of the consent theory as stated by Paras Diwan[23] is two-fold: It makes divorce very easy and it makes divorce very difficult. As regards the first assumption it may be stated that spouses do not seek divorce at the drop of the hat. There are several constraints like social taboos, dim prospects of second marriage, the existence of children who may be of young and tender age where it becomes necessary to protect them. The spouses under such circumstances may sacrifice and may not think of divorce for the sake of the children. As respects the second assumption it is very correct that if one of the party wants to divorce by mutual consent, the other party may veto and may not agree for divorce. In such a case, divorce becomes impossible because divorce by mutual consent requires the consent of both the parties.

Yet another hurdle in the way of obtaining any remedy under the Hindu Marriage Act is Section 23. Under this section even if the Court is satisfied that the ground for granting relief exists, the relief cannot be given unless the petitioner is not in any way taking advantage of his or her own wrong or disability for the purpose of relief. Where the ground of relief is based on adultery the Court must see whether the offence has not been connived at or condoned or accessory to the commission of the matrimonial offence.

There is a controversy about the question as to what amounts to taking advantage of his or her own wrong. It has been held by the full bench of Punjab High Court in *Bimla Devi v. Singh Raj*[24], that Section 23(i)(a) does not apply where a husband had obtained a decree of restitution of conjugal rights against his wife and if the wife did not comply with the decree it will not amount to taking advantage of a wrong. Therefore the petition for divorce was granted. In similar circumstances the Bombay High Court took a contrary view in *Lakshmi Bai v. Lakshmi Chand.*[25] The Supreme Court finally approved the decision of Bimla Devi's case in *Dharmendra Kumar v. Usha Kumar*[26]. It was argued in the Supreme Court that the wife did not agree to proposal for reunion by the husband and this conduct amounted to taking advantage of her own wrong. The Supreme Court rejected the contention and granted divorce under Section 13(1-A).

The other discretionary bars to granting the remedy under the Hindu Marriage Act and in other divorce laws are that the petition has been filed after unnecessary and improper delay. And to top it all the section says that only when there is no other legal why relief should not be granted, then and in such a a case but not otherwise the Court shall decree such relief accordingly. An obligation is also placed upon the Court to make efforts at reconciliation.

IRRETRIEVABLE BREAKDOWN OF MARRIAGE

As early as in 1978 the Law Commission in India recommended the inclusion of divorce on the ground of irretrievable breakdown of marriage along with other grounds. The Hindu Marriage Act, 1955 provided that the divorce would be obtained by a petition firstly when a decree in favour of restitution of conjugal rights had been passed and the respondent had not complied with it for a period of two or more years and secondly when a decree of judicial separation has been passed and no cohabitation had been resumed for a period of 2 or more years, these grounds being the indication to the marriage having been broken-down irretrievably. However the Amendment of 1964, recognised breakdown of marriage as a ground allowing either party to sue for divorce.

Since refusing the decree to the respondent may give rise to hardship or difficulties, for instance, if the petitioner alone is allowed to file a petition for divorce and not the respondent, in this situation the petitioner whether husband or wife may not go to obtain divorce and keep the spouse in a matrimonial limbo, therefore the amendment of 1964 allowed either party to sue for divorce on failure to comply with the decree of restitution of conjugal rights or judicial separation or reconciliation after judicial separation.

The concept of breakdown of marriage has of late been judicially recognised in cases where the petitioner applied for any remedy under the Act such as adultery or cruelty is not able to prove the matrimonial offence, but the marriage of such spouses has lost the flicker of life and has failed to achieve the object and purposes of the marriage and where no reconciliation is possible between the parties the courts have granted the remedies under the Act. Kusum's comments on the subject are very instructive.[27] Not only have the courts recognised a theory of marriage breakdown but in some cases have dissolved the marriage by invoking Art. 142 of the Constitution.[28] In *Romesh Chand v. Savitri*[29] the marriage was dead for all practical purposes, though parties had lived together for 25 years. The husband had agreed to transfer the house. The Supreme Court dissolved the marriage on husband's transfer his house to the wife exercising its power under Art. 142 of the Constitution. Also in *Kanchan Devi v. Pramod Kumar*[30] the court held that " In view of the peculiar facts and circumstances of the case and being satisfied that the marriage between the appellant and the respondent has irretrievably broken-down and there is no possibility of reconciliation, the court exercised its power under Art. 142 and directed that marriage may be dissolved by a decree of divorce.

The Supreme Court has observed in a case that irretrievable marriage is not itself sufficient to dissolve the marriage however where exigency demands the court should end the agony and bitterness by granting the divorce.[31]

As respects the ground of divorce by mutual consent, we have already sufficiently offered our remarks on the drawbacks of the consensual divorce. We will now hasten to comment on the breakdown of marriage as a ground of divorce along with the guilt or fault grounds as suggested by some writers we have referred to above. We may recall that the Commission in its seventy first report has recommended the inclusion of breakdown of marriage as an additional ground of divorce. The Commission is of the view that there is no inherent contradiction or fallacy in having both the new and the old grounds. It is stated that since no proof of an irretrievable breakdown as a result of adultery, cruelty or desertion is required under its scheme, the retention of fault notion would be in order. With great respect we differ from the views expressed by some writers as also of Law Commission. The million dollar question relating to breakdown of marriage is how to prove breakdown. What is the yardstick to measure the magnitude of breakdown. Examples of breakdown of marriage or the reasons for breakdown may be incompatibility of temperament, petulance of manner, irreconcilable differences, serious marital discord, living separate and apart for a reasonable period of time may evidence marriage breakdown. There is a danger that a conservative judge may not consider the above mentioned reasons to presume breakdown, whereas a liberal judge may conclude that the idiosyncrasies of the husband and the silly nothings of the wife can result in the breakdown of marriage. Then the principle of breakdown will become an unruly horse running helter and skelter. Since we are in the end suggesting reforms of divorce law on a totally different philosophy we are not in favour of even adopting breakdown of marriage as a sole ground for divorce.

THE INADEQUACY AND ILL-EFFECTS OF THE DIVORCE LAW BASED ON THE ABOVE STATED THEORIES

The divorce law in India applicable to all the communities namely Hindus, Christians, Parsis and the law applicable to inter-religious marriages is a codified law. And all the three theories of divorce i.e. Guilt or Fault Theory, the breakdown theory and the consensual theory find a place in these enactments.

We will now critically examine each theory in order to expose inherent weaknesses and the manner in which the theories are applied in practice. Off course while placing these theories in the proper perspective, we have by way of passing remarks stated how these theories have been applied in deciding cases. We will now go into some specific problems to prove inadequacy and the irrationality, the hardships, the technicalities of the law in its application.

The first theory of divorce which we have addressed is the Guilt theory. A few observations by the Anglo-American judges will leave no one in doubt the evils of the adversary system, the perjury percolating in the courts and the discrepancy between the law in the books and law in action does not satisfy anybody. George Squire commenting upon the evils of adversary procedure declared: [32]

> The adversary principle is the Gibraltar of Anglo-American procedure. Embedded in it are the standards of juridical functions such as the rules of evidence ... block any major change in divorce or any other civil litigation.

Paul W. Alexander, judge of the Family Court, Toledo lamented ...[33]

> No one is more painfully conscious than the legal profession of the utter imbecility of our present divorce procedure and pernicious and almost wicked philosophy upon which it is based. Every honest lawyer is ashamed of the atmosphere of hypocrisy and lies in which he usually must handle a divorce case.

Again Paul Sayre observed[34]

> This scheming of the parties themselves in an atmosphere of falsehood as well as fraud on our courts, works a degrading influence on the quality of our civilization and bring our whole system of justice into disrepute.

The above observation apply with equal strength to the Indian situation. The grounds on which parties file petitions for divorce is not the real reasons or causes. The causes may be psychological, economic, social intolerance or even invisible repugnance. There are a plethora of cases where parties in collusion or by force or fraud try to obtain divorce like "hotel cases" in England where one spouse in order to obtain divorce on the ground of adultery asks the wife to be present with a stranger or friend in a particular hotel. The husband gatecrashes and takes a sparkling picture of his wife with a friend in a compromising posture in order to prove adultery. In India too there are cases where the husband took the photograph of his wife sitting with a stranger near Qutub Minar and produced the photograph as proof of adultery. In another case the husband forcibly compelled the wife to write a letter before the Guru Granth Saheb admitting the birth of a child before marriage in order to obtain a decree of nullity for fraud. In short, these cases particularly relating to adultery is nothing less than washing the dirty linen in the courts.

The spouses where a legal battle for years, sometimes more than 15 years and fight like gladiators. We can gauge the heat, the acrimony, the agony and disappointment in the matrimonial proceedings.

A RATIONAL DIVORCE LAW FOR ALL[35]

After having pointed out the concealed traps, the pitfalls and the stumbling blocks in the present divorce law we make a strong plea for an honest, sincere, rational divorce law on the lines on which the Family Law Act of 1996 in England has been enacted. We strongly advocate that it is not the court or the state that should decide whether to continue the marriage or separate the spouses. The matter must rest with the parties themselves. When both or one of the parties want to liberate himself or herself from the shackles of married life they should be allowed to do so. Law must recognise what is a fact and relieve the parties from the burden of married life. Conjugal life should be lived in trust, happiness, sharing the joys and sorrows of life. Marriage is a holy wedlock and not an unholy deadlock. In the words of Law Commission of England, a good divorce law should achieve two objectives, to buttress rather than to undermine the stability of marriage and when regrettably a marriage has broken down irretrievably to enable the empty shell to be destroyed with maximum fairness and minimum bitterness, distress and humiliation.

When we are suggesting a rational or rather a radical divorce law, we must also be extremely mindful and cautious to safeguard that the law should provide for the party who is unwilling to agree to a forced divorce. The law may lay down that the petition for divorce either by one or both the parties cannot be entertained unless a period of one year has elapsed after marriage. It may also provide an exception to file a petition for divorce before such period in case there are exceptional hardships on the part of the petitioner or exceptional depravity on the part of the respondent. A certificate must be obtained to the effect that reconciliation or mediation processes have been gone through with the assistance of the family members or lawyers or by the persons who are interested in the welfare of the family. The parties must be made to understand the seriousness of the consequences of divorce. In addition to this, the party or the parties should provide a statement of what arrangements financial, social, custody of the children etc have been made. The court will examine and sit as an overseeing participant and after being convinced of the truth of the arrangements may dissolve the marriage. Even after making all these arrangements another six months period should be given to the parties as a 'cooling off' period so that they can decide whether to drop the guillotine on the marital tie or save the marriage if possible. The principle of law and the philosophy of divorce is to give a decent burial to a defunct marriage.

The increase in literacy, the assertions of individualism, the passion for freedom and liberty, the change in the cultural and social ideas and values not to speak of the women's liberation movement, the empowerment of women by the instrumentality of the law, the awareness to excise the rights by both men and women have all contributed to look to the marriage relationship in a different perspective. Dignity, self-respect, economic independence among women too compel us to alter the basis of divorce law.

At the same time we must realize that the state is interested in the stability of marriage, the society is concerned in happy marriages. Married life is to be lived with mutual love and trust and in conjugal harmony. If the marriage has floundered on the rocks of disharmony, when there is no flicker of life in marriage, when there are no prospects of reconciliation, when the spouses have plucked the fruits of matrimony and left the stones, then the relationship should come to an end. Courts of law cannot enforce conjugal bliss between the spouses, they can alleviate human sufferings.

NOTES

1. Law Commission of India, Fifty ninth report on the Hindu Marriage Act, 1955 Para 1.14 p. 9 March 1974.
2. Cheshire (1945) 61 L.Q. Rev. 352.
3. See S. J. Hussain, A look at the Divorce Law Reform in England, Kurukshetra Law Journal, Vol. 2. 1976. pp. 80-83.
4. The Law Commission, Reform of the Grounds of Divorce: The Field of Choice 3123, (1966).
5. S. Chatterjee v. Nilima, 74 CWN (1969) 168.
6. Supra note 4.
7. Divorce Reform Act 1969, Sec. 291) (a) to Sec. 2(1)(e). The Act provided under Section 2(3) If the court is satisfied on all evidence such as mentioned in sub-section(1) of this section then, unless it is satisfied on all evidence that the marriage has not broken down irretrievably, it shall ... grant decree nisi of divorce. See generally Bromley Family Law (1998) on the subject.
8. See Roper v. Roper [1972] 3 All. E. R. 668.
9. See Goodrich v. Goodrich [1971] 2 All. E. R. 1340.
10. As quoted by Rosenbaum in Divorce Law Reform in England [1972-73] 12 J. Fam. L at 371.

11. V.S. Jaya, Irretrievable Breakdown of Marriage As An Additional Ground For Divorce (2006) Jl. I. L. Vol. 4813 at P. 439
12. B.D. Aggarwal, Irretrievable Breakdown of Marriage as Ground of Divorce Need for Inclusion (1997) SCC (J) 11. See further Paras Diwan, Studies in Hindu Marriage and Special Marriage Act (1978) p. 32, Kusum, Irretrievable Breakdown of Marriage: A Ground for Divorce (1978) 20 JILI. 288.
13. See N.V. Lowe and G. Douglas Family Law (1998) Ninth Ed. From p. 235-240.
14. *Ibid.* 36.
15. Supra note 12 at 240.
16. Hansard H. L. Debs, 30 Nov 1990. Col (Lord Mackay L. C).
17. Sec. 8 of the Family Law Act, 1996.
18. Ibid. Note 16 S. 20(1) and subsequent sections of Family Law Act, 1996.
19. The conflicts and controversies among the courts have been placed in Subba Rao, Family Law (2004) pp. 197-200.
20. Romesh Londhe, A.I.R. 1976 Bom. 566.
21. Santosh Kumari v. Virendra Kumar A.I.R. Ker. 166.
22. Suresh Devi v. Om Prakash, A.I.R. 1976 SC 1100.
23. See Paras Diwan (2nd. Ed) 2004 at 560.
24. Bimla Devi v. Singh Raj (1977) P & H 167.
25. Lakshmi Bai v. Lakshmi Chand (1968) BOM. 332.
26. Dharmendra Kumar v. Usha Kumar A.I.R (1977) SC 2218.
27. See Kusum, Family Law Lectures (2003) 148 where she has collected cases where marriage breakdown theory has been judicially recognised. Some of the cases are : Saroj Rani v. Sudarshan Kumar A.I.R (1984) SC 1502; Bhagwat v. Bhagwat A.I.R 194 SC 710; Smt. Kanchan Devi v. Pramod Kumar A.I.R (1996)(1) HLR . 280. See at p. 151 and 152 of her book cited above.
28. Article 142 of the Constitution states that the Supreme Court has the power to pass any decree or order as is necessary for doing complete justice in any case or matter pending before it.
29. Romesh Chand v. Savitri A.I.R. (1995) SC 851.
30. Kanchan Devi v. Pramod Kumar see supra note 23.

31. Durga Prasanna Tripathy v. Arundhati Tripathy, A.I.R. 2005 SC 3297.
32. George Squire, The Shift From Adversary to Administrative Divorce, (1953) 33 Boston U.L. Rev. 141 at 143
33. Alexander, Family Life Conference Suggest New Juridical Procedures and Attitude Towards Marriage and Divorce, (1948) 32 J. Am. Jud. Society, 38 at 40.
34. Paul Sayre, Divorce For Unworthy: Specific Grounds for Divorce (1953) 18 Law & Contem.Prob at 28
35. We have not dealt with the Islamic Law of divorce for the subject needs a separate discourse. It may be pointed out here that the Islamic Law of divorce is almost very similar to the divorce law reforms we have suggested.

POSITION OF WOMEN UNDER MUSLIM PERSONAL LAW: SOME OBSERVATIONS

*Subhash Chandra Singh**

INTRODUCTION

The issue of women's rights in Islam is highly controversial. Any materials on this subject should be used with caution because of the lack of objectivity. While it is generally agreed that the rights granted to women in the *Qur'an* were a vast improvement in comparison to the situation of women in Arabia prior to the advent of Islam. Before the advent of Islam, women were treated like slaves or property. Women were used for one purpose, and then discarded. They had no freedom, could own no property and were not allowed to inherit. In times of war, women were treated as part of the prize. Outside Arabia conditions for women were no better. In Egypt, India and all European countries in the Dark Ages, women were treated worse than slaves.

The rights of women have assumed an enhanced significance in modern times in general, and in the Islamic world, in particular. Historically, women have remained subordinate to men. The traditional Islamic societies were patriarchal in character. Islam brought a significant change in the status of women despite the deeply entrenched patriarchy of seventh-century Arabia. The *Qur'an* provides

* Head, Department of Law, Mahatma Gandhi Kashi Vidyapith, Varanasi-2210002 (U.P.)

explicit rights to inheritance, independent property, divorce and right to testify in a court of law. It prohibits wanton violence towards women and girls and is against duress in marriage and community affairs. Islam considered a woman to be equal to a man as a human and as a partner in his life. A Muslim woman is not permitted to change her family name to her husband's name upon marriage. She is always known by her father's name as a mark of her own identity.

In the period immediately following the death of the Prophet women were active participants at all levels of community affairs—religious, political, social, educational and intellectual. They played key role in preserving traditions, disseminating knowledge and challenging authority when it went against their understanding of the *Qur'an* or the prophetic legacy. But with the passage of time the condition of women in Islam began to decline and reverts back to pre-Islamic norms. Women came to be discussed in law in the same terms as material objects and possessions. It was not until the post-colonial period women reemerged as active participants in all areas of public life.

Recent legislative changes and judicial pronouncements show that at least some parts of the Islamic personal law are not considered, either by courts or legislatures, to be in conformity with the present day constitutional norms or requirements of justice, equity and good conscience seems to be a question which has to be decided quite apart from religion. Gender-related Islamic norms are also considered to be against the norms of international human rights law. This paper critically examines the status of Muslim women in the context of Islamic personal law and its conformity with the Constitution and international human rights law.

WOMEN'S RIGHTS AS HUMAN RIGHTS

Equality of sexes is now recognized as a human right. The United Nations, since its inception, is working in the direction of achieving this concept. Women, who represent more than half of the world's population and the vast majority of them, are subject to subjugation of their tradition and religion, in every sphere of human activity. The concept of equality is no longer a characteristic of a particular culture but as a universal principle and a human right. Article 1 of the Universal Declaration of Human Rights (1948) states, "All human beings are born free and equal in dignity and rights". The importance of the status of women is also reflected in the resolution of the United Nations General Assembly passed unanimously on 7 November 1967. It states that the full development of nations, the world's general welfare and the cause of peace require full equality of both sexes everywhere. The resolution in particular calls upon nations to take "all appropriate measures" to abolish any law or custom that discriminates against women."[1]

The information on the phenomenon of violence and discrimination against Muslim women reveals the powerful impact of religion, customs and tradition in fostering and intitutionalising extreme forms of discrimination against women in the family and community. Here I would particularly refer to the Convention on the Elimination of All Forms of Discrimination Against Women (CEDAW) 1979, and international instrument providing the ethical and legal basis for protection and promotion of human rights of women under United Nations framework. This is considered as the International Bill of Rights for women. The CEDAW has been ratified by 161 countries. Out of these, except few Muslim countries, most of the Muslim majority countries have ratified the Convention with reservations.[2] Article 28 of the Convention permits State Parties to make a reservation. India also made a reservation.[3] One of the major obstacles in the way of actualising the human rights of women faced by the CEDAW committee is the reservation on the Convention which are incompatible with the object and purpose of the Convention. CEDAW has been subjected to more reservations than any other major international treaty. Over 50 countries have made reservations to some substantive articles of the Convention including India and most Muslim countries (except Indonesia and Yemen) which have ratified the Convention. Such substantive reservations have the potential to limit significantly the obligations undertaken by the reserving state in protection and promotion of women's rights as prescribed under the Convention.[4]

It is noted that reservations made by the Islamic countries have followed a several pattern. The reasons for entering reservation to specific provisions of the article/articles are those being, "Contradictory to the principles of Islamic Sharia law." In private sphere, Muslim women are discriminated in all matters relating to marriage, divorce, guardianship and child custody and inheritance and ownership of property. An important area of discrimination against women is equal inheritance rights. Reservations entered by Muslim countries as well as by India on Article 16 (or part of it) deals with these rights are considered as a serious violation of human rights of Muslim women.

SEX EQUALITY AND THE CONSTITUTION

Equality of sexes is also guaranteed by the Indian Constitution. The Preamble to the Constitution affirms the objective of equality. Article 14 in Part III of the Constitution declares the fundamental right to equality before law and equal protection of laws within the territory of India. And Article 13(1) lays down that "All laws in force in so far as they are inconsistent with the provision of this part shall to extent of such inconsistency, be void." The equality provision has been used more extensively in all countries including India in promoting state accountability for protecting women from violence and discrimination by state and non-state actors.

The Constitution of India imposes on the State a duty to respect freedom of conscience and religion, and recognise the right to profess, practice and propagate religion. Yet the rights to profess and practice religion as manifested in the Constitution of India are subject to 'public order, morality and health'. Where the right to manifest religion is limited, restrictions imposed by Governments to protect women from violence and domination can be justified by reference to the Constitution. Similarly civil society groups can challenge laws and policies that seek to reinforce religious or customary norms that either discriminate against women or encourage violence against women. These restrictions provide the State with an opportunity to balance what may be perceived by some as conflicting interests of religious ideologies and human rights. The constitutional provisions can be used to legitimize intervention.

There are few provisions of Islamic law which are not in consonance with the provisions of the Constitution. We have referred to a few instances such as polygamy, unilateral repudiation of the wife by the husband and a daughter's share of inheritance. These are the provisions which impinge upon the concept of equality between the sexes contemplated by the Constitution. It is often said that personal laws are outside the purview of challenge under Article 13 of the Constitution of India. The judgments in *Narasu Appa's* case[5] and *Dwarka Bai's* case[6] indicate three arguments made in support of the discriminatory personal laws: first, that discrimination against women in the personal laws is beyond the purview of Articles 13 and 14 as 'laws in force' do not include personal laws; second, inequality of sexes in law can be upheld on the ground of reasonable classification; and third, that even if it is held that personal laws are covered by Article 13(1) their provisions permitting polygamy do not amount to a discrimination on the ground of sex only. In the modern world polygamy may seem to be an anachronism and may seem to be based on outdated and outworn ideas.

In *State of Bombay* v. *Narasu Appa Mali,*[7] a view was expressed that even if personal laws fell within the purview of Article 13(1) of the Constitution, the provisions of personal laws permitting polygamy did not amount to discrimination on the ground of sex only. Gajendragadkar, J. stated:

> Even assuming that personal law was included (in the words 'laws in force') the question still remains to be considered as

to whether polygamy discriminates against women only on the ground of sex. This argument in our opinion overlooks the history of polygamy as a social institution. Polygamy is justified if at all on social, economic and religious grounds and hardly over on grounds like sex. In the modern world polygamy may seem to be an anachronism and may seem to be based on outdated and outworn ideas. When, however, it is found recognized in any personal law, it is based on considerations which were very vital and compelling to those who believed and who still believe in the sanctity of their personal law. Therefore, it would be difficult to say that the institution of polygamy would constitute a discrimination against members of one sex only on the ground of their sex.[8]

RIGHTS IN RESPECT OF MARRIAGE, DIVORCE AND CHILD CUSTODY

Let us take the status of Muslim women in respect of marriage, divorce, and child custody. Though marriage is a contract under Muslim law, this is one sided contract. Muslim women traditionally have been married at an extremely young age, sometimes even before puberty. This practice is related, of course, to the historical fact that fathers and other male relatives generally have been chosen the grooms themselves, despite the guarantee of the *Qur'an* that marriage is a contract into which male and female enter equally. While it is true that technically a girl cannot be forced into a marriage she does not want, pressures from family and the youth of the girl too often have made this prerogative difficult to exercise.[9] Often, the consent is not even asked for or considered important, and sometimes marriages take place despite the girl's objections.

The practice of child marriages is common in Muslim society in all parts of the Islamic world, in particular in the poor urban and rural areas. The reasons behind child marriage are usually economic. The child is sold off into marriage to ease the burden of the family. Indian law specifies a minimum age of marriage in the Child Marriage Restraint Act (1929). Most of the girls sold or forced into marriage are under the age of 18 which is the minimum age. Therefore offenders who violate the law can be dealt with under the Child Marriage Restraint Act. However, it has been pointed out that this legislation is merely a symbolic and inoperative in real practice. This Act defines a "child" as a female under 18 and a male under 21 and makes it an offence to either marry a child or to allow such a marriage or to solemnize it. However, the penalty for an infringement is very minimal.

Furthermore, a conviction under this law does not make the marriage 'null and void'. Consequently, the Act has not had a deterrent impact. However, a girl who has been married off before the age of 15 has the right to repudiate the marriage before she turns 18. The law on minimum age of marriage, though it is weak and ineffective to prevent child marriage has met with much resistance from the clergy who state that Islam sets no age-limit on marriages and thus the law is not acceptable. Both CEDAW and the Convention on the Rights of the Child (CRC) contain provisions creating commitment to abolish this practice. India therefore continues to face a serious problem of child marriage as both Hindu and Muslim communities practice child marriage without any fear of penal law.

Under Muslim personal law when a marriage was contracted for a minor girl by any guardian other than the father or father's father the minor had the option of repudiating the marriage on her attaining puberty. This is technically called option of puberty. Certain changes have been effected by the Dissolution of Muslim Marriages Act, 1939 regarding a girl's right to option of puberty. This Act entitles her to exercise the option of puberty even if she was given in marriage by her father or father's father. According to Section 2 (vii) she is entitled to obtain the decree of the dissolution of her marriage on the ground that:

(1) She was given in marriage by her father or other guardian;

(2) She had not attained the age of fifteen years at that time;

(3) She repudiated the marriage before attaining the age of eighteen years; and
(4) The marriage has not been consummated.

According to the *Qur'an*, a man may marry up to four wives, so long as he is able to provide for each equally.[10] He may marry a Muslim woman or a member of the Jewish or Christian faith, or a slave woman".[11] A Muslim woman, however, may marry only one husband, and he must be a Muslim. Contemporary Muslim women apologists are quick to point out that these restrictions are for the benefit of women, ensuring that they will not be left unprotected. In Islam, marriage is not a sacrament but a legal contract, and according to the *Qur'an* a woman has clearly defined legal rights in negotiating this contract. She can dictate the terms and can receive the dowry herself.[12]

It is to be mentioned here that in all the pre-Islamic civilizations—Persians, Israelites, Athenians, Hindus—all practiced polygamy with no restrictions whatsoever.[13] For the first time, the *Qur'an* restricted the number of wives to four with the condition of equal justice between co-wives. Of course, polygamy is not the normal condition of Muslim society. The *Qur'an* allowed it under restrictions only to meet those contingencies of life wherein polygamy alone could check incontinence, which Islam would not allow in the slightest degree.[14] Polygamy is practiced by only a small percentage of the contemporary Muslim population, and a man with more than two wives is extremely rare. Many countries are now taking steps to modify the circumstances in which a husband may take more than one wife, although only in two countries, Turkey and Tunisia, are multiple marriages actually illegal. Other countries have made such moves as requiring the husband to have the permission of the court (as in Iraq and Syria) or to get the permission of the first wife (as in Egypt), or permitting the wife to write into her marriage contract that she will not allow a co-wife (as in Morocco and Labanon).[15]

Though no reforms have been made in India either to restrict or abolish polygamy among Muslims, the courts have made a contribution towards controlling this practice. The two ways by which the courts have done so are: first, by recognizing the right of delegated divorce (*talaq al-tafwid*) in favour of the wife in the event of the husband marrying or taking another wife; and second, by refusing restitution of conjugal rights to the bigamous husband.[16] Treating Muslim marriage as a contract, the courts have held that any agreement entered into by the parties, if not opposed to public policy or the spirit of Muslim law, would be enforceable.[17] Thus both pre-nuptial and post-nuptial agreements which gave a right to the wife to get a divorce if the husband took a second wife, were held to be valid.[18] Here it is to be noted that polygamy was never encouraged in Islam. It was merely tolerated. This was clearly illustrated in *Itwari* v. *Ashgari*.[19] In this case the husband sued for restitution of conjugal rights against the first wife, after contracting a bigamous marriage. The court refused relief to the husband.

Let us now consider the question of unilateral divorce in Islamic law. What is perhaps unjust and unpleasant to women in Islamic law is the case with which a Muslim wife may be repudiated by a *talaq*. Unilateral divorce was always been detested as harsh and unjust to women; but strange enough it has never been discontinued and still hangs as the sword of Damocles over the head of any Muslim woman. J.N.D. Anderson has aptly observed:

> It is the Islamic law of divorce not polygamy which is the major cause of suffering of Muslim women.... The Muslim wife indeed has always lived, so far as the law is concerned, under the ever present shadow of divorce, a shadow mitigated only in comparatively rare cases by certain precautionary devices.[20]

Some jurists hold that in an archaic society where the ideas of honour and decency are at low ebb and the human values are not well defined, the laws regulating the relation between the sexes take their imprint from a coarse imperiousness of male desires and favour the stronger sex. Instances of such laws are the Herbraic law, the laws of Manu, and to great extent the matrimonial law of pre-Islamic Arabia.[21]

There is a large and influential body of Muslim jurists who regard *talaq* emanating from the husband as really prohibited except for necessity and only with the sanction of a judge administering the Muslim law.[22] A similar view has been expressed by Justice V. R. Krishna Iyer of the Kerala High Court, authority for which is found in the texts and writings of some Muslim scholars.[23] The *Qur'an* enjoins: If they (women) obey you, then do not seek a way against them.[24] On this Galwash Comments:

> The *Qur'an* expressly forbids a man to seek pretexts for divorcing his wife, so long as she remains faithful and obedient to him. The law gives to the man primarily the facility of dissolving the marriage. If the wife by her indocility or bad character renders the married life unhappy; but in the absence of serious reasons no man can justify a divorce either in the eyes of religion or the law. If he abandons his wife or puts her away in simple caprice, he draws upon himself the divine anger—for the curse of God, said the Prophet, rests on him who repudiates his wife capriciously.[25]

The All India Muslim Personal Law Board proclaims that *triple talaq* is a social evil, but it is equally assertive that this social evil should not be removed by legislative reform. The Board claims: "Our laws are based on divine inspiration and *triple talaq* comes from the same inspiration that is *Shariat*. We have no powers to amend or abolish it. So the *triple talaq* is irrevocable".

Under the Muslim law, it is only the husband who can pronounce *talaq* on his wife, the wife cannot pronounce on her husband. But the husband can delegate the power to his wife or to a third party by an agreement. This is known as divorce by delegation (*talaq-i-tafweez*). Thus an agreement made before or after the marriage by which it is provided that the wife should be at liberty to divorce herself from her husband under certain specified conditions is valid if the conditions are of a reasonable one and not opposed to the policy of Muslim law. The husband marrying a second wife is such a condition.

A Muslim woman, however, can also secure a divorce on the grounds stipulated in the Dissolution of Muslim Marriages Act, 1939. The act comprises two main provisions. First, it abolishes the traditional principle under which apostasy by a Muslim woman could *ipso facto* dissolve her marriage. Secondly, it specifies and illustrates a large number of grounds, basically derived from the *Maliki* school of Islamic law, on which a Muslim wife can seek dissolution of her marriage by the Court. Though the Act is comprehensive in itself, certain amendments in and additions to its existing provisions are called for. For instance, incompatibility of temperament between the spouses may be recognized as another ground for dissolution of marriage.

In accordance with Islamic law, custody of the children traditionally has gone to the father at some time between the age of 7 and 9 for boys and between 7 and puberty for girls, depending on the legal school. This practice too is slowly changing, and in most areas, women who have been divorced by their husband are allowed so keep their sons until puberty and their daughters until they are of an age to be married.

RIGHT TO INHERIT AND OWN PROPERTY

The legal position of women is closely tied to the rights over property a woman acquired at marriage from her parents and from her husband as well as at the death of those same individuals. In ancient Egypt, writes Hopkins, women commonly owned property; they could legally inherit property and also testate it to others; they could hold property independently of their husbands; they have the same legal capacity to transact business as men; in sum, the status of women was high.

The *Qur'an* provides women with explicit rights to inheritance and independent property rights. Historically, there is no evidence for the exclusion of women from property in per-Islamic times[26] nor is this suggested by a careful reading of the *hadith* with the possible limitation on their ownership of agricultural land in Medina.[27] In post-Islamic times the situation was changed by the intervention of a religious text. While the position regarding women may not have changed all that much, the general legal situation altered because of the nature of the sectarian activity. Islamic law does not emerge directly from the religious text. It took shape only after long discussion of legal scholars which were embodied in *fiqh* and which absorbed local custom as well as developing particular lines of arguments to form distinct schools.[28] The difficulties entailed in understanding the verses of the *Qur'an* referring to inheritance and succession gave rise to a number of differing interpretations associated with the main schools of Islamic law, *Hanbali*, *Shafi'i*, *Hanafi*, *Maliki*, and their component groups and scholars. Some of the differences arise from attempts to work out general principles, leading in turn to judicial disagreements.

The general position regarding women's right to inheritance and ownership became clearer when Islam gave them clear rights in property that were considered revolutionary 1400 year ago. Sunni law recognized two kinds of rights of women to property. First, she was entitled to a portion of the inheritance equal to half that of a male of the same degree of relationship to the deceased. If there were no sons, the daughter became the recipient of the bulk of the property.[29] Although daughters were otherwise entitled only to a half share of the inheritance they also received a dowry at marriage. This dowry came from two sources, indirectly from the groom and directly from her parents. The amount of the groom's contribution was the subject of pre-marital bargaining and was specified in the marriage contract known as the writ (*al-kitab*), though it was not always written down. Two-thirds of this amount was generally payable immediately before the marriage contract was made; the remaining third was held in reserved to be paid to the wife if she was divorced without her consent or in the case of the death of her husband.[30]

Now we can see that it is one of the great innovations of the *Qur'an* over earlier practices that women are permitted to inherit and own property. In this context, Islam was much progressive, as over fourteen years ago, it made women a shareholder in the wealth of her husband, father, brother, sons and daughters. Non-Muslims have generally found great difficulty with the *Qur'anic* stipulation that a woman is allowed to inherit property but that the inheritance should be only half that of a male. According to Islamic understanding, however, the rationale is precisely related with the difference of responsibility between man and woman. When she is young her father is responsible for her maintenance and after marriage her husband has to maintain her. On the other hand the man has to bear the responsibility for himself, his wife and children, and his parents. This is why the man gets double the share of a woman in inheritance. Besides, in a way the woman gets double advantage: as a daughter she gets a share in the father's wealth and as a wife in her husband's wealth also. This is obviously a very weak argument since men also inherit from as many sources and in many cases women have to partly or fully bear responsibilities for their children and family.

RIGHT TO BIRTH CONTROL AND ABORTION

Birth control is yet another important question of our times. The purpose of marriage, according to Islam is not only the satisfaction of sexual impulse but also multiplication of the contribution to the maintenance and growth of human population. Therefore resort to birth control is not permissible in Islam without genuine reasons.

On the basis of some rather obscure references in the *Qur'an*, birth control has generally been frowned upon by Muslim religious leaders, and abortions and sterilization are strictly forbidden. The only ground on which family planning is opposed by any religion is sanctity of life. Catholic Christians also oppose it on this ground. Basically there are two groups, namely, pro-choice and pro-life. The former argues that the mother, who bears the entire brunt of giving birth to a child and subsequently to rear it, should have a choice in the matter, i.e. to retain or the abort the foetus. The mother's choice, from this perspective, is more important than anything else. Pro-life people on the other hand argue that sanctity of life is more fundamental than anything else.

Briefly speaking, Islam does not permit abortion under normal health conditions, and considers it a deliberate act of killing an innocent person, which is heinous crime under any law. Abortion could be allowed for a woman's sake and that too when properly suggested by some responsible physicians. Under normal health conditions, and particularly when the foetus is developed enough (that specialist considers it a living body), abortion amounts to deliberate killing and therefore, not allowable. Abortion or even prevention of conception for fear of economic hardships is the negation of the basic principles of Islam that God is sole provider and sustainer of every living soul. That is the reason, the act is un-Islamic. If even the conception is the result of extra-marital union or forced rape, abortion is not allowed, because the (innocent) baby to be has the right to life that cannot be denied. The biological parents—both or either one—or else the society/state is responsible to take care of even "unwanted" or illegal births.

CHALLENGES OF RELIGIOUS FUNDAMENTALISM

Religious fundamentalism has been a major challenge to give effect to international human rights instruments especially those relating to women's rights. Although the history of human rights reveal that underlying values of human rights are found in elements of the world's religions and ethics, emergence of religious fundamentalist doctrines relating to all major religions explicitly entail curtailment of human rights of women and impose standards of subordination of women. Saudi Arabia presents an interesting case study of the confrontation of Islamic ideals with contemporary reality. Women in Saudi Arabia are greatly inhibited in the labour arena; because of conservative religious attitudes that they must be veiled and covered, are not permitted to drive or even ride in a taxi with a strange man, and in general are unable to participate on the social and professional work with males. We have already seen how during the Taliban regime in Afghanistan women and girls no longer have access to education, health care services, jobs and other means of gaining an economic livelihood or the right to freedom of movement in the name of Islam.

It may be noted that Islamic *Sharia* law is being followed in a number of Muslim countries as a general framework of the legal system. Important areas, in which Muslim women are faced with severe discrimination, fall both within public and private sphere of their life. To strengthen women's religious duty of submission and obedience to men, the Muslim fundamentalists support the traditional gender segregated spheres of women requiring confinement at home, caring for family which severely affect their economic independence and role in public decision-making. In private sphere, women are discriminated in all matters relating to marriage, divorce, guardianship and child custody, inheritance and ownership of property. Patriarchy is one of the greatest obstacles in the way of achieving gender justice. Islamic gender laws reflecting patriarchal values are sought to be legitimized by invoking religious scriptures and it is argued that religious laws being divine origin and sacred, cannot be changed. Any attempt to change laws is dubbed as a human endeavour and hence unacceptable.

Several Islamic countries in recent years have witnessed two simultaneous developments: First, the states-making anti-women laws in the name of *Shaira* (Muslim law); second, articulate and powerful women's movement in the respective countries fighting against fundamentalist forces and anti-women laws.

CONCLUSION

It is clear from the above discussion that under the Islamic law women have a legal position superior than that of their counterparts under other religions. The quest for Muslim woman's rights within the framework of Islamic laws should be seen as a starting point. It is true that the law of Islam vests in her all the rights of an independent human being. It is clear to me that the *Qur'an* aimed to erase all notions of women as subhuman. There are more passages that address issues relating to women as individuals in the family and as members of the community. The *Qur'an* provides women with explicit rights to inheritance, independent property, divorce and the right to testify in a court of law. However, much more is needed to be done for the welfare of Muslim women. The combined and coordinated efforts may enable them to step out of a world of ignorance, inequality and indignity.

Rights and empowerment are interconnected. It is obvious that the debates on rights cannot be raised by Muslim women in the absence of empowerment. There are over a billion Muslims in the World. Roughly half of that number is women, who are adversely affected by laws and customs which serve the interests of a male elite. It is imperative to take the subject of Muslim women's rights out of the hands of self-appointed male guardians of Islam. It is said that the rights no longer lie with women in the absence of empowerment. The empowerment tool in the 21st century is knowledge. It is through education and knowledge that even marginalized Muslim women can become permanently empowered. The empowerment movement must come from women themselves. Unless a substantial number of women in a Muslim community come to believe they have rights under the Islamic law and demand to exercise them, rights to Muslim women remain an abstraction.

NOTES AND REFERENCES

1. B. Sivaramayya, Equality of Sexes as a Human and Constitutional Right and the Muslim Law, in Tahir Mahmood (ed.), *Islamic Law in Modern India*, 69 (N.M. Tripathi Pvt. Ltd., 1972).
2. It is important to note that of the fifteen Muslim countries around the world that have signed CEDAW, there is no clause on which they have a consensus, illustrating the importance of

religion and culture in the application of international human rights law.

3. When India ratified CEDAW in 1993–having sıgned the document in 1980–it introduced two declarations. The first permits a local interpretation of Article 5(a) 'measures to modify prejudicial social and cultural customs' and 16(1) 'in conformity with its policy of non-interference in the personal affairs of any community without its initiative and consent'. More than fifty years on, this policy continues to stand in direct conflict with constitutional declaration that the State would move towards a uniform civil code. India also declared in relation to Article 16(2), that 'though in principle it fully supports the principle of compulsory registration of marriages, it is not practical in vast country like India with its variety of customs, religions and level of literacy'. India also maintains a reservation to Article 29 of CEDAW.
4. Article 10 of the CEDAW obligates states to eliminate discrimination in education and Article 11 recognizes the right to work as a human right. In Islam, the segregation of women from men and use of *hejab* not only create a barrier between sexes, but also disallowed women to pursue education and economic independence by restricting her mobility.
5. AIR 1952 Bombay 84.
6. AIR 1953 Madras 792.
7. AIR 1952 Bombay 84.
8. *Id*. at 89.
9. Jane I. Smith, Islam, in Arvind Sharma (ed.), *Women in World Religions*, 238 (Sri Satguru Publications, New Delhi, 1995).
10. *Surah* 4:3.
11. *Surah* 5 :6.
12. *Surah* 65 : 4.
13. Ameer Ali, *The Spirit of Islam*, 222-26 (1904).
14. Bashir Ahmad, Status of Women and Settlement of Family Disputes under Islamic Law, in Tahir Mahmood (ed.) *supra* note 1 at 187.
15. Jane I. Smith, Islam, *supra* note 9 at 237.
16. S. Jaffer Hussain, Judicial Interpretation of Islamic Matrimonial Law in India, in Tahir Mahmood (ed.), *supra* note 1 at 176.

17. See *Abdul Kadir* v. *Salima* 1886 ILR All. 149; *Ghulam Fatima* v. *Khaira*, AIR 1923 Lah. 674; *Aziz* v. *Mst. Naro*, AIR 1955 H.P.32.
18. See *Saiduddin* v. *Latifunnisa* (1918) 46 ILR Cal. 141; *Saifuddin* v. *Soneka*, AIR 1955 Assam 153. It is notable that such stipulation is not valid under the *Shia* law.
19. AIR 1960 Allahabad 684.
20. J.N.D. Anderson, *Islamic Law in the Modern World*, 51-52, (London, 1959).
21. M.R. Zafer, Unilateral Divorce in Muslim Personal Law, in Tahir Mahmood (ed.), *supra* note 1 at 168.
22. *Id.* at 170.
23. *A. Yusuf* v. *Sowramma*, AIR 1971 Kerala 261.
24. The *Qur'an*, IV : 34.
25. Galwash, *The Religion of Islam*, 104.
26. A Beeston, The Position of Women in Pre-Islamic Saudi Arabia, Proceedings XXII Congress of Orientations Vol. 2 : 101-6, Leiden (1957), at 103.
27. G. Stern, Marriage in Early Islam, 158-68 (London, 1939).
28. Jack Goody, The Oriental, the Ancient and the Primitive : Systems of Marriage and the Family in the Pre-Industrial Societies of Eurasia, 369 (Cambridge: Cambridge University Press, 1990).
29. *Sunni* Schools allowed a daughter a maximum of half of estate. In Shia law a man might bequeath a further third to an entitled heir, bringing the total to five-sixths. If there were no competing heirs, the daughter would be equally entitled to increase her share.
30. E. W. Lane, An Account of the Manners and Customs of the Modern Egyptians Written During the Years 1833-34 and 35 (5th edn.), (London, 1871) at 202.

SOME ASPECTS OF GOND WOMEN WITH REFERENCE TO EMPOWERMENT: A STUDY IN SAMARBOH VILLAGE UNDER CHHINDWARA DISTRICT OF MADHYA PRADESH

*Mosume Bose Roy Datta**

THE VILLAGE AND POPULATION

The village Samarboh is located about 42 kms. away from Chhindwara Town of Madhya Pradesh. In Samarboh village, out of total 121 households 55.4% belong to Raj Gond Tribe, Scheduled Castes (18.2%) and others (26.4%). The family size of the Gond of Samarboh is larger (6.5). It emphasizes that the Gond women used to have more family burden like performing more household chores, looking after children and other works for family.

Actually, 32 Gond households out of total 67 comprising 199 population were enumerated during field survey. The percentage of women is comparatively more (52.3%) than men (47.7%) and the sex ratio has been more being 1095. A substantial percentage of women are in up to 10 years age group (30.0%), 23.0% in 11-20 years age group (Table 1).

* Junior Research Fellow, Ministry of Tourism & Culture, Department of Culture, New Delhi.

Table 1
Gond women according to age in Samarboh, 1999

(Percentage Distribution)

Age group (in years)	*Population*
Upto 10	30.0
11 - 20	23.0
21 - 30	19.2
31 - 40	11.5
41 - 50	9.6
51 - 60	3.8
61 and above	2.9
Total Number	104
Percentage	100.0

Source: Field survey, 1999.

OCCUPATION AND WOMEN

Indeed, 48.04% of Gond in Madhya Pradesh are returned as workers, in which majority (65.26%) are involved in cultivation and 27.76% as agricultural labour. Sex-wise, of the total Gond workers, 60.64% are men and 39.36% women (Singh: 1991). So, it may be said that women share a substantial percentage of Gond labour force in the state.

Similarly, agriculture is the basis of Gond economy in the village. 43.3% of total 104 women are engaged in agriculture either primarily or secondarily (Table 2). In case of agriculture the men mainly plough the land. While, being expert Gond women used to undertake agricultural

Table 2
Distribution of Gond women by occupation, 1999

(Percentage Distribution)

Type of occupation	*Number of woman*	
	Primary	*Secondary*
Cultivation	4.4	20.0
Agricultural labourer	6.7	68.9
Household	88.9	11.1
Total Number		45
Percentage		100.0

Source: Field survey, 1999.

operation which amount to almost 70% of the total agricultural activities (as reported).

Besides, they have a role in animal husbandry, collection of fuel and potable water, and other economic activities. It was reported during field survey that they have common desire to be educated and also prefer to marry a man who is educated and employed in government service. If so, then the women need not to do a huge work in agriculture. Few cases in this context were reported that the wives already left their husband as they could not tolerate the heavy burden of hard working in husbands' large agricultural field along with other household work.

On the whole, women are involved both in household and other gainful occupations viz. agriculture and agricultural labour. So the Gond women in the village play a substantive role in sustaining the family. This substantiates that the Gond women have the burden of hard working both in domestic and agricultural field. Even then, the women particularly in case of agriculture labour work are deprived of getting wage equally with men in the village. Like, the men normally get Rs. 25/- to Rs. 30/- per day wage for agricultural labour work and for the same work women get Rs. 20/- to Rs. 25/-. Therefore, the inequality in wage for agricultural/daily labour work by sex has been common in the area.

Though the traditional occupations of agriculture and animal husbandry have sustained their economy since time immemorial and many of them still are continuing thè agriculture as their main source of livelihoods. But, at present the Gond men and women are also engaged in various service sectors as observed during field survey.

MARRIAGE AND WOMEN

Gonds of Samarboh strictly follow the exogamy at the phratry (*'deo'*) level. That is, a man can not marry a woman of any sept which worships the same number of Gods as himself. Such marriage is being prohibited among them. They practise cross cousin marriage and preference is given to the mother's brother's daughter. The most distinctive feature of Gond marriage is that the procession usually starts from the bride's house, in contradiction to the Hindu practice. After marriage, the woman acquire the clan name of her husband. Polygamy is also common among the Gonds of Samarboh. During field survey, such polygamy has been found in 4 cases among the Gond.

Bride price (*'hunda'*) used to be paid in cash and kind to the bride's father is common among the Gonds. But it was reported that instead of bride price there has now been started the demand of dowry ('dahej'). For instance, a Gond bride's family had given a black & white Television set and one Motor Cycle as dowry to a bridegroom. In another case, a colour Television set and a cycle was given as dowry. Moreover, it has become a common practice to some extent that the payment of conveyance cost for bridegroom's procession to bride's house has to be made by the bride's parents. So, there is now a significant change in Gond society of Samarboh that instead of getting bride price the bride's family has to pay the dowry. Moreover, there is significant demand that the bride should be educated. Because, an educated bride (having matriculation and above level of education) can get job as teacher in Anganwadi center and primary school etc.

Pre-marital sex has not been a curse and in case of such happenings that woman can marry another man only after having her head being shaved because of no prohibition for marriage of that woman. Even nobody can raise any objection or question in her husband's house in this regard after marriage. The divorcee/widowers are normally allowed to remarry in the society. Taking the aforesaid situation it may be said that the Gond society is positive and favourable towards the remarriage, pre-marital sex if happened, divorce etc. of women, except the problem of growing emergence of the cases of 'dowry' instead of 'bride price'.

EDUCATION AND WOMEN

Scope and access to formal education available for Samarboh Gonds

Gonds in the area are having greater availability and access to modern formal education due to availability of number of schools (including Adivasi Ashram School and Hostel) in the village, various schools including college in its very nearby (3 kms. away) Bichhua Block Development Office areas which played greater role to spread formal education among the Gonds in the areas. Such greater availability and access to educational facilities obviously has influenced the outlook and attitudes of Gond much favourably towards formal education. As a result, the number of Gond students no doubt has increased significantly.

Educational Background of Gond Women of Samarboh Village

A good 26.0 per cent of female population has been reading at various educational levels. Excluding female student, the majority among women (70.1 %) are illiterate. While in such case the illiteracy has been 26.5% among men. Therefore, illiteracy has been comparatively much higher among women than men (Table 3). It has been observed that the education is mostly in present generation. There has been a good trend of development in the field of education and Gond women at present are getting the benefits of education to some extent. Though there has been low level education among the present generation Gond women as compared to men in the village.

Though everybody has equal access and opportunity for education and Gonds are having much better availability and access to educational opportunities, but all they could not avail such access due to some common constraints in turn resulted into the educational wastage among them too. Such wastage has been comparatively more among females. For instance, it was found that due to sharing of burden of domestic work including occasional work in agriculture as well as mothers' participation in agriculture and agricultural wage labour work 11 girl were not sent to school for enrolment in any of the available school, and 14 girls were being dropped out of the school from early classes (III to VI).

Table 3
Educational Distribution Among the Gond Women of Samarboh

(Percentage Distribution)

Educational level		*Women* *Student*	*Other*
High School		3.7	2.6
Middle School		22.2	6.5
Primary		33.3	14.3
Anganwadi (Pre-primary)		40.7	3.9
Can sign only		-	2.6
Illiterate		-	70.1
Total	Number	27	77
	Percentage	100.0	100.0

Note: Total women population is 99 (excluding 5 very minor girl child) of 32 Gond households enumerated during field survey, 1999.
Source: Field Survey, 1999.

Educational Aspiration for Girls

Nearly cent per cent have favoured the necessity of education for their girl children. Only 3.0% do not favour to educate girl child as it hampers the household work of the family. Undoubtedly, the overwhelming majority have aspired and favoured the education of girls. Because, the educated girls can get better job in government sectors, school teacher job, etc. Moreover educated girls can achieve more respect in society, and in their respective husbands' family after marriage. Besides, education of girls is necessary to get them married with educated person in a good family. Educated women can educate her children and others. Interestingly, after seeing educated female teachers in various schools the respondents have aspired that their girl children should be educated.

Table 4 substantiates that there is visible inequality in the context of respondents' aspired educational achievement for sons and daughters. Like 53.2% of them aspired higher level of educational achievement for their sons i.e. 'graduate and above' including technical education. While this has been only 18.7% for their daughters. Even those who did not mention any level of educational aspiration for their children but opined that they would educate children 'as much as they can', their percentage in this case are 25.0% for sons and 18.8% for daughters respectively. Moreover, a good 37.5% aspired to educate their daughters from primary to high school level. While such low level educational aspiration for sons has been nominal 6.2%. So. it may be said that the respondents are having higher aspiration of educational achievement for sons and but low in cases of their daughters. As the

Table 4
A comparative analysis of Respondents' level of aspiration towards their Sons' and Daughters' educational achievement

(Percentage distribution)

Respondens' level of aspiration	*Sons' educational achievement*	*Daughters' educational achievement*
Primary (I – V)	-	9.4
Middle School (VI – VIII)	3.1	15.6
High School (IX - X)	3.1	12.5
Secondary	3.1	9.4
Higher Secondary	12.5	12.5
Graduate	21.9	12.5
Post -graduate	25.0	3.1
Technical Degree	6.3	3.1
As much one can	25.0	18.8
No aspiration	-	3.1
Total Number	32	32
Percentage	100.0	100.0

Source : Field survey, 1999 .

aspiration of the parents ultimately influence the educability of children, thereby there might have adverse effects on their daughters' educability and continuity of education towards higher level.

POSITION OF WOMEN

Traditionally, the women in Gond family had comparatively low status. They did not have a share in the family property, female education was almost non-existent. They were hardly even consulted in family affairs at the time of taking any important decision including decision for educational future of children.

However, with the spread of modern education in the areas, the Gonds are now having favourable attitude towards education of women as seen earlier. So, an attempt also has been made to find out the respondents' attitude towards *consultation with women* in relation to educational future of children as well as other family affairs. In this context, it was observed that the majority (78.1 %) favoured the consultation with women in relation with the educational future of the children and other family affairs. Even then, a considerable 21.9 % of them also did not favour in this direction.

The Gonds of Samarboh are mainly patrilineal, and their residence is patrilocal. In case of *property sharing*, traditionally male equigeniture was the rule of inheritance in Gond society and the eldest son always succeeds as the head of the family. There are a greater number of nuclear families found among the Gonds, though vertically extended families also are found. So, the respondents also were asked to specify whether they favour the sharing of property by women? The analysis in this regard shows that a majority (62.5 %) of them do not favour any sort of sharing family property by women. Though a considerable 37.5 % are having positive attitude and favour the sharing of property by women as a whole. But, it is also important whether this has been in practice during real situation. In such case, it was observed that those who are having daughter only and no son, they are intended to give the share of their family property to daughters. Moreover, in very few cases the share of family property was given to daughter, but in such cases the percentage of share had been very low as compared to sons (as reported during field survey).

In many cases the men are still the decision-maker and inheriting the family property in actual situation as observed during field survey. Whatever the changes in this regard that has been the changes in the attitude of men towards women which may be considered positive and that ultimately may bring about the changes towards equal position of women with men in near future to a extent. Because, the process of attitudinal changes is likely to affect the role performances and behaviour patterns of the individuals, and the thought pattern of the individuals are manifested in their attitudes.

TATTOOING AND WOMEN

Significantly, *Tattooing* among the Gonds seems to have been originally a magical means of protecting the body against real and spiritual dangers. Indeed, the tattoo is the symbol of Adivasis/Bhumijans as believed by the Gonds. Traditionally both men and women Gonds were formerly tattooed, though the custom is no more present among the Gond men in the village. But women are still tattooed with a superstition that the God will remain with them if tattooed, and any magic directed to them by enemy will certainly fail. It is common that the women should be tattooed in her father's house. In this context, it was found very interesting that the young generation women who have either been going to school or have gone through modern formal education along with having exposure to Television are not interested any more in tattooing and do not desire to get any parts of their body tattooed. Even if tattooing is done under very compulsion from their parents, then they do not want to show it while feel shy for such tattooing as they have the experience and seen the educated tribal women do not tattoo in this regard. Even they try to erase the mark of tattoo by continuous rubbing the tattooed part of their body.

HEALTH AND HYGIENE AND WOMEN

The Gonds of this village though make use of both the traditional and modern medicine for treatment. But in reality, majority of them were observed preferring to undergo treatment first by the traditional medicine-man locally known as 'Bhumka'. Because, they had have strong believe in spirits and black-magic as observed during field survey. But interestingly they have now positive attitude towards family planning to a some extent, and the cases of sterilization had been reported during field survey. Besides, the role of traditional mid-wife in the village has been still important as the delivery of child being done mostly at home, though there is one Block Hospital very nearer to the village. Moreover, the pregnancy wastage has also been an important problem for women in the areas. Data collected from Bichhua Block Hospital on such cases among the tribe has been shown in Table 5.

Table 5
Record of Conception, Pregnancy Wastage and Fertility among the Tribe in the Areas

(Number of cases)

Details	*Year* 1994-95	1995-96	1996-97	1997-98	1998-99
Number of pregnant woman	26	20	23	-	10
Delivery at Hospital	-	-	1	-	-
Delivery at Home by mid-wife/ live birth	21	16	15	-	4
Abortion/miscarriage/birth of still baby	5	4	7	-	5
Sterilization	10	7	3	-	1
Use of modern contraceptive methods	21	-	25	28	19

Source: Bichhua Block Hospital, Bichhua, 1999 .

CHILD MORTALITY

Table 6 shows that pregnancy wastage and child mortality has been significant in the village.

Table 6
Child mortality in Samarboh Village, 1999

(Number of cases)

Detail Sl.No.	Number of child Male	Female	Total
1. Abortion/Miscarriage	-	-	2
2. Still birth	1	1	2
3. Immediately after birth	3	3	6
4. Within 1 year	-	2	2
5. In between 2-3 years	3	3	6
6. In between 3-4 years	2	1	3
7. Above 5 years	3	-	3

Source: Field survey, 1999.

NUMBER OF CHILDREN IN THE FAMILY AND THE WOMEN

Majority of the families are having more than two child in the family. Interestingly, the largest part of the total families are having 4 to 8 children in the family. It substantiates that due to having more number of children the women have to provide more domestic labour in child nutrition and rearing in the family, which has been ultimately a great burden to them. All these may result into the deterioration of health condition of women in the family (Table 7).

CHANGES IN DRESS PATTERN

There has been changes observed in dress pattern among Gond women. Specifically, the young generation women along with using some sort of modern dresses also are using undergarments, which was not so in the past. Besides, there are also some changes in the style of wearing *'shari'* by women among the Gonds of the village.

Table 7
Number of Children According to Number of Family in Samarboh

Number of child	*Percentage of family*
1	9.4
2	6.3
3	15.6
4	28.1
5	15.6
6	12.5
7	3.1
8	3.1

Note: 1. One family does not have any child.
2. One family does not have any child at present due to death of the child. 3. Number of total family enumerated 32 .

Source: Field survey, 1999.

PARTICIPATION OF WOMEN IN POLITICS

In Samarboh-Murrah Gram Panchayat the number of total members has been 14 including the *'Sarpanch'* (head of the gram Panchayat). Out of which 9 are men and 5 women. In fact, 33% of the total Panchayat seats are reserved for women. Moreover, out of 5 women Panchayat members, 2 of them belong to Gond tribe.

CONCLUSION

On the whole, it may be said that the position of women in terms of empowerment and increase in their self-reliance is yet to be achieved significantly by the Gond women in the area. Though there has been changes to some extent due to spread of education and modernization. Yet, the empowerment of women can be realized through some specific women's needs and interest. This means, there is required equal organization of society in terms of both the structure and nature of relationship between men and women. It certainly includes removal of discrimination such as rights to own land/property, abolition of sexual division of labour, better education and participation in gainful employment for self earning as well as access to credit, equal status in decision-making and resource control in the family, decrease of the burden of domestic labour and child care, and to overcome the constraint like the trend vis-à-vis reproductive activity only for begetting the more number of children (mainly son) in the family etc. It may also be said that only the laws and any sort of reservation for women can not do betterment for them until the equality of women with men starts in each family.

On the whole, this study suggests that an in-depth study is necessarily required to be made particularly on the position and empowerment of women in Gond society with a view to throw light intensively on this aspect.

REFERENCE

Singh, K. S. (1991), *People of India : Scheduled Tribe,* Volume 3, Oxford University Press.

HUMAN RIGHTS VIS-A-VIS WOMEN'S RIGHTS: INTERNATIONAL AND NATIONAL PERSPECTIVE

*Zubaird Ahmad Khan**

INTRODUCTION

Human beings are rational beings. They by virtue of their being human possess certain basic and inalienable rights which are commonly known as human rights. Since these rights belong to them because of their very existence, these become operative with their birth. Humans right being the birth rights are, therefore, inherent in all the individuals irrespective of their caste, creed religion, sex and nationality. These rights are essentially for all the individuals as they are consonant with their freedom and dignity and are conducive to physical, moral, social and spiritual welfare. They are also necessary as they provide suitable conditions for the materials and moral uplift of the people. Because of their immense significance to human beings, human rights are also sometimes referred as fundamental rights, basic rights, inherent rights, natural rights and birth rights. The idea of human rights is bound up with human dignity. Thus all those rights which are essential for maintenance of human dignity may be called human rights.

* M.A. (History) LL.M., Ph.D., Reader (Associate Professor) Department of Law, A.M.U. Aligarh.

International human rights is the world first university of ideology, religious, political, philosophical and economic ideas. Human rights are not merely ideas or aspirations nor are these some rights granted to us by the existence of particular set of laws. These claims are made by virtue of the fact that we are the human beings with inalienable rights of human dignity. These rights cannot be delegated to any authority either to legislature or judiciary to define and illustrate. These are non deligateable and non transferable. As such these human rights have been violated not only by unjust acts of individuals but also by national and international structures; we are witnessing such violation daily.

A woman is the central figure in our society which inspires confidence in children, inculcates values in them and prepares them to persue their goals relentlessly. History bears testimony to the fact that height of patriotism, selflessness and determination are inhabited in children through the persistent efforts of mother. As it was said by Napoleon, "Give me good mothers I will give you a good nation." The human rights of women are inaliënable integral, and indivisible parts of human rights. The full and equal participation of women in political, civil, economic, social and cultural, life at national and international levels and the eradication of all forms of discrimination on ground of sex are priority objectives of the international community, concluded by World Conference on Human Rights 1993

In view of the indispensably pivotal role played by women in sphere of family and society, the human right effecting women in particular call for urgent and foremost attention in the interest of justice, equality and human dignity. Women are considered the weaker sections of society are more vulnerable to such violence. In a world reacted by violence women face rape, mutilation and death at the hands of not only common men but also of those in power including armed men. They are beaten by their husbands, stipped by upper caste men, subjected to rape and finally forced to die in a helpless society. They are sexually harassed. *Their suffering continues despite an historic declaration by the international community that women's rights are human rights.* In modern times the affirmation, protection and implementation of human rights have virtually became a (Sine qua non) of a just and fair society and these issues are neither confined to the area of international law nor are mere platitudes for the purpose of academic debates any more. For centuries, the women have been subjected to various forms of exploitation, harassment and torture both physical, mental and sexual. While India is about to complete 60 years of its independence and women still are treated as second class citizen and sexual subject and being exploited by the society even in present era. The darkest and ugliest form of their exploitation is either in the form of sexual harassment at workplaces, dowry death and dowry demands or in any other form. Society has witnessed numerous forms of women's victimization, dowry death, eveteasing, rapes, assaults, abduction, sexual harassment at work places forced prostitution, pornography on internet are manifest form of exploitation and criminalization of women in India .Despite the dignified and enumerated position and status stated in various religious and social texts position of women is not at par with male. The concept of equality between male and female was almost unknown to us before the enactment of the Constitution of India. Preamble of the Constitution besides other articles seeks to secure its citizens equality of status and other opportunities.

HISTORICAL PERSPECTIVE AND CONCEPT OF HUMAN RIGHTS

The roots for the protection of the rights of man may be traced as for back as in the Babylonian laws, Assyrian laws, Hittites laws and the Dharma of the Vedic period in India. Writing of Plato and other Greek and Roman philosophers also depict for protection of human rights though they had a religious foundation. Similar rights were secured to the Romans by the Roman law. The origin and the concept of human rights are usually agreed to be found in the Greco-Roman natural law doctrines of stoicism which held that a universal force Prevails. All action and the human conduct should, therefore, be judged according to the law of nature. Since the advent of human civilization, the quest for peace, prosperity and development has been common to all mankind. Law regulating societies do vary from country to country, however, philosophers and jurists, world wide have always asserted the brooding omnipresence of a higher law. It was termed as *Jus Naturale* by the Romans, *Lex Natura l is* by medieval Christian thinkers, *Rita and 'Dharma'* by ancient Hindus, and Christend *'Natural Law'* by modem jurists i.e. the law higher than the positive laws of states[1]. According to Natural Law theory individuals were entitled to certain immutable rights as human beings.

The promotion and protection of human rights has been a major preoccupation for the United Nation (1945), when the Organizations founding nations resolved that the horrors of the *Second World War* should never be allowed to re-occur. *The Charter of the United Nations Organisation adopted in June* 1945, declared one of" its objects as to reaffirm faith in fundamental human rights and its purpose of 'promoting and encouraging respect for human rights. Modem historians credit the origin of the concept to *Magna Carta* A.D. 1215. On close examination it would be seen that the Magna Carta was a petition urging the king to concede certain rights to a particular section of the people. The term Human Rights was introduced in the U.S. Declaration of Independence in 1776 and the U.S. Constitution embodied a Bill of Rights (1789). French Revolution gave birth to the Declaration of Rights of Men and Citizens in 1790. In 1929, Institute of International Law, New York, U.S.A., prepared a *Declaration of Human Rights and Duties.* In 1945, the Inter-American Conference passed a resolution-seeking establishment of an international forum.

An elaborate list of Human Rights was formulated by adopting the *Universal Declaration of Human Rights. After three years* the General Assembly, declared in the *Universal Declaration of Human Rights* that, *"Respect for human rights and human dignity, in the foundation of freedom, justice and peace in the world" In* December, 1966, UN General Assembly adopted two Covenants, namely, *Covenant on Civic and Political Rights* and the *Covenant on Economic, Social and Cultural Right*[2] and some fifty international instruments covering all aspects of human endeavour have developed out of the original document.

HUMAN RIGHTS OF WOMEN: AN INTERNATIONAL PERSPECTIVES

The rights of women along with those-of men have been recognised in major human rights instruments since the formation of United Nations Organisation. In fact, the U.N. Charter itself reaffirms its faith in fundamental human rights, equal rights of men and women. Article-l of the *'Universal Declaration of Non Discrimination'* proclaims that all human beings are born free and equal in dignity and rights, without any distinction including that of sex.[3] The Declaration represents a milestone in the history of mankind a veritable *Magna Carta which spells out precise Civil, Political, Economic, Social and Cultural Rights* which are valid for all members of the international community. It covers the whole range of activities from the rights of indigenous people to economic and social rights which include rights of women. The declaration also deals with the mechanism available to ensure these rights are respected and fulfilled.

The inclusion of Women's right in key United Nations document however, has not brought about equality. Consequently a number of the human rights instruments had to bc passed both by the United Nations General Assembly and by U.N. Specialized Agencies with regard to various aspects of Women's Rights. The two Human Rights Covenants i.e. *International Covenant of Economic, Social and Cultural Rights* 1966 and the International *Covenant on Civil and Political Rights,* 1996 reinforce the equality concept and forbid discrimination on account of sex.[4] These Covenants refer to the equal rights of men and women to the enjoyment of all Civil and Political Rights including the right to marry and found a family. In 1951 the *International Labour. Organization* (ILO), adopted a convention concerning, Equal Renumberation for Men and Women workers for work of equal values besides adopting two other conventions to improve the working conditions for women namely: *Convention on Prohibition of Night Work forWomen Employed in Industry,* 1948 and the Convention providing *Maternity Protection* (revised) in 1952. The other conventions of special importance to women are the *Convention on the Political Rights of Women,* 1952, the *Convention on the Consent to Marriage in Minimum age for Marriage and Registration of Marriage* (1962) and the *Convention on the Nationality of Married Women* (1957) which directly address issues related to the status of women. In addition the *United Nations Education Scientific and Cultural Organisation* (UNESCO) had adopted the *Convention against Discrimination in Education* (1960) which prohibits "any distinction, exclusion, *limitation Or preference*" on account of sex.[5]

A number of regional rights Charter, viz., *European Convention for the Protection of Human Rights and Freedoms,* 1950, *'African Charter on Human and People's Rights.* 1981 and *'American Convention on Human Rights.* 1969, all include provisions for progressive protection and guarantees for women. The major international instruments relating to the women's human rights issued apart from information Bill of Rights are:

1. Convention on the Political Rights of Women 1953.
2. First world Conference of Women, held at Mexico i.e. the begining of the UN decade for woman in 1975.
3. Convention on the Elimination of All forms of Discrimination against women, 1979, (CEDA W)
4. Second World Conference of woman, at Copenhagen 1980
5. Third World Conference of Women at Nairobi 1985
6. Un Conference on Human Rights at Vienna 1993
7. Fourth World Conference on Human Rights at Beijing 1995
8. UNIFEM 1998 (UN body for compaign against gender based violence)

ESTABLISHMENT OF INTERNATIONAL STANDARDS

International Human Rights standards were developed to protect people's human rights against violations by individuals, groups or nations. The following declarations adopted by the international community are not legally binding: The *Universal Declaration of Human Rights* (1948), The *Declaration on the Right to Development* (1986), and The *Declaration on The Protection of All Persons from Enforced Disappearance* 1992.[6] Many countries have incorporated the provisions of these declarations into their laws and Constitutions. Some other convention includes The Convention on the *Prevention and Punishment of the Crime of Genocide* (entered into force in 1951); The International *Convention on the Elimination of All Forms of Racial Discrimination* (entered in to force in 1969). The *Convention on the Elimination of All Forms of Discrimination Against Women* (entered into force in 1981); The *Covention Against Torture & Other Cruel, Inhuman or Degrading Treatment or Punishment* (entered into force in 1987)[7].

The U. N. General Assembly unanimously adopted a *'Declaration of Elimination of Discrimination Against Women'* in November 1967, resolving to abolish sex discriminatory laws & practices to grant women equal right with men in matter *of* civil law. However, the *Convention on the Elimination of all forms of Discrimination Against Women,* adopted by General Assembly in 1979, is the most comphrensive international Legal instrument on the human rights of the women and contains more concrete provisions aimed at the real implementation of the rights already recognised. The Convention has twin objectives: to prohibit discrimination and ensure equality (Articles 2-4). The essence of the Convention is that for the first time it provides an extensive definition of the term *"discrimination against women"* as any distinction, exclusion of restriction made on the basis of sex which has the effect or purpose of impairing or nullifying the recognition, enjoyment or exercise by women, irrespective of their marital status on the basis of equality of men and women, of human rights and fundamental freedoms in the political, social, cultural, civil and in any other field.

The U.N. General Assembly, in order to strengthen and complement the processes initiated under the *Convention* on *the Elimination of All Forms of Discrimination Against Women,* has adopted a Resolution (No. 48/1 04) on 23rd February, 1994 consists *of* 6 Article & defines violence against women[8] as follows:

'Any act of gender based violence that results in, or is likely to result in physical, sexual or psychological harm or suffering to women including threats of such acts, coercion or arbitrary deprivation of liberty, whether occurring in public or in private life. Violence is to include interalia dowry related violence, traditional practices harmful to women, trafficking in women, forced prostitution, sexual harassment, violence occurring in the general community and violence perpetrated or condoned by the state.

Beside these conventions and resolutions. World Conferences were also held to highlight the women's issues. The first Conference of Women was held in Mexico, in 1975 and the U.N. General Assembly declared it as *'International Women's Year'*. Second World Conference of Women was held in Copenhagen in 1980 focusing on three sub-themes, *Education, Employment and Health*.

Nairobi housed the Third World Conference on Women in 1985, reviewed and appraised the achievements of the decade for women and to develop strategies for overcoming obstacles still remaining. Fourth world conference on women was held in Beijing with three main objects:

1. to equip the women to meet the challenges of 21st century for scientific, technological, economic and political development;
2. to empower the women so as to enable them to take part in decision making and,
3. to draw up a platform of action for the completition of unfinished works.

In addition to this, the Second World Conference on Human Rights held at Vienna in June 1993 called for full and equal participation of women in all aspoects of public life. The issue of women's right to health and to control their reporductive capacities was recognized in Cairo's *'International Conference on Population and Development'*, 1994. The International Convenant on Economic, Social and Cultural Rights under Article 7 recognises *'women's right to fair conditions of work'* which reflects that women shall not be subjected to sexual harassment at the place of work which may vitiate the working environment.

HUMAN RIGHTS OF WOMEN AND INDIAN CONSTITUTION

It is necessary to observe the position of women under Indian Law, otherwise the present chapter remains incomplete. Being a signatory to various international conventions, covenants and protocols on human rights, India has 'assumed the responsibility to provide and protect various rights of women. Therefore, as regards the Indian Constitution it guarantees not only the equality before law and equal protection of laws to women but also confers certain affirmative rights. Articles 14, 15, 16 have been provided with equality provisions. India has adopted a clear polity on human rights and these human rights set forth in different groups *viz.* (a) right to equality (b) right to freedom (c) right against exploitation (d) right to freedom of religion and worship (e) cultural and educational rights (t) right to constitutional freedom. Article 14 of the Indian Constitution ensures equality before law to all persons within the territory of India. The strict compliance with rule is obligatory on the part of the state and a citizen can not waive this right. The expression "equality before law" finds a place in almost all written Constitution that guarantees fundamental rights and also has been used in the Universal Declaration of Human Rights. Article 15 (1) and (2) prohibits discrimination between citizens on the grounds only of religion, race, caste, sex, place of birth or any of them. The word "discrimination" means to make an adverse distinction or to distinguish unfavorable from others. If a law makes discrimination on any of above grounds, it can be declared invalid. The preamble's; aim is at equality of status and opportunity for "We, the people", obviously including the women also. Clause (3) of Article 15 is special provision for women and children & exceptions to the general rule laid down in clause (1) & (2). It says that nothing in Article 15 shall prevent the state from making any special provision for women and children. Because the woman's physical structure and performance of material functions place her at a disadvantage in the struggle for subsistence and her physical well being becomes an object of public interest in order to preserve the strength and vigour of the race. Thus under Article 42, women workers can take special maternity leave and a law to this effect will not infringe. Consequently the state has introduced reservation for women in public employment, in admission to educational institutions and the legislature at least at the local self-government level, among other schemes for their benefit. Even the fundamental duties contained in part IV–A of the constitution also enshrine the principle of dignity for women. Similarly Article 16, no citizen is subjected to any disability or restriction to hold public offices or in matter of public employment. The right to freedom under Article 19; guarantees freedom of speech, expression, peaceable assembly, association, practice of any occupation. The right against exploitation prohibits forced labour and child labour, cultural and educational rights concerned the protection of the interest of minorities.

The Directive Principle of State Policy contained in part IV of the Constitution, directs the state to protect the human rights of women including the right to equal pay for equal work for men and women both, the right to health and work in hygienic conditions, the right to maternity benefit and the right to gender justice etc. Equal Remuneration Act was passed in 1976. In 1961 Maternity Benefits Act was passed in order to give effect to ILO convention on maternity benefits. Many *other* laws have also been passed and progressively interpreted to prevent the exploitation of women, especially family related laws i.e. marriage, divorce, property, inheritance and adoption in an effort to develop women's personality and to raise their status in the society. The rights of women includes the right to equality before the law; the rights against gender discrimination; the right against harassment; right to abortion; right to privacy and the right to economic empowerment. In modern time, right against domestic violence has also gained recognition as a human pursuant to the enactment of the National Commission for Women Act 1990. Even, women of easy virtue are entitling to right of privacy and that no one can invade her privacy as and when he likes.

In addition to constitutional provisions some *other* measures have also been taken to improve women's need and to raise their status. The first step in that direction is the drafting of the National Perspective Plan for Women, 1988-2000 A.D. The prospective plan for women is an effort at a long term over all policy for Indian women, linked to national targets determined for the end of the century in respect of certain basic indicators especially of health, education and employment. Second important step is setting up of the Commission for Women Act, 1992. The Commission is an autonomous body, set up at the apex level to fulfill the critical objectives of achieving equality of status and opportunity for women, safeguard their interest and culminating all forms of discrimination against them.

It is, however, the domestic relation where the inequality against women is a state reality. Though the Universal Declaration of Human Rights and the different conventions on women made it compulsory to accord complete equality on matters of marriage, divorce, inheritance, ownership of property etc. The law and practice in India is at variance with regard to these matters. The reason for this is' Indian personal laws, as followed by Hindus, Muslims, Christians and Parsis, are different from each other and each applies in-equally against women.

HUMAN RIGHTS OF WOMEN: INDIAN SCENARIO

Human rights of women have been defined as "collective rights for a woman to be seen and accepted as a person with the capacity to decide or act on her own behalf and to have equal access to resources and equitable social, economic and political support to develop her full potential, exercise her right as a full human being and to support the development of others[9]. If we analyse this definition we can understand that every right that helps women to become full flaged human being is her human rights and denial of any such rights amounts to violation of women's human rights. Violation of women's human rights includes[10]:

I. Sexual or Physical assault and mental harassment;
2. Female foeticide and infanticide,
3. Female circumcision,
4. Dowry death, Sati, Forced prostitution, and
5. Denial of her autonomy and authority over her body.

This list is only to mention some violations, but it may extend to unlimited humiliations and violence against women, for example, wife beating, stripping of women in public, economic exploitation of women, exploitation of women labour by less payments, like that the list goes on and on. Deeply rooted societal and customary rules have further impeded their progress to a great extent. The sex based discrimination and deprivation are premised to a large extent on the arbitrary division of male and female roles in the society. It is heartening to note that the difference in sex roles begins from the time when the female child is identified in the womb of the mother. By chance she survives and takes her breath on the earth; she is put in chains at every step of her life which makes her generic status also at stake.

Being a Signatory to various International Conventions, Covenants and protocol on human rights, India has assumed the responsibility to provide and protect various rights of women. Therefore, the concept of *"equality and non discrimination" finds* its due place in the Indian Constitution and to ensure these principles Article 14, 15, 16 have been provided with equality provisions. India has adopted a clear policy on human rights and 'these human rights set forth in different groups, viz. right to equality.[11] State is also empowered to make special provisions in favour of women.[12] There are also other fundamental *rights viz, right to freedom*[13] *right to life and liberty*[14], *right against exploitation*[15], *right to freedom of religion and worship.*[16] cultural and educational right[17], right to constitutional remedies[18]. Resorting to judicial activism, the Supreme

Court has expanded the scope or 'right to life' to new horizons by reading many more right to it as integral and essential part thereof. Thus women also have fundamental rights of human/feminine dignity[19], to privacy[20], to health[21], to primary education[22], to free legal aid[23], to speedy trial[24] as adjuncts to right to life. The Indian Parliament has enacted The *Protection of Human Rights Act* 1993; Section 2 (d) of the Act defines *"human rights"*, to mean "the right relating to life, liberty, equality and dignity of the individual guaranteed by the Constitution or embodied in the International Covenants and enforceable by courts in India".

At this juncture its seems pertinent to make a brief sociolegal review of human rights in India on certain issues.

RIGHTS OF WOMEN AGAINST EXPLOITATION AND ABUSE

(a) Women as Labour and Industrial Workers

India is a signatory to ILO convention and has enacted a plethora of labour and industrial laws aimed at interalia securing health and favourable conditions of work. However, all laws providing for equal remuneration, maternity relief and leave, healthy and safe working conditions, minimum wages and overtime wages, fixed working hours etc. are flagrantly violated with impunity of tacit enforcement agencies[25].

(b) The Girl Child

Abuse of the girl child is yet another facet of female exploitation. Survey conducted by some NGO's reveal that children are. raped, sodomized and sexually exploited in many other ways. The law fails to provide relief to a victimized girl-child owing to an insensitive legal procedure and subsequent ostracizing by the society. The National Commission for Women laments the serious contradiction in the existing laws which tend to inhibit women as well as children from reporting crimes of sexual abuse against them. Such abuse sometimes has even commercial undertones. The current trend of high consumerism worsens the situation for vulnerable girl-children who under them became an alternative source of sexual gratification.

(c) Custodial Abuse

A person, being a public servant, a superintendent or manager of a jailor or remand home, or a member of management or staff of a hospital may deprively take advantage of his official position and induce or seduce women under his custody to have sexual intercourse with him. This may not amount to rape but is obviously an abuse of the women's subservient position, and is also her physical exploitation. The Indian Penal Code declares the above as offences and lay down punishment of 5 years imprisonment in each case. However, fear of moral stigma and social or court-room harassment and an insensitive approach of the police generally prevents victims from reporting their exploitation by such authortative approach of the police generally prevents victims from reporting their exploitation by such authorities. As a result, the law is rendered a mere dead-letter.

WOMEN'S RIGHT TO HEALTH AND NUTRITION

"The State shall regard the raising of the level of nutrition and the standard of living of its people and the improvement of public health are among its primary duties," directs Article 47 of the Indian Constitution under Chapter IV, Directive, Principles of State Policy. In a trend setting judgement, the Supreme Court in *Consumer Education and Research Centre* v. *Union of India*[26], declared the right of a worker to good health, medical care and safe hygienic workplaces as embodied in a person's fundamental right to life. Similarly, right to a healthy environment[27] and to emergency medical aid[28] have also been declared a fundamental right *for* being essential facets of right to life.

But in a country where around 40% of the population is living below the poverty line, it is not surprising that a considerable population of its female population suffers from acute problem of health and nutrition. Mothers in India continued to be the most vulnerable section of the population craving *for* primary health care. To quote a report by the Commission on the Status of women, "because women need *more* iron than men and because they tend to receive a lower share in the distribution of food, globally 43% of women and 5% of pregnant women suffer from anemia. In developing countries, 56% of the women 'are anemic. Because their mothers lack iodine, 30,000 babies, are still born every year and over 1,20,000 are born cretins[29]. The judiciary, especially the Supreme Court, has been playing an effective and meaning ful role towards protecting human rights of women. A part from securing several non-justiciable socio-economic rights *for* women are guaranteed fundamental rights, the Apex Court has frequently resorted to evolving novel measures such as compensatory jurisprudence with the view to secure gender justice.

A new era is said to have begun with the setting up of 'National Human Rights Commission, *'National Commission for Women'* and several state-level Human Rights Commission in early nineties in our country[30]. As sentinel of Human Rights of the common citizen, these Statutory Institution have so far done a commendable job despite their inherent limitations. There are also numerous independent human rights watch groups in India viz., *'people's Union for Democratic Rights'* (PUDR), *'People's Union for Civil Liberties'* (PUCL). *'Common Cause', 'Women's Initiative' etc.* who have done a service to the protection of women's rights.[31]

Thus, we witnessed that the U.N.O. from the very beginning is concerned with the plight of women. This is significant in itself as it not only accepts the prevalence of discrimination against women but also becomes a major instrument to eliminate discrimination in all forms. However, these instruments lay down the international norms to be adhered by the State at the national and internationallevels. But it is the implementation which is crucial to judge the progress to wards the realization of human rights. Human Rights should be developed as way of life but not mere slogans.

CONCLUSION AND SUGGESTIONS

From the above discussion it can be inferred that the sex inequality, discrimination and exploitation against women remain a persistent and un-solving problem. Women have suffered and been oppressed by the society from the time immemorial and are still victimized in every walk of life, socially, culturally, economically, legally and religiously.

India has an elaborate system of laws to protect the rights of women like Hindu Marriage Act 1955, Hindu succession Act 1956, Hindu succession (Amendment) Act, 2005, Dowry Prohibition Act 1961, Sati Act, Widow Remarriage Act 1856, Immoral Traffic Act 1956, Equal Remuneration Act which have been enacted from time to time to remove gender discrimination and protect women's rights. There is visible gap between the law as it stands and the law as it operates. This is the reason why the plethora of laws that were passed to combat dowery deaths, cruelty, rape, eveteasing, female foeticide, sexual harassment etc proved ineffective.

The current economic situation and the imbalances within the monetary and financial system playa major role in the development prospects and effective participation of women in the society. Women should be provided with an equal opportunity for access to resources. The concerned action should be directed towards establishment of a system of sharing responsibilities. Women's opportunity to enjoy their rights are often hindered by cultural or religious norms that discriminate against women. Sometimes such violations are evidenced in the treatment of women in the society due to their social, legal and economic condition as a general phenomena.

The position of women attracted social reforms with the coming of modern period. Efforts have been made in 19th and 20th centuries for the betterment of women. These attempts have succeeded to some extent but failed to change the social attitude and still the women are facing various miseries, exploitations and oppressions. Under the present system the position of women is miserable and exploited one. Innumerable crimes are committed against them and women are criminally assaulted, raped, enticed, kidnapped and abducted for immoral and illegal purposes. They are raped and molested by custodian of law and often forced to be a prostitute. Women also face various other offences apart from the sexual offence. They are beaten and killed by their husbands and relatives. Most distressing is the fact that these crimes are increasing day by day. It has rightly been pointed out by Rotert Ingersol, "There will never be a generation of great men until there has been a generation of free women-of free mothers". To protect the Human Rights violations relating to gender in equality and discriminations some drastic measures are the need of the hours. Collective efforts are required from social workers, legislature, women's organization and youths and then such atrocities can be prevented. The following suggestions may be useful to deal with the problems:

We have to redefine the concept of violence against women. It means to see the crimes like rape, abduction wife beating, dowery death and murders are the acts of violence motivated by the powers and authority. .Violent acts can occur in many circumstances where people will not acknowledge them normally. Women have to say things publicly which they dared not to say before.

Women organization should be strengthened. Voice of single women does not carry weight. If a group of women of like minded joined together, form an organization and raise voice, can make an impact. The social norm can be attached by the organization only. The organization should create awareness among women to struggle against their oppression and to fight the persons who exploit, humiliate and torture them.

The humanistic rational approach should be developed to the victims of crimes against women. These may include rethinking of roles, rehabilitation of victims and evolution of organizational procedures of the police, courts, rescue homes etc.

There should be a change in attitudes and values of judicial officials, the establishment of family court and change in police attitude. Re-orientation of magistrates is necessary. Instead of raising the technical points and acquitting the accused the circumstantial evidence should be given importance.

The image of police has deteriorated due to irresponsibility, corrupt as well as unlawful practices. A police officer should give proper treatment to the complainant, also co-operate, and create confidence rather than ill-treating him/her. The role of police is very important relating to cases concerning cruelties against women.

Sensitive lawyers can play a significant role in achieving equal legal status to women in India. It is their duty to challenge the discrimination. In the legal aid movement the women should be mobilized in co-operation with voluntary organizations and legal aid agencies for propagation and promotion of legal literacy. Knowledge of laws and access to the judicial system would strengthen the position of women and enable them to seek remedies and relief available under the law. It includes legal literacy, awareness about the machinery, providing legal assistance and actual litigation in court as well as in pre-trial stages. The work in this field must necessarily start with a programme of legal literacy of voluntary social workers and organizations and trough them for women in their respective areas. Mass media and particularly the press,

All India Radio and Doordarshan can play an important role to spread legal literary. In addition to all these things, the economic, social, cultural and political conditions of women should be improved. Priority emphasis .can be placed upon income generating opportunities. Urgent attention is necessary regarding the educational and vocational training of women in all fields of occupation.

NOTES AND REFERENCE

I. D.K. Ghatt, *Human rights and Gender Issues: A Socio-legal Perspective;* Indian Bar Review, vol. 27 (1) 2000, p-24.

2. Kashmir Singh; *Human Rights in India;* Ami-User Law Journal (1998), p-6

3. Dr. K. Uma Devi, *Human Rights are Women's Rights: A Review,* Supreme Cout Journal; vol. 2, 1998; p. 10

4. Article 30 of the Covenants

5. Article 54 of the Convention

6. The United Nations and Human Rights

7. Ibid.

8. Supra note 5; p. 13

9. 1968 APWLD Codes of Values

10. *Supra note.5;* p-ll

11. Article 14, *India Constitution*

12. Article 15 (3), *Indian Constitution*

13. Article 19, *Indian Constitution*

14. Article 21, *Indian Constitution*

15. Article 23, *Indian Constitution*

16. Article 25, *Indian Constitution*

17. Article 29, *Indian Constitution*

18. Article 19, *Indian Constitution*

19. Francis Coralie v. *Union Territory of Delhi;* (AIR) 1981 SC 746

20. People;s Union for civil liberties Vol. I AIR 1997, SC. 568.

21. Indian council for Euro legal Action Vol. I (1996), 35 Scc. 212.

22. J.P. Unnikrishnan V state of Andhra Perdash. AIR 1993 SC 2178

23. Kadrapalladia V state of Bihar AIR 1981 SC 939.
24. *Ibid.*
25. The apex court has also taken note of these harsh realities in its Judgement in People's Union for Democratic Rights Vol. I, A.I.R 1982 SC, 1473.
26. (1995) 3 SSC, 42.
27. Dr.B.L.Wadhera Vol. I (1996) SCC. 594.
28. Permanand kataria Vol. I AIR 1989 SC.2039 see also Plahun, Banga Khet Majdoor Samita stste of West Bengal (1996) 4 SCC. 37
29. Commisssion on the Status of Women, 39th Session New York, March 15, April 14, 1995;
30. Supra note 3, p. 34
31. *Ibid.*

STATUS OF CHRISTIAN AND MUSLIM WOMEN'S WORK PARTICIPATION IN INDIA

Nahid Sarikhani *

INTRODUCTION

Women as mothers, daughters, sisters and wives play very significant roles in men's lives. They are equal to men in all fields, but unfortunately, today, we see in the structure of any society, women are considered as second grade citizens without any freedom and they are consciously or unconsciously forced to perform all their duties without any rights of their own. In traditional societies women had always worked in economic units of the family when their works were under-estimated. These societies have taken many opportunities from them. As women's role and their freedom depend on men a lot. Men decide about women's education, their works outside home, equal property rights etc.

One of the traditional societies is India. In India, the husband is superior and the wife is his subordinate. The entire role – complex of their relationship in the family is based on this hierarchy. As Aleen Ross says that the women's tasks in all societies have less prestige than those of men, women talking over male business or professional roles are moving at a higher level of job prestige (Anuradha, Bholte. 1988).

* Department of Sociology, Mysore University, Manasagotri, Mysore, Karnataka, India

Harriet Bradley has argued that the culture of masculine deforms this affect both men and women. As individuals we are all trapped and constrained by gender stereotypes. He has emphasized the way in which sex-typing of jobs has hushed women into inferior places in the hierarchy and into economic dependency, that doesn't mean that men, do not suffer from the pressures of having to live up to ideas of masculine behaviour which may be alien to them as individuals. (Harriet, Bradly. 1989)

Malavika Karlekar with a study on sweeper women in Delhi has said it is possible to make a woman's life easier only within the matrix of a superior-subordinate relationship. This is due not only to the domination of men but equally to the women's acceptance of their inferior position. "As my work among the Balmikis showed women accepted the superiority of their husbands under all circumstances. Husbands were the unquestioned maliks of the hearth and home irrespective of whether they were unemployed men, private sweepers or clerks".(Karlekar, Malarika. 1987)

The Indian Constitution has conferred equal opportunities, rights and duties on all its citizens, irrespective of their caste, class, race and religion. In this condition, people belonging to different religious groups have utilized the facilities, which are provided by the government. Nowadays women are coming forward to achieve something in the competitive world. They are working in all fields like men and are competing with them too. Many studies have indicated that Hindu and Christian women work participation rate is higher than that of women from other religions, especially, Muslim women. However, Muslim women in some countries are also being educated and are working in different fields, like men, but their number is very negligible. When compared to that of Christian women, Muslim women's work participation rate is very low in India.

According to the census of 2001, the work participation rate of women is only 25.6% in India; Work participation rate for Muslim women is 14.1%, while among Christian women it is 28.7 % (COI, 2001). The lowest work participation rate among Muslim women is caused due to the following factors:

The Purdah system; the structure of the Muslim family is not yet conducive to women's freedom; early marriage; many males have a negative attitude against women's professions after marriage (like doctors, engineers and technicians); illiteracy and so on.

Safia Ipbal (1986) indicates years of set patterns of the thinking of men, influence of Non-Muslim Communities, a virtual famine of moral values, a wide chasm between actual Islam and Muslims and intolerance between the communities, are the main causes of Muslim women falling behind. (Arvind Sharma. 2002)

While Christians stand against polygamy, purdah, sati and child marriage. They emphasize the importance of women equally sharing education and opportunities of education and progress too. The largest factor affecting the status of women today is the changing family pattern coupled with the increased access to formal education. The girl's education might diminish their marital prospects. In addition, lead women towards equal status and equal participation in social and economic development of the communities.

The present study attempts to explore Muslim women's work participation rate in major economic sectors and their education. Also, Muslim women compare with Christian women in India.

STUDY OF THE POPULATION

According to the census 2001, at the national level of 1028 million populations, 13.4% are Muslims and 2.3 per cent are Christians.

Table 1 shows, population of Muslims is steadily increasing, as unadjusted growth rate would increase from 22.9 per cent to 36 per cent during 1991-2001, while for Christians it would increase from 21.5 per cent to 22.6 per cent during 1991-2001. Sex ratio among Muslim population at national level is 936 which is just above the national average of 933for all religions that it probability indicates that the position of women has worsened considerably, a decline in the sex ratio due to absolute conditions of health and survival among women. While Christians have the highest sex ratio of 1009 females per thousand males in the census of 2001.

Table 1
Population and Proportion of Muslim Population by sex, sex ratio, Per centage Increase, India 2001

Census Year India	*Persons*	*Males*	*Females*	*Sex ratio*	*Per centage Increase*
Muslim	138,188,240	71,374,134	66,814,106	936	(1991-2001)=36
Christen	24,080,016	11,984,663	12,095,353	1,009	(1991-2001)=23

Source: Census of India 2001, The First report on Religion Data, New Delhi, registrar general & census commissioner, 2004.

EDUCATION OF MUSLIMS AND CHRISTIANS IN INDIA

Education is an indispensable means for helping women out of their economic misery because economic dependency is another factor contributing to low status of women. Educated Muslim women everywhere show the tendency towards increasing economic independence. In fact, the awareness of the need to become financially independent and to supplement family incomes, forces women to accept jobs outside home.

According to the census of 2001, literacy rate for the population age 7 years and above for the country as a whole stands at 64.8%. As Muslim literacy rate is lower than the national average literacy rate at 59.1%, while among Christians are 80.3%.

Table 2 shows, in the rural and urban areas literacy rate among Christians is more than the Muslim population. Table

2 also explain that of the total Muslim population 7 years over, 40.9 % are illiterate, while the rate among Christians 19.7 % the illiteracy rate among Muslims is more that Christians in rural and urban areas.

Table 2
Literates rate of Muslims by residence, India -2001

Residence	*Total Population 7 age over*	*Literates*	*Illiterates*
	Muslim		
Total	112,295,181	66,396,634	45,898,547
Per cent	100	59.1	40.9
Rural area	70,864,447	37,367,715	33,496,732
Per cent	100	52.7	47.3
Urban area	41,430,734	29,028,919	12,401,815
Per cent	100	70.1	29.9
	Christen		
Total	20,840,407	16,724,465	4,115,942
Per cent	100	80.3	19.7
Rural area	13,573,130	10,118,361	3,454,769
Per cent	100	74.5	25.5
Urban area	7,267,277	6,606,104	661,173
Per cent	100	90.9	9.1

Source: Census of India 2001, The First report on Religion Data, New Delhi, registrar general & census commissioner, 2004.

In addition, in table 3 shows, when there is deep gap among literacy rate of Muslim men and women than Christian men and women. As difference between literacy rate of men and women among Muslim population is 17.5% while among Christians it is 4.2%. This pattern similarly blinks among rural and urban areas. The statistics above indicate Muslim women have not been able to take full advantage in society. Because in between Muslim society governing traditional attitude then Muslim women and also there is social, structural and institutional factors in Muslim communities such as early marriage, veiling, segregation etc.

Table 3
Literates rate of Muslims by residence, sex, India -2001

Residence	*Literates*		*Illiterates*	
	Male	*Female*	*Male*	*Female*
		Muslim		
Total	39,248,081	27,148,553	18,846,513	27,052,034
Per cent	67.6	50.1	32.4	49.9
Rural area	22,624,881	14,742,834	13,678,138	19,818,594
Per cent	62.3	42.7	37.7	57.3
Urban area	16,623,200	12,405,719	5,168,375	7,233,440
Per cent	76.3	63.2	23.7	36.8
		Christen		
Total	8,720,395	8,004,070	1,615,127	2,500,815
Per cent	52.1	47.9	39.2	60.8
Rural area	5,374,410	4,743,951	1,387,772	2,066,997
Per cent	53.1	46.9	40.2	59.8
Urban area	3,345,985	3,260,119	227,355	433,818
Per cent	50.6	49.4	34.4	65.6

Source: Census of India 2001, The First report on Religion Data, New Delhi, registrar general & census commissioner, 2004.

WORK PARTICIPATION RATE OF MUSLIM AND CHRISTIAN WOMEN IN INDIA

The work participation rate is defined as per centage of total workers (main and marginal) to total population. This is considered as a very crude measure since this does not take into account the age structure of the population.

According to Indian census of 2001, the total population of 138,188,240 the number of Muslims returned as workers is 43,396,093. Or, in other words, 31.3 per cent of Muslim population of India constitutes workers. Of these workers, 33,886,213 are males and 9,409,880 are females (table 4), sex ratio in between them is 278. In other words, the 2001 of census has recorded Muslims working population sex ratio of 278 Muslim women per 1000 Muslims males.

Of the total population of 24,080,016 the number of Christians returned, as workers are 9,551,397. In other words,

39.7% of Christian population of India constitutes workers. The lowest WPR at the national level are seen for the Muslim population. Of the total Christian workers, 6,077,963 are males and 3,473,434 are females (table 4), sex ratio in between them is 571. Statistical analyses have shown Christian women WPR are higher than Muslim women workers. The gap between Christian male and female WPR (27.2%) is lower than Muslim male and female WPR (56.6%).

Table 4
Work Participation rate of Muslim Population by sex, sex ratio, and residence: India, 2001

Residence	*Persons*	*Males*	*Females*	*Sex ratio*
		Muslim		
India	43,296,093	33,886,213	9,409,880	278
per cent	100	78.3	21.7	
Rural area	29,151,524	21,559,619	7,591,905	352
per cent	100	74	26	
Urban area	14,144,569	12,326,594	1,817,975	147
per cent	100	87.1	12.9	
		Christen		
India	9,551,397	6,077,963	3,473,434	571
Per cent	100	63.6	36.4	
Rural area	6,669,593	4,075,179	2,594,414	637
Per cent	100	61.1	38.9	
Urban area	2,881,804	2,002,757	879,020	439
Per cent	100	69.5	30.5	

Source: Census of India 2001, The First report on Religion Data, New Delhi, registrar general & census commissioner, 2004.

A majority of target population are employed in the rural areas, women workers have risen in the rural area, as sex ratio of Muslim women worker is 352 and Christian women is 637. Of course, in the urban area, sex ratio of Muslim women workers (147) is lower than Christian women workers (439).

Table 5
Work Participation Rate of Muslim and Christian Communities by Sex: India, 2001

India / States / Union terrritories	*Muslim*			*Christian*		
	Total	*Male*	*Female*	*Total*	*Male*	*Female*
India	31.3	47.5	14.1	39.7	50.7	28.7
Jammu & Kashmir	35.1	47.2	22.0	50.6	67.6	22.1
Himachal Pradesh	45.9	56.3	32.9	47.6	60.1	32.5
Punjab	40.3	56.7	19.7	35.7	51.5	18
Chandigarh	39.6	60.6	7.3	41.7	52.5	30.1
Uttaranchal	27.5	46.0	6.4	37	49.2	24.2
Haryana	37.8	45.2	29.4	39	53.3	23.4
Delhi	30.9	51.3	4.8	44.9	54.1	36.3
Rajasthan	34.7	46.7	21.7	42.9	49.7	36.1
Uttar Pradesh	29.1	44.6	12.4	33.9	46.7	20.6
Bihar	30.9	45.8	15.1	39.2	46.3	31.9
Sikkim	53.4	70.9	13.6	47.4	55.4	39.1
Arunachal Pradesh	45.0	61.6	18.4	43.5	45.3	41.7
Nagaland	43.6	60.5	16.2	42.2	44.4	39.9
Manipur	36.8	43.7	29.6	44.2	46.5	41.8
Mizoram	76.1	86.5	37.9	51.7	55.6	47.8
Tripura	29.2	46.2	11.2	38.7	43.6	33.9
Meghalaya	31.4	48.9	11.8	41.9	46.2	37.5
Assam	29.1	47.2	9.7	41.7	48.2	35
Weast Bengal	32.9	50.5	14.0	38.9	48.6	29.2
Jharkhand	31.6	43.5	18.8	45.6	50.1	41.3
Orissa	26.9	45.9	6.8	44.6	50.5	38.9
Chhattisgarh	32.3	48.5	15.0	46.1	51.8	40.5
Madhya Pradesh	32.8	47.6	16.9	40.5	48.2	32.7
Gujarat	32.7	51.1	13.0	45.9	54.1	37.5
Daman & Diu	37.5	61.6	7.3	43.2	59.2	26.3
Dadra & Nagar Haveli	42.5	64.3	11.0	47.4	52.2	42.1
Maharashtra	32.4	50.0	12.7	38.9	52.4	25.3
Andhra Pradesh	33.8	50.1	16.8	42.8	53.3	32.7
Karnataka	36.4	52.1	19.9	39.5	53.7	25.8
Goa	34.3	54.6	10.9	32.4	45.6	20.4
Lakshadweep	23.0	38.9	7.1	81.5	90.5	37.9
Kerala	23.2	42.0	5.9	33.9	52.1	16.3
Tamil Nadu	31.8	52.0	11.9	39	53.2	25.2
Pondicherry	24.4	46.5	4.2	34.9	50.3	20.9
Andaman & Nicobar Islands	34.5	53.8	12.1	40.3	54.8	24.3

Note: 1. Population figures for India and Manipur exclude those of Mao Maram, Paomata and Purul sub-divisions of Senapati district of Manipur.

Source: Census of India 2001, The First report on Religion Data, New Delhi, registrar general & census commissioner, 2004.

According to table 5, the highest work participation rate of Muslim women of over 30 % has been returned from Himachal Pradesh (32.9%) and Mizoram (37.9%). While the highest Christian Female WPR of over 30 per cent has been returned in 21 states of India which 6 states are over 40 %. These consist of Arunachal Pradesh (41.7%), Manipur (41.8%), Mizoram (47.8%), Jharkhand (41.3%), Chhattisgarh (40.5%), Dadra and Nagar Haveli (42.1%).

The lowest work participation rate of Muslim women less than 10 % has been recorded in 9 states and Union Territories. While, the lowest Christian Female WPR is over 20 % except in 2 states (Punjab18% and Kerala 16.3%).

In general, data of table 5 shows Christian male and female WPR is lower than the Muslim male and female WPR in all states, especially in big cities.

Table 6
Work Participation Rate of Muslim Women and housewife by residence: India, 2001

Residence	*Women*	*Workers*	*House wife*
	Muslim		
India	66,814,106	9,409,880	57,404,226
Per cent	100	14.1	85.9
Rural area	43,321,253	7,591,905	35,729,348
Per cent	100	17.5	82.5
Urban area	23,492,853	1,817,975	21,674,878
Per cent	100	7.7	92.3
	Christen		
India	12,095,353	3,473,434	8,621,919
Per cent	100	28.7	71.3
Rural area	7,950,417	2.594,414	5,356,003
Per cent	100	32.6	67,4
Urban area	448,027	103,716	344,311
Per cent	100	23.1	76.9

Source: Census of India 2001, The First report on Religion Data, New Delhi, registrar general & census commissioner, 2004,

On the other hand, table 6 has been shown, of the total Muslim women population of 66,814,106 the number of

Muslim women has been recorded as Non-workers (House keeper) is 57,404,226 or 85.9 %, and only 14.1 % of them are workers, while among the Christian women 71.3 % were Non-workers (House keeper) and 28.7 % has been returned as workers.

Also, the number of Muslim women house keepers in rural and urban areas are higher than Christian women house keeper and Christian female workers are higher than Muslim female workers in rural and urban areas.

Table 7 shows, a majority of Muslim and Christian women workers in India are employed as agricultural labourers and cultivators. Participation of Christian female workers than Muslim women workers were less in household industry workers. But, Christian female WPR than when compare to their counterparts among Muslim women have been employed more in petty trades and services, building and construction etc.

Table 7
Work Participation rate of Muslim Population by category of work, sex, India, 2001

India	*Sex*	*Total Workers*	*Cultiva-tors*	*Agricultures Labourers*	*Household Industry workers*	*Other workers*
			Muslim			
	T	43,296,093	8,979,686	9,545,976	3,520,467	21,249,964
		100	20.7	22.1	8.1	49.1
	M	33,886,213	6,910,438	6,645,706	1,708,121	18,621,948
		100	20.4	19.6	5	55
	F	9,409,880	2,069,248	2,900,270	1,812,346	2,628,016
		100	22	30.8	19.3	27.9
			Christen			
	T	9,551,397	2,793,646	1,458,380	260,745	5,038,626
		100	29.2	15.3	2.7	52.8
	M	6,077,963	1,624,320	783,228	105,583	3,561,832
		100	26.7	12.9	1.7	58.2
	F	3,473,434	1,169,326	672,152	155,162	1,476,794
		100	33.7	19.4	4.5	42.5

Source: Census of India 2001, The First report on Religion Data, New Delhi, registrar general & census commissioner, 2004.

In general, results above show a significant part of population of the study are recorded as unskilled work source in the country. On the other hand, many women workers are deprived of professional training especially Muslim women.

CONCLUSION

According to the census of 2001, at the national level 13.4 % are Muslims and 2.3 % are Christians. There is a deep gap among literacy rate of Muslim men and women compare to Christian men and women. As difference among Muslim population is 17.5 % while among Christians it is 4.2 %. In fact, absence of education put the Muslim women in a disadvantageous position. While data reveals Christians emphasize importance of education and opportunities of education for women. This matter affects their marriage; it increases age of marriage among Christian girls. In addition, education provides extra prestige and represents an important asset to their marriage. Whereas Muslim girls are deprived of this chance.

Data has shown Christian women WPR is 28.7 % and Muslim women WPR are 14.1 %. Christian women WPR are higher than Muslim women workers. The gap between Christian males and females WPR (27.2%) is lower than Muslim males and females WPR (56.6%).

Sex ratio is 278 among Muslims, and Christians are 571. Numbers of Muslim women housekeepers in rural and urban areas are higher than Christian women housekeepers.

Generally, comparison census of 2001 among Muslim and Christian women has indicated women WPR than men WPR as low. Unfortunately, position of Muslim women is worse. Muslim women suffer from polygamy, Purdah, Sati and child marriage. These factors have a damaging effect on status of Muslim women. Christians stand against them.

Equal education opportunities have provided greater chances of progress and development for Christian women. These opportunities finally lead Christian women towards equal status and equal participation in social, economic and cultural development of societies, while Muslim women are deprived from such situations. It is true that traditional norms, cultural and patriarchal values have shaped the role of Muslim women in India.

RECOMMENDATIONS

Today, various legislations, policies and programmes have been implemented to protect the interests of women and to improve their status, especially that of Muslim women. Unfortunately, many times they are not properly implemented or they are not adequate.

- The largest factor affecting the status of women is the changing family pattern coupled with the increased access to formal education, even though the per centage of women in higher education is still considerably low.
- According to the social situation of Muslim women in India, we should implement proper programmes related to improvement and to increase awareness level of Muslim women about equal status of women with men. This belief should be translated into actual practice through several institutions, customs and programmes. Certainly, the majority of these men know that their attitudes and practices in these matters don't have the support of the Quran or the Hadith. This can being about a change in Muslim women's attitude towards the Muslim women positions and rights.
- We should increase self-confidence in Muslim women by encouraging them to accept jobs and promotions without any fear and hesitation.
- Self-employment opportunities must be adequately extended to Muslim women.
- It is essential to implement legislations that protect Muslim women's rights by advertisement, plays, films etc.
- There is a need to develop Muslim women's organizations and Muslim women's activities in society.

- There is a need for the establishment of sufficient and proper baby-sitting and child-care centers for working women in the offices.

REFERENCE

Anuradha, Bholte (1988), "Employed Women: A Sociological Perspective" Delhi. Discovery Publishing House. p. 235.

Arvind, Sharma (2002), "Women in India Religions"New Delhi. Oxford University Press. pp. 178-179.

Census of India (2001), The First Report on Religion Data. New Delhi. Registrar General & Census Commissioner, 2004.

Harriet, Brably (1989), "Men's Work, Women's Work: A Sociological History of the Sexual Division of Labour in E mployment" USA. Polity Press. p. 239.

TRIBAL WOMEN IN INDIA

Pranati Datta[*]

INTRODUCTION

Women in India are subject to discrimination and exploitation. The status of women in a society is a reflection of social justice in that society. Low status of women in India is the consequence of the overarching patriarchal state structures and other perspectives, followed by abject poverty, illiteracy, social discrimination, lack of awareness and backwardness of women.The defective social and religious values and norms, biases and discriminating social perspectives towards women and the age-old tradition have hampered progressive development. The basic indicator of status of women is their level of income and education, participation in the economically productive activity, health status, and fertility behavior. Role played by a woman in the family, society and community is also reflection of her position.

The status of tribal women in patrilineal societies seem to be better than that of women in other communities in patrilineal society. In tribal society women are not treated as inferior citizens. Females are complement to men. Women are important part of family life and their role in the society is important. They help husband in agriculture, gathering

* Associate Scientist B, Population Studies Unit, Indian Statistical Institute.

forest ingredient, selling and buying from the market, child care and cooking and taking care of the house. But it must, however, be pointed and agreed that the status of women in tribal societies and their egalitarianism have often been over emphasized. Freedom of economic activity or participation does not always speak of their better status, as it is often done out of compulsion or necessity. Not only women are burdened with work.(Singh and Rajyalakshmi,1993), or given the responsibilities of children and arranging for food, fuel and water, they are considered fit only for certain specific works and not the important ones of political, economic and social nature.

STUDY OBJECTIVE

The present study attempts to assess status of tribal woman in India. Several demographic indicators e.g sex ratio, female literacy rate, girls enrolment per boys, gender parity index, age distribution, dependency ratio, parity progression ratio, have been utilized to evaluate the position of tribal woman in India.

General Demographic Feature of Tribal Population in India

Before discussing tribal women it would not be irrelevant to have an idea of general demographic feature of tribal population in India.

Higher infant mortality rate in the tribals compared to the national average,

Low nutritional status of the tribals,

Lower life-expectancy in the tribals than the national average,

High incidence of disease in some tribal groups,

Higher fertility rate in tribal women compared to the national average. (Basu S., 1993)

The literacy rate of the rural tribal female is the lowest of all groups.

There is gender bias in the literacy of tribal population as in other groups, the female literacy being lower than the male literacy. Though there has been five-fold increase in the literacy of tribal females it still is much lower than the national average for the females.

There are wide variations in the literacy rates of various of tribal groups. There are tribes with zero per cent literacy and there are tribes with literacy rate as high as 40 per cent (Nagas). The female literacy rates also vary from zero per cent in some tribes to 33.4 per cent in Khasis, Jaintias, etc

RIGHTS OF TRIBAL WOMAN

There are many studies on tribes, their culture,. But there is paucity of studies on status of tribal women, their socio-cultural problem, educational development etc in India (Mann.1987; Singh, Vyas, Mann, 1988); (Chauhan,1990).

Among the best part of tribal women right is that she is equal partner in the house and society though the male head of the family has right to maintain house. She has right to be involved in rituals, social ceremonies, running house, participation in social activities. As women their responsibility is more and in some cases they have more rights than men.

Women are never forced to marry to unknown or objectionable. If she dislikes, she can say no and that is final. Most good part of women rights of tribal women is that her parent does not have to give dowry as it is prevailing in Indian Hindu and other modern societies. Instead of dowry there is high bride price which imply higher status of women in their society. Girl children are valuable to parents so they get equal or in some cases better treatment from parents There is no stigma on widowhood. Child marriage is discouraged and never happens in this society. She has the right to decide her marriage. Most marriages in the tribal group take place between ages 16-21(Ahuja, 1965) A higher social status of women was reported by Furer - Haimendorf [1943] Hutton

[1921], Hunter [1973], and Firth [1946] among Tharus of U.P., and Nagas and Garos of the North East.

However it is found that there are some facts that indicate lower status of tribal women relative to tribal men. She is often deprived of her actual wage. She does not have property rights except in a matrilineal society. Tribal woman can not hold the office of a priest. In certain tribes only the males can participate in ancestor worship (Satyanarayan and Behra, 1986). The Toda and Kota women in southern India cannot cross the threshold of a temple. The Santal women cannot attend communal worship.

Rivers (1973), Dalton (1872) and Grigson (1938) have reported low status of women among Todas, Kharies and Mariya Gonds with reference to certain taboos during certain periods and ceremonies.

BASIC FEATURE

Sex Ratio

Sex ratio can be used as a broad index of gender in-equality. One of the indicator of discrimination against Indian woman is skewed sex ratio. Sex Ratio is a measurement of balance between males and females in human population (Sinha, 1990) and one of the important aspect of demographic profile for any Population. Large imbalance in this respect affect social, economic, community life in many ways. A higher or lower sex ratio reflect the status of the socio-cultural, maternal and child health care available in the population. The sex composition of population in India is found to be favourable to males. There were 933 females per 1000 males, where as for tribal population it is slightly higher (978 females for 1000 males) as per 2001 census. As compared to general population, there appears to be more even distribution of males and females among the Scheduled tribes. Sex ratio of scheduled tribe are relatively higher than that of general population. This suggests that females in the tribal society are not neglected. The social and cultural values protected their interest. A relatively balanced sex ratio indicates both better women's status and lesser anti-female discrimination in Indian tribal population, as a whole, compared to non tribal. But it started to show declinir g trend from 982 in 1971 to 972 in 1991 again it has increased slightly to 978 in 2001. This decline could be attributed to higher mortality amongst females of scheduled tribe community due to their nutritional deficiency and limited access to health services. Slight increase in 2001 may be the positive impact of special health and family welfare drive for them. Among tribes male and female population maintain a balancing position and enjoy equal status which is a rare event in present so-called modern upper caste patrlineal society.

Table 1
Sex Ratio of General Population and Scheduled Tribe: 1961-2001

	Sex Ratio : no of female per 1000 males	
Census years	*Total Population*	*Scheduled Tribe*
1961	941	987
1971	930	982
1981	934	984
1991	927	972
2001	933	978

Source: Census of India, 1961, 1971, 1981, 2001 Series - 1 India, part 2B—Primary Census Abstract (ST)

EDUCATION

Literacy Rate

Education for the tribal is an input to them for their economic development, promoting self confidence and inner strength to face challenges. Female literacy is significant indicator of educational development within any social group. Female education is highly important for upliftment of socio-economic parameter of the society. Literacy is a qualitative attribute of the population and is one of the most important indicators of socio-economic and political development of a society. It is a major component of human resource development index and is basic to social and economic progress. India inherits large scale inter-caste variation in literacy.Educational inequality was aggravated by economic inequality, gender disparity and rigid social stratification.

The level of literacy is one of the most important indicators of social, cultural, and health improvement among the tribal communities (Madan, 1951). The Indian tribes are exposed to literacy only in recently (Raza Moonis, et al.,1990). By and large their response to programmes of literacy and of formal education varied significantly between tribes and regions. Their responses depended on their socio-cultural and demographic characteristics and on the magnitude and direction of the forces of modernization, such as urbanization and industrialization (Bose,1970). Female literacy is a powerful instrument for social change. Female literacy among tribals are low compared to general population (Chauhan, 1990). Literacy rates for ST males and females register increasing trend during 1981 to 2001. Female literacy for scheduled tribe is still very low.

Table 2
Literacy Rates among General and Scheduled Tribe Population

	General Population			*Scheduled Tribe*		
	1981	*1991*	*2001*	*1981*	*1991*	*2001*
Total	36.23	52.21	65.38	16.35	29.65	47.10
Male	46.89	64.13	75.3	24.52	32.50	59.17
Female	24.82	39.29	54.16	8.04	14.50	34.76

Source: Census of India, 1981, 1991, 2001, Primary Census Abstract, General Population, Scheduled Castes and Scheduled Tribes.

The ST literacy rate which was 29.65 in 1991 increased to 47.1 % in 2001. It means literacy rate increased 17.5%. The male-female literacy rate for scheduled tribe was 59.71% and 34.76% respectively in 2001.

However, the difference between the literacy rate of scheduled tribes and that of the general population is quite large.

The status needs to be improved and for this serious effort is required for raising the level of literacy of the Scheduled Tribe population both males and females. There are historical and socio-economic reasons for having this wide gap between one section of society and the rest.

However, it is seen that where educational facilities are provided they are not accessible in the real sense of the term to the targeted group. So far as Scheduled Tribes population and in particular the ST Girls are concerned, it is fret that lack of residential facilities in educational institutions deters, Scheduled Tribe families to send their children to such institutions. Considering the important role of women in shaping the size of the family and outlook of its members, and also as an active agent of economic and social development, investment in providing education to the women of these communities is required not only to improve their social and economic status, but also to help in accelerating the pace of development of these communities and the nation as a whole.

LITERACY BY EDUCATIONAL LEVEL

Literacy status of Scheduled Tribe by educational level as per 2001 census can be explained by following figure 1. Female literacy without educational level (6.4 per cent) is slightly higher than male(4.9per cent). Highest per centage of female literate having below primary level education is observed and it is higher than male literate below primary level. Literacy status is low for female with other educational levels i.e primary, middle, matriculation, higher secondary / Intermediate/ Pre-University, Technical diploma or certificate, graduate and above.

There is variation in Rural-Urban literacy level for scheduled tribe female and this can be viewed from the

Fig. 1: Per centage of Scheduled Tribe literate by Educational Level and Sex: 2001

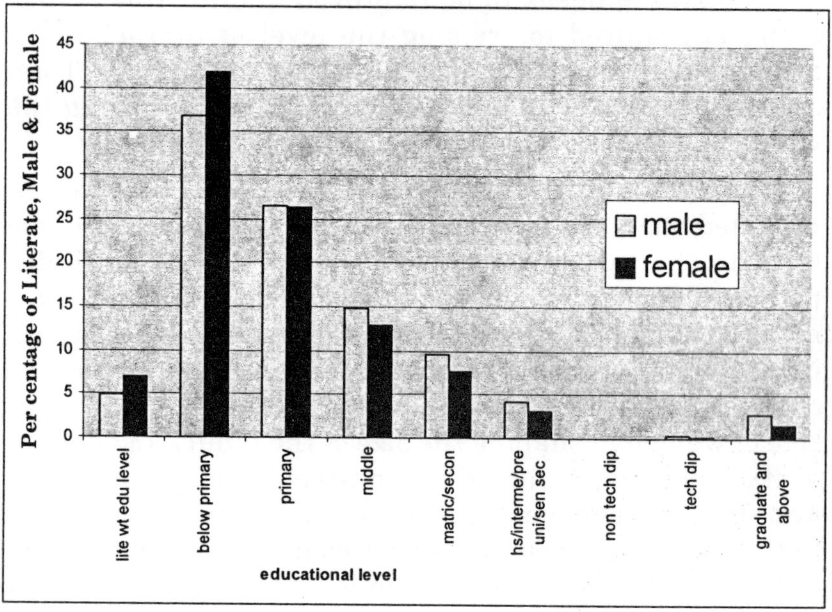

following figure 2. Literacy without educational level and below primary level is higher in rural areas compared to urban areas. But for middle, matriculation/secondary, and Higher secondary/ Intermediate/Pre-University/Senior secondary level urban areas experience higher female literate than rural areas. There is higher per centage of female graduate+ in urban areas in comparison with rural areas. There is no non-technical diploma or certificate holder in either rural or urban areas of India. Female technical diploma holder is more or less same in rural and urban areas.

Following educational levels have been used in the Fig 2.

1. literate without educational level
2. below primary
3. primary
4. middle

Fig. 2: Literacy of Scheduled Tribe Female by Educational Level and Residence: 2001

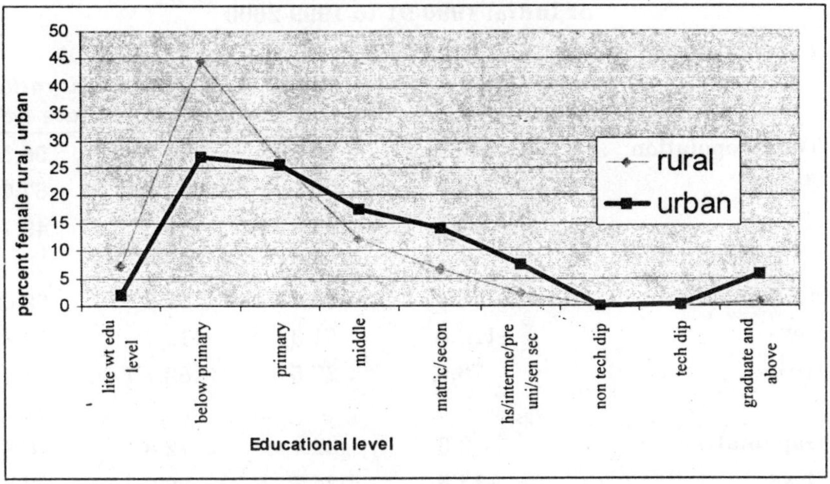

5. matriculation/secondary
6. higher secondary / intermediate/pre-university/senior secondary
7. non technical diploma
8. technical diploma
9. graduate and above.

GROSS ENROLMENT

Gross enrolment for female is very low compared to male tribes.

Gross enrolment ratio (table 3) for classes 1-5 and classes 1-8 has declined for boys and improved for girls of 1-8 classes of general population during 1990-91 to 1999-2001. In case of ST boys gross enrolment ratio has decreased for classes 1-5 but has improved for classes 1-8 during the period 1990-91 to 1999-2000. Improvement in gross enrolment ratio is observed for ST girls during the period 1990-91 to 1999-2000. The improvement in enrolment of ST children can be attributed to large scale government effort to universalize education, and growing demand among the tribal communities to access formal education.

Table 3
Gross Enrolment Ratio of ST and General Population of India: 1990-91 to 1999-2000

TotalPopulation / ST / sex	*1990-1991*		*1999-2000*	
	Gross enrolment ratio		*Gross enrolment ratio*	
	Class 1-5	*Class 1-8*	*Class 1-5*	*Class 1-8*
Total Population	100.1	62.1	94.9	58.8
Boys	114.0	76.6	104.1	67.7
Girls	85.5	47.8	85.2	49.7
ST Population	103.4	39.7	97.7	58.0
Boys	126.8	51.3	112.7	70.8
Girls	78.6	27.5	82.7	44.8
Gap total	+ 3.3	-22.4	+2.8	-0.8
Boys	+12.8	-25.3	+8.6	+3.6
Girls	-6.9	-20.3	-2.5	-4.9

GIRL-ENROLMENT

Number of girls enrolment per hundred boys enrolled for Scheduled tribe is an index of status of ST women in India. In primary education number of girls enrolment per hundred boys has increased from 39 in 1950-51 to 79 in 2001-02. For middle level education it has enhanced from 18 to 72 for the same time period. Number of girls enrolment per hundred enrolled boys for secondary education has increased from 16 in 1950-51 to 65 in 2001-02. All these are surely an indicator of improvement of status of tribal women in India. This also reflect gender bias in education. Female enrolment is still lower relative to male. This is represented in the following figure 3. Girls enrolment per 100 boys for primary, middle, secondary level follows upward rising trend.

Table 4
Number of Girls enrolment per hundred boys enrolled

Year	*Primary (I-V)*	*Middle (VI-VIII)*	*Secondary (IX-X)*
1950-51	39	18	16
1960-61	48	32	23
1970-71	60	41	35
1980-81	63	49	44
1990-91	71	58	50
1991-92	72	62	52
1992-93	72	61	51
1993-94	76	66	57
1994-95	75	65	57
1995-96	76	65	57
1996-97	76	66	58
1997-98	77	67	58
1998-99	77	68	62
1999-2000	77	68	65
2000-01	78	69	63
2001-02	79	72	65

Source: Educational Statistics, Govt of India

Fig. 3: Number of Girls Enrolment per 100 Enrolled boys for Scheduled Tribe Population, 1950-51 to 2001-02

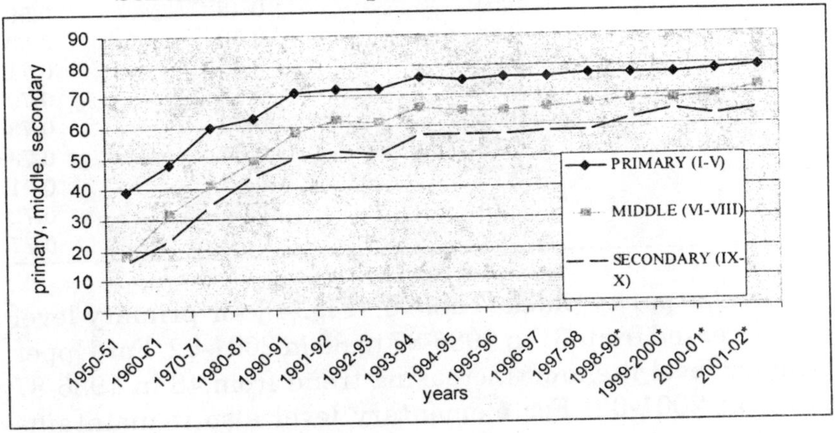

GENDER PARITY INDEX

Gender Parity Index (GPI) has been calculated by dividing girl's gross enrolment ratio(GER) by boy's gross enrolment ratio GER for a given level of education. It measures progress towards gender equity in education. GPI varies between 0 and 1. When the GPI shows a value equal to 0 it means that there is no gender equity in education, there is maximum discrimination against females. When GPI is 1 at any level of education it shows that there is no gender disparity at that level and learning opportunities are available for girls equally to that of boys. From the available figure it is clear that there is no perfect gender equity in education for any level of education, but gender equity is gradually improving towards female tribes.

Table 5
Gender Parity Index for Scheduled Tribes in India: 1986-87 to 2001-2002

Year	*Gender Parity Index Scheduled Tribe Students*		
	Primary (I-V)	*Upper Primary (VI-VIII)*	*Elementary (I-VIII)*
1986-87	0.61	0.48	0.59
1990-91	0.65	0.50	0.60
1995-96	0.70	0.61	0.71
1996-97	0.69	0.63	0.70
1997-98	0.76	0.62	0.73
1998-99	0.76	0.64	0.73
1999-2000	0.73	0.63	0.71
2000-2001	0.73	0.66	0.72
2001-02	0.80	0.70	0.77

Gender parity index [Table 5, (Fig. 4)] for primary level has increased from.61 in 1986-87 to.80 in 2001-02. For Upper primary level it shows increasing trend from.48 in 1986-87 to.70. in 2001-02. For elementary level also it maintains upward trend.

DROP OUT

Drop out is a universal phenomenon in Indian educational system which results in considerable wastage. A dropout has been defined here as one who having enrolled in a particular trade either leaves it mid-way or leaves after failing in the final examination.

Fig. 4: Gender Parity Index for Scheduled Tribe Students in India

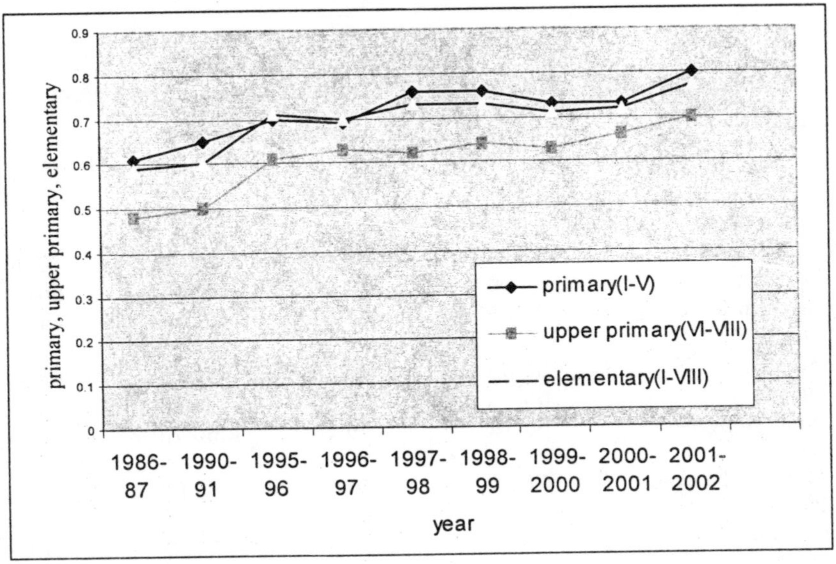

The drop out rate among indigenous and tribal people is very alarming. Various steps taken by the State governments to check drop out including free distribution of books and stationery, scholarship, reimbursement of examination fee, free bus travel etc have failed.

Drop Out Rate for tribal boys and girls in India and different states are presented in the following table 6

Drop out rate for boys and girls increase sharply as their educational level increases. Drop out is lowest in Kerala in classes I-V. At lower level of education gender discrepancy is relatively low but as level of education increases the gender inequity in drop out becomes much more pronounced. The drop out rate among tribal boys in classes I-VII is 66.86% where as it is 71.17% among girls. Cost of education and need to work as child labour due to poverty contribute to high drop out rate in higher education for tribal family. Girl child is engaged in domestic work also. Though education is free at lower level, poverty stricken tribal family can not bear the burden of other cost including books and learning materials. Hence supply of human capital is constrained by poverty, lack of resources, shortage of schools, inadequate infrastructure etc.

Table 6
Drop Out Rates for Scheduled Tribes in India: 2002-2003

States	*Drop Out Rates*			
	Classes I-V		*Classes I-VIII*	
	Boys	*Girls*	*Boys*	*Girls*
North East				
Meghalaya	61.42	59.29	81.11	80.30
Mijoram	55.90	54.90	59.89	56.34
Nagaland	37.38	37.01	42.81	44.19
East				
Bihar	66.60	65.39	82.43	85.57
Orissa	58.03	53.50	77.45	79.12
West Bengal	53.70	59.26	60.73	42.42
Central				
Madhya Pradesh	51.90	50.51	65.56	70.16
West				
Gujarat	36.13	43.10	58.26	67.04
Maharashtra	28.79	40.23	61.03	66.43
Rajasthan	50.61	59.87	52.58	73.17
North				
Uttar Pradesh	31.19	30.02	36.97	36.45
Himachal Pradesh	16.23	21.70	26.79	37.43
South				
Andhra Pradesh	63.29	68.71	78.59	84.34
Kerala	2.20	5.96	33.63	40.03
Tamil Nadu	27.24	21.01	56.98	54.36
India	50.82	52.10	66.86	71.17

Source: Selected Educational Statistics 2002-2003(as on 30th September, 2002) Dept of Secondary and Higher Secondary Education, Ministry of Human Resource Dvelopment, Govt of India

Gender discrepancy in the drop out rate is relatively lower in north eastern states Meghalaya, Mizoram, Nagaland. The drop out rates among tribal girls in classes 1-VIII are comparatively low and far below national average (71%) in Himachal Pradeshand Uttar Pradesh followed by Kerala, and West Bengal.

OBSTACLES TO GENDER EQUITY IN EDUCATION

In the context of ST women in India prevalence of high illiteracy is limiting their engagement with the main stream society. Literacy campaign generated social mobilization which affected social sectors, women's empowerment, health, population stabilization and environmental awareness, It served to promote equity, justice, foster scientific temper, sense of belonging to India's great composite culture and consciousness, unity in diversity. But what is done is not up to the requirment and mark.

Inequality in gender is one of the most crucial and yet one of the most persistent disparities in India where male-female literacy differential are more glaring in the rural areas. Acute economic deprivation and social disability accentuate the problem of illiteracy amongst the ST. The main problem arises from lack of communication, inaccessibility of their habitation, scattered population, lack of adequate institutional infrastructure and the variety of tribal dialect make problem of illiteracy more acute.

AGE DISTRIBUTION

Age distribution is shown to point out the nature of population structure. In general, a population with more than 35 per cent under the age 15 is considered young and the population with more than 10 per cent aged 65 and above considered old.

From the following table it can be concluded that tribal population experience young age structure. There is not much gender difference with respect to age distribution of tribal population. Tribal Dependency ratio is high compared to non tribal. Ageing index is low for tribals compared to non tribals in India.

Table 7
Age Distribution of Tribal Population in India : 2001

Age group	*Tribal population*			*Non tribal population*
	person	*male*	*female*	*person*
0-14	39.49	39.95	38.87	35.08
15-59	54.07	54.06	54.43	57.33
60+	5.81	5.69	6.46	7.59
Dependency ratio	83.78	84.42	83.28	74.42
Ageing index	14.71	14.24	16.61	21.63

Note: Dependency ratio is a ratio of population aged 0- 14 and aged 60+ to population in age group 15-59. Dependency ratio : $[(p_{0\text{-}14} + p_{60}) / p_{15\text{-}59}] * 100$

Ageing index is Ratio of population aged 60 years and above to the population aged 14 years and below i.e Aging Index: $(p_{60+} / p_{0\text{-}14})* 100$

Gender differential with respect to age among tribal population in India is presented in the following Figure : 5. Gender differential in 0-9 age group is negligible. Among other age group there is some gender differential among tribal communities in India.

MARRIAGE

The pattern of marriages in India is characterized by three types of regulation, namely (a) Endogamy (marrying within the group of birth (b) Exogamy (marrying out) and (c) consanguineous or sapinda marriage. The regulation of consanguineous marriages does not permit marriages between two individual related through a common male ancestor upto the seventh generation on the father's side. There is a greater incidence of consanguineous marriages specially among the population of the southern States, Muslim groups, Parsees and various tribal communities(Basu,1985).

In tribes most marriages are in four ways. (1) arranged marriage, (2) love marriage, (3) Widow marriage, (4) Dharanjia marriage Under this system when a boy of poor family expresses willingness to marry a girl of his liking, the boy has to work as domestic servant to satisfy girl and her parents.

Fig. 5: Age Distribution of Tribal Male and Female

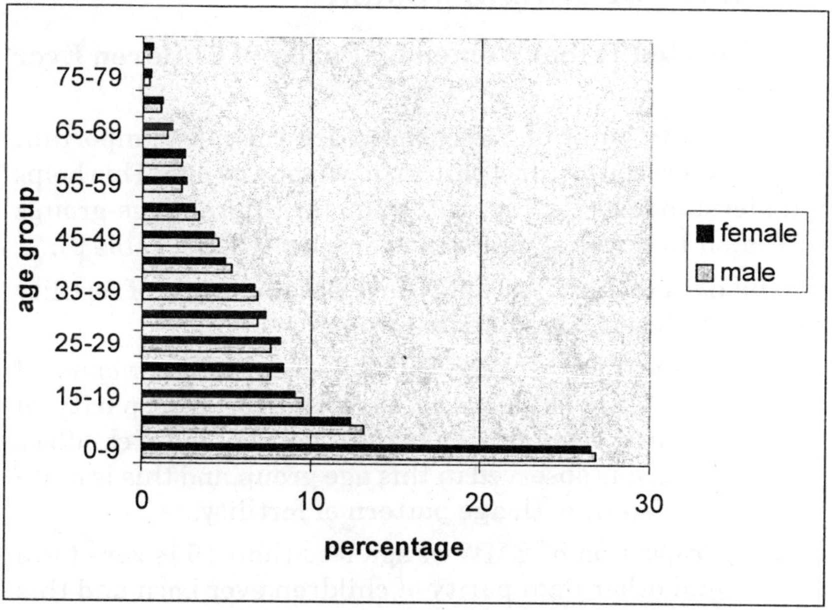

In many tribal communities, cross-cousin marriages were preferred and practiced. The system of cross cousin marriage had proved to be beneficial to the females in terms of care and treatment at husband's place. It also avoided high bride price/dowry and maintained the property of the household.

Consanguineous marriages may, however, result in an increased probability of abortions, miscarriage, still births, neo-natal deaths, infant and juvenile deaths physical and mental defects susceptibility to infections diseases etc.

Many of the tribal societies were lax towards pre-marital sex relations which were considered as a training in the art of love and sex life and often ended in marriage (Vidyarthi and Rai, 1977).

Girls in tribal societies were given in marriage generally after puberty.

FERTILITY OF TRIBAL WOMEN

Ever Married Tribal Women by Parity of Children Ever Born

From fertility point of View, these are the most Important Data to Know the fertility pattern of women by age. This helps to understand the fertility rates among different age-groups of Women In terms of children ever born (CEB) (Table 9).

The data on parity (Table 9) reflect the levels of fertility rates for different ages of tribal women.

1. Highest per centage (80%) of ever married women of less than 15 years is observed for zero parity of children ever born. i.e highest per centage of childless women is observed in this age group.and this is quite consistent with age pattern of fertility.
2. Proportion of EMW of age less than 15 is zero for 3 and other high parity of children ever born and this is logical since women with age less than 15 can not be expected to have more than two children.

   No significant changes are noticed for per centage for EMW of age 50 and above and this is only for the reasons that fertility reaches its end point in this age group.
3. Proportion of women of age 15-19 for parity 3 and 4 of CEB is very insignificant and this proportion is zero for parity 5,6 and 7 and this seems to be consistent.
4. Proportion of childless women (0 parity women) are comparatively low in the age group of 30-34, 35- 39, 40-44, 45-50, 5-54 and 55-59 respectively.
5. The high per centage of EMW of higher age group for higher parity i.e 5,6,7+ reflects an important feature of high fertility among tribal woman

Table 9
Per centage of Ever married Woman by parity of children ever born

Age group of ever married women	*Per centage of ever married tribal women by parity of children ever born in India*							
	Parity of children ever born							
	0	*1*	*2*	*3*	*4*	*5*	*6*	*7+*
All ages	14.654	12.89	16.35	16.98	13.88	9.62	6.33	9.25
Less than 15	80.26	9.58	10.16	0	0	0	0	0
15-19	66.92	24.84	5.63	1.24	1.35	0	0	0
20-24	28.8	32.8	24.07	9.64	2.85	0.78	0.27	0.77
25-29	12.36	15.71	26.91	24.17	12.67	4.9	1.69	1.59
30-34	7.87	8.20	18.48	24.41	19.34	11.32	5.64	4.74
35-39	6.73	6.95	14.82	21.28	19.28	13.51	8.39	9.03
40-44	6.78	6.76	12.84	18.62	18.38	14.00	9.57	13.03
45-49	7.07	7.12	11.95	16.62	17.45	14.05	10.14	15.6
50-54	8.53	7.80	11.25	14.92	16.17	13.76	10.3	17.27
55-59	8.65	7.66	10.36	13.46	15.35	13.88	11.02	19.62
60-64	11.42	8.58	10.03	12.21	13.96	13.12	10.74	19.96
65-69	11.58	8.21	9.31	11.22	13.23	13.01	11.21	22.23
70-74	14.18	9.19	9.37	10.55	12.36	12.16	10.54	21.64
75-79	13.82	9.03	9.08	10.23	11.60	11.89	10.57	23.78
80+	15.92	9.40	9.36	10.72	11.66	11.29	9.83	21.82

Per centage of Scheduled tribe ever married woman by parity of children ever born has been presented in the following Fig 6. Per centage of childless woman (0 parity woman) is highest (80%) for age group less than 15. This per centage gradually diminishes with higher age group. Tribal woman with more than 7 children (parity 7+) gradually increases with higher age group implying high fertility of tribal woman.

Parity Progression Ratio (PPR) indicates the extent to which woman progress from one parity to the next. In a probabilistic sense, one can say that PPR indicates the chance of a woman of parity 1 to go for higher parity(to have additional child in a year. This ratio can directly be calculated for real cohorts which have crossed the reproductive age group. PPR for parity I.

a_i = (women of parity (i+1) and above/women of parity i and above)

= No. of women of atleast (i+1) parity/No. of women atleast i parity = $w_{(i+1)+} / w_{i+}$

Fig. 6: Scheduled Tribe ever Married Woman by Parity of Children ever Born in India: 2001

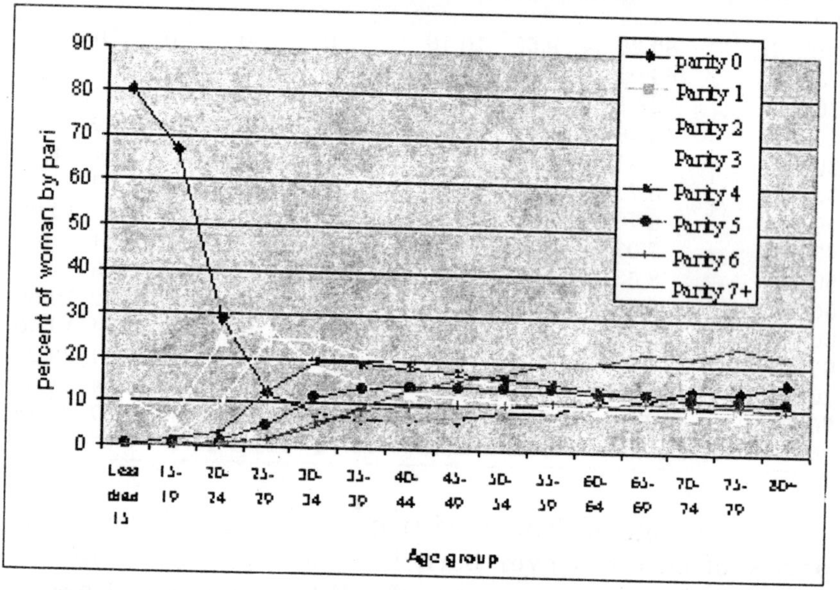

PPR is always less than one. Knowledge of PPR helps to understand and to assess the propensity of women, in a population, to go for higher order of births.. In a probabilistic sense one can say that PPR indicates the chance of a woman of parity I to go for high parity. Thus the chance of having one child is a_0, two children is a_0a_1, and three children is $a_0a_1a_2$ and so on.

In the table 11, a_0, a_1, a_2, a_3........ are the parity progression ratio corresponding to parity 0,1, 2,....i respectively. For tribal population where generally fertility is not controlled, PPR is high

In table 10 Number of ever married woman with parity of children is shown. Table 11 presents parity progression

Table 10
Number of ever married women with exact number of Children Ever Born

CEB	*Number of ever married women with exact number of children Ever born* 0	1	2	3	4	5	6	7+	*Total no. of ever married women*
No. of Married Women	3158215	2779651	3525850	3660744	2993517	2073368	1365278	1995046	21551669

Table 11
Parity Progression Ratio for Tribal Women in India : 2001

Women by parity wi	*No of women*	*Parity progression ratio, a_i*	*Chance of a woman for high parity*
W_0 +	21551669		
W_1 +	18393454	a_0 =.85345	a_0 =.85345
W_2 +	15613803	a_1 =.8488	a_0a_1 =.7244
W_3 +	12087953	a_2 =.7741	$a_0a_1a_2$ =..5607
W_4 +	8427209	a_3 =.6971	$a_0a_1a_2a_3$ =.3909
W_5 +	5433692	a_4 =.6447	$a_0a_1a_2a_3a_4$ =.2520
W_6 +	3360324	a_5 = 6184	$a_0a_1a_2a_3a_4a_5$ =.1558
W_7 +	1995046	a_6 =.5937	$a_0a_1a_2a_3a_4a_5a_6$ =.0925

ratio for tribal woman. Propensity of woman to go for first, second and third child is.85345,.7244,.5607 respectively.

POLICY

The greatest challenge to government of India since independence is proper provision of social justice to the ST population, the poorest of India's poor, by improving their socio-economic condition. A strategy for development would require intensive approach in terms of their geographic and demographic concentration. Constitutional gurantee declared a new feature of the India's poorest of the poor, to become a dignified human being. Long years of government intervention has not made any significant impact in improving the conditions of the tribals. In human development index, the tribal regions and people are at the bottom of the table in every state and districts. No one can question the basic fact that the tribal people in India are the poorest of all.

Following course of action is recommended for upliftment of tribal women.

Innovative educational programmes at the micro-level for the tribal group specially for females is required.

It is necessary to conduct statewise and district-wise surveys to find out causes of non-enrolment of girl child in tribal communities in order to achieve the goal of universalisation of elementary education.

Studying the problems of drop-outs, wastage and stagnation among tribal girls in school should be emphasised

There should be committee to evaluate ongoing integrated tribal development programme in tribal areas

The role of mass media in educational development of tribals required to be assessed.

In view of the high incidence of illiteracy and high drop out rate especially among female tribes there are urgent need for medium of instruction in tribal dialects, participation of local community in educational activity, proper commitment of teachers, adequate orientation of teachers and other administrators about tribal life and culture, adequate and timely supply of text books and note books, provision of incentives, proper monitoring mechanism to motivate continuation of education without drop out

Unless the state, civil society and the intelectuals become aware of and concerned about gender in-equality and social justice, it will be impossible for women to fight out the problems and challenges. While empowering tribal female major emphasis will be on social empowerment, economic empowerment, political empowerment and social justice.

REFERENCES

Ahuja, R. (1965), Religions of Bhils—A Sociological Bulletin, XIV, 1, 21-33

Basu, S. K. (1985), Inbreeding in India: Its Genetic Consequences and Implications in Health Care (In) Population Genetics and Health Care: Issues and Future Strategies: NIHFW Technical Report 8. New Delhi. pp. 71-77.

Basu, S.K. (1993), Health Status of Tribal Women in India, Social Change, Vol. 23, No. 4, pp. 19-39.

Bose, A. B. (1970), Problems of Education Development of Scheduled Tribes, *Man in India* Vol. L (1) pp. 26-51.

Chauhan, Abha (1990), *Tribal Women and Social Change in India.* A.C. Brothers, Etawah.

Dalton, E. T. (1872), Descriptive Ethnography of Bengal Calcutta.

Firth, R. (1946), Human Types. London: Nelson.

Furer-Haimendorf, Von. C. (1943), The Chenchus: Jungle Folk of Deccan, London: Macmillan and Company.

Grigson, W. V. (1938), The Maria Gonds of Bastar. Oxford: Oxford University Press.

Hunter, W.W. (1973), Orissa. London: Smith Elder.

Hutton, J. H. (1921), The Sema Naga. London: Macmillan

Vidyarthi, L. P. (1983), Tribes of India. In *Peoples of India: Some Genetical Aspects.* XV International Congress of Genetics, Dec. 12-21, ICMR, New Delhi.

Vidyarthi, L. P. and Rai, B. K. (1977), *The Tribal Culture of India.* Concept Publishing Company, Delhi.

Mann, K. (1987), Tribal Women in a Chaging Society. Mittal Publications, Delhi.

Madan, T. N. (1951), Education of Tribal India. *Eastern Anthropologist* Vol. V (4) pp. 179-82.

Raza Moonis, Ahmad Aijazuddin and Nuna Sheel Chand. (1990), Special Pattern of Tribal Literacy in India. In Demography of Tribal Development (eds. Bose, Sinha and Tyagi). B. R. Publishing Corporation, Delhi.

Rivers, H. H. (1973), The Todas. London: Macmillan.

Satyanarayana, R. & Behera, D. K. (1986), Socio-economic Responsibility of Tribal Women: A Micro-study of the Kissan of Western Orissa. Tribal Women and Development. Agenda Papers, Theme I, p. 15.

Singh, J. P. Vyas N. N. and Mann R. S. (1988), *Tribal Women and Development.* Rawat Publications, Jaipur.

Singh, A. K & Rajyalakshmi, C. (1993), Status of Tribal Women in India: Social Change. 23(4). p. 3-18.

Sinha, U.P. (1990), Demographic Profile of Tribal Population in India. *In Demography of Tribal Development* (eds, Bose Ashis, Sinha U.P. and R.P. Tyagi) B.R. Publishing Corporation, Delhi.

LAW RELATING TO FEMALE FOETICIDE AND HUMAN RIGHTS OF WOMEN IN INDIA

*Devinder Singh**

INTRODUCTION

The International Conference on Population and Development recognized, the Programme of Action, which provides,[1]that full attention should be given to the promotion of mutually respectful and equitable gender relations and particularly to meet the educational and service needs of adolescents to enable them to deal in a positive and responsible way with their sexuality. Taking into account the rights of the child to access to information, privacy, confidentiality, respect and informed consent, as well as the responsibilities, rights and duties of parents and legal guardians to provide, in a manner consistent with the evolving capacities of the child, appropriate direction and guidance in the exercise by the child of the rights recognized in the Convention on the Rights of the Child- 1989(CRC), and in conformity with the Convention on the Elimination of All Forms of Discrimination against Women-1979. The Convention on the Rights of the Child recognizes that States Parties shall respect and ensure the rights set forth in the present Convention to each child within their jurisdiction without discrimination of any kind, irrespective of the child's or his or her parent's or legal

* Reader, Department of Laws, Panjab University, Chandigarh, Pin–160014. *e-mail-thakur_dsingh@yahoo.com, thakur_dsingh@indiatimes.com*

guardian's race, colour, sex, language, religion, political or other opinion, national, ethnic or social origin, property, disability, birth or status.[2] In all actions concerning children, the best interests of the child shall be a primary consideration. Among the other rights of the child under the CRC one of the main high lights of the convention is that every child has the inherent right to life, and the states shall ensure, the maximum child survival and development. Therefore, right to take birth is the inherent right of the unborn child under the convention.

Female–foeticide & Infanticide are Human Rights Issues

Female-foeticide[3] and infanticide[4] are human rights issues. With the advances in the medical science now it is possible to know the sex of child in the womb of mother. People adopt this method to kill female child. It causes many problems. Abortion at any a stage is harmful to the mother's health. Early childhood care and education rights–and all the underlying protections and entitlements needed for the first 5 years of life–begin with the assurance of three simple essentials: the right to be born, the right to survive birth, and the right to stay alive through infancy and to the fifth birthday. For half of India's children, this assurance is at grave risk, simply because they are girls—and daughters are not wanted. The first early childhood right for them is to live –and both negative social attitudes and new technologies are conspiring to deny them this. Population law has responded to the immediate challenges presented by the rapid population growth, its ultimate concern is human rights. Family planning is a mean to achieve a set of basic human right, which include adequate food, health, clothing, shelter, education, and work, recreation and old age security. These inherent rights or fundamental rights are synonymous with the law of nature. United Nations recognized the family planning as the basic human right only in May 1968, when the United Nations Conference on Human Rights in Tehran proclaimed, "parents have a basic human right to determine freely and responsibly the number and the spacing of their children". A unanimously adopted resolution added the language "a right to adequate education and information in this respect" for all "couples". An examination of the conference proceedings revealed that the term "couples" instead of "parents" or "families" was used in the resolution in order to ensure that couples may decide to have no children at all, one delegation even stressed the fundamental right of women to conscious motherhood.[5] At the same time it causes imbalance in population. Most importantly it brings to an end the life of a born or unborn child. In India with a population of more than one billion people, the number of legal abortions is much less than unreported cases. Therefore, destruction of the female foetus at any stage is necessarily a human right issue not only of unborn unborn child but also of the mother.

In traditional society the birth of the female is traditionally less favoured than that of the male. Being born a boy is itself a privilege. Investment in the upbringing of a girl is relatively less; as the major goal being marriage, she is looked upon as a transitory member of the family in contrast to the boy. He is the transmitter of the family name to future generations and occupies the significant role in conducting family rites. She is usually regarded as a liability, to be married of well and as early as possible. After marriage the mother's status increase with the birth of a boy.[6] Birth of a child is celebrated everywhere but not that of a baby girl. Couples want male issues and not female and the advance in medical science seems to have come to their assistance, ultrasound tests help in the termination of the pregnancy if the foetus happens to be female. IVF embryo transfer techniques now can produce the male heir-apparent to any couple. Doctors who indulge in such practices do not care for Prenatal Diagnostics Techniques Regulation and Prevention Act. Advertisements appear like 'Plan Your Family by X-Y separation of sperms" in every English and local language media and videocassettes etc. Huge hoardings at important junctions both in the rural and urban areas implore you to 'Plan your family by X-Y separation' and even offer seasonal reduction in the cost. Competition is cutthroat and no body seems to be worried as long as one has a son.[7] These are all violation of human rights of women, namely–right to health.

Girl children who escape foeticide, infanticide, or neonatal denial are still in the 0-6 high-risk frames for early disposal. She is less fed, less encouraged to explore the world, more likely to be handed jobs to do, given less health care and medical attention, socialised not to ask. Most of Indian children aged below 3 years suffer from anemia; no one has cared to investigate whether girls predominate among these under-nourished children, but chances are that they do. Outpatient data from hospitals shows lower admissions of girl children, and girls in more serious condition than boys when brought for treatment.[8]

Magnitude of the Problem in India

In India, there are less than 93 women for every 100 men in the population. The accepted reason for such a disparity is the practice of female foeticide and infanticide in India, prompted by the existence of overall male dominance in the society.[9] For a poor family, the birth of a girl child can signal the beginning of financial ruin and extreme hardship. According to a recent report by the United Nations Children's Fund (UNICEF) up to 50 million females are missing from population of India, as a result of systematic gender discrimination. In most countries in the world, there are approximately 105 female births for every 100 males. But in India, in almost all the states[10] the population of female is less than the male in all age groups.[11] The child sex ratio (0-6 years) declined from 945 to 927 girls per 1,000 boys in 2001 from 1991 census. In the 1991 census, there was one district with a sex ratio below 850:1,000. There were 45 such districts in the 2001 census. The sharpest declines in sex ratio were in Punjab, Haryana, Gujarat, Uttaranchal, Maharashtra. The ten districts with the worst sex ratios in the country – all below 800–are all in Haryana and Punjab.[12]

Reasons of Bias Against the Girl Child

(i) Girls are often treated as inferior and are socialized to put themselves last, thus undermining their self-esteem. Discrimination and neglect in childhood can initiate a lifelong downward spiral of deprivation and exclusion from the social mainstream. According to Hindu texts, there are three values relating to the girl, which does not apply to the boy, and over the years the interpretation of these texts, always dangerous practice, where dogma is laid down in any society, has worked against women. A girl was thus *dana;* gift, *vikrya* payment as a dowry, the *atisarga,* which means abandonment.[13]

(ii) In almost every society the girl child is discriminated against from the earliest stages of life, through her childhood and into adulthood. In some societies, men outnumber women by margin. The reasons for the discrepancy include, among other things, harmful attitudes and practices, such as female genital mutilation, son preference - which results in female infanticide and prenatal sex selection - early marriage, including child marriage, violence against women, sexual exploitation, sexual abuse, discrimination against girls in food allocation and other practices related to health and well-being. As a result, fewer girls than boys survive into adulthood.

(iii) In our country, personal laws, (in the matters of marriage, divorce, maintenance, succession, adoption etc.) are practiced by all the communities – Hindus, Muslims, Christens and Parsis. These personal laws are based on the cultural and religious heritage of the respective communities, which is driven by the fanatics. These laws recognize the secondary role of women in the affairs of the family. This the main reason for the bias against women in our country.

(iv) Gender-biased educational processes, including curricula, educational materials and practices, teachers' attitudes and classroom interaction, reinforce existing gender inequalities. Girls are less encouraged than boys to participate in and learn about the social, economic and political functioning of society, with the result that they are not offered the same opportunities as boys to take part in decision-making processes.

LAW RELATING TO FEMALE FOETICIDE AND INFANTICIDE

Indian Penal Code, 1861 (IPC)

Medical Termination of Pregnancy Act, 1971 (MTPA)

The Pre-Natal Diagnostic Techniques (Regulation and Prevention of Misuse) Act, 1994 (PNDT)

Indian Penal Code, 1861 (IPC)

The IPC makes adequate provisions for the protection of mother and unborn child. It has provision to save the women from miscarriage and quick with child. Sections 312,[14] 313[15] and 314 if IPC.[16] deals with the law on abortion and miscarriage Section 312 provides that if any person causes a miscarriage of woman, he shall be punished with the imprisonment up to three years and fine or with both, and if the woman be quick with child, he shall be punished with imprisonment up to seven years and fine also. Under this section a woman who causes her miscarriage or gives consent to miscarry is also liable for punishment. Although this section makes an exception for causing miscarriage in good faith for saving the life of woman. Section 313 provides the punishment for life or ten year and fine, who causes the miscarriages of a woman without her consent. In *Moideen Kutty Haji v. Kunhikaya,*[17] the accused took the woman to the doctor who caused abortion. The woman consented to cause miscarriage. No offence was made out against man because he was only accompanying the woman and it could not be established that the man has requested the doctor to cause the abortion. Section 314 makes a provision for the imprisonment up to ten years and fine also, who intends to causes miscarriage of a woman by doing any act.

Miscarriage means the expulsion of the child or foetus from the mother's womb at any period of pregnancy before the term of gestation is completed. The term "miscarriage" is not defined in the I.P.C. in its popular sense. It is synonymous with abortion, and consists in the explosion of the embryo or foetus, i.e. the immature product of conception. The stage at which pregnancy has advanced and the form which the ovum or embryo may have assumed are immaterial.[18] Quickening is the name applied to the peculiar sensations experienced by a woman about the fourth or fifth month of pregnancy. The symptoms are popularly ascribed to the first perception of the movement of the foetus. But quickening is not a constant uniform and well-marked distinction of the pregnant state.[19] The MTPA uses the work 'termination of pregnancy' which has not also not been defined by the Act. In the absence of statutory definition, one may, for it meaning advert to dictionary and lexicon. Legally, miscarriage means the premature expulsion of the product of conception and ovum or a foetus from the uterus, at any period before the full term is reached. Medically, three distinct terms, viz. abortion, miscarriage and premature labour, are used to denote the expulsion of a foetus at different stage of gestation. Thus the term, 'abortion' is used only when an ovum is expelled within the first three months of pregnancy, before the placenta is formed. Miscarriage is used when a foetus is expelled from the fourth to the seventh month of gestation, before it is viable, while 'premature labour' is the delivery of a viable child possible capable of being reared, before it has become fully mature. It is stated that children born at or after 210 days or 7 calendar months of uterine life are viable, i.e. are born alive and are capable of being reared.[20]

However the IPC permits abortion for saving the life of the pregnant women. Section 312 provides that termination of pregnancy in good faith for saving the life of the pregnant woman. Similarly Sections 5(1) and 8 of the MTPA allows the medical practitioner to terminate the pregnancy in case the opinion is formed in good faith and protection from the legal proceeding. Good faith has nowhere defined in MTPA. The General Clauses Act 1897[21] defines good faith as a thing shall be deemed to be done in good faith where it is, in fact done honestly. I.P.C.[22] defines good faith, as nothing is said to be done or believed in good faith it is done or believed without due care and attention. The term good faith is not a constant term but it varied from case to case. The standard of care and skill to satisfy the duty in fact is that of the ordinary competent medical practitioner exercising the ordinary degree of professional skill.[23]

Medical Termination of Pregnancy Act, 1971 (MTPA)

The provisions regarding the termination of pregnancy in the I.P.C., which were enacted about a century ago, were drawn up in keeping with the then British law on the subject. The English law on this issue is that-abortion can be done for the betterment of man's genetic inheritance. This will lead to the welfare of the parents, where lives may well be blighted by having to rear a grossly defective child and perhaps also it will be a burden on national economy. The doctor must decide where there is a substantial risk that child if born would be seriously handicapped. Advances in knowledge and medical skills make it more and more possible to attach a precise weight to the chance of the foetus being affected by genetic defects on by what happens to it in the womb.[24] In India, abortion was made a crime for which the mother as well as the abortionist could be punished except where it had to be induced in order to save the life of the mother. Furthermore, most of these mothers are married women, and are under no particular necessity to conceal their pregnancy. In recent years, when health services have expanded and all classes of society avail of hospitals to the fullest extent, doctors have often been confronted with gravely ill or dying pregnant women whose pregnant uterus have been tampered with a view to causing an abortion and consequently suffered very severely. The object of the Act, besides the elimination of the high incidence of illegal abortions, is perhaps to confer on the woman the right to privacy, which includes the right to space, limit or reject pregnancy, the right to decide about her own body. Another important feature of the Act is to encourage reduction in the rate of population growth by permitting termination of an unwanted pregnancy of a married woman on the ground that a contraceptive device failed. After the liberalization of Indian abortion law the courts face some issues to decide the problems arising out of abortion.[25]

Main Provisions of the Act

(i) ***How a pregnancy can be terminated***– the Act[26] provides as under section 3 provides that the registered medical practitioner on the following grounds can terminate a pregnancy:

(a) If the pregnancy is less than 12 weeks and a medical practitioner is of the opinion and if the pregnancy exceeds twelve weeks the opinion of the two medical practitioners is that the pregnancy of the woman involves a risk of life or injury to her physical of mental health or if there is a risk to the health or child which is to be born.

(b) If the pregnancy is caused by rape which causes injury to the mental health of the woman. In *Kamalavalli v. C.R. Nair,*[27] the permission was asked from court and court granted the permission to the 28 years old rape victim to cause the abortion, subject to the doctor's permission. If the rape is not reported to the competent authority it will go unreported and the victim may visit the doctor for abortion. The record in such a case shall be kept secret.

(c) If the pregnancy is caused by the failure of any contraceptive method which is used by the married couple, which causes injury to mental health of the woman.

(d) If the pregnant woman is minor or lunatic taking the consent of her guardian in writing shall terminate her pregnancy.

It is also provided in this section that the pregnancy at No. (a) above can be terminated when the opinion of the medical practitioner is formed in good faith and pregnancy at No. (b), (c) and (d) can be terminated when the consent of the pregnant woman is there.

(ii) Where pregnancy can be terminated– Section 4 provides that pregnancy shall be terminated at the government hospital or any hospital approved by the purpose of this Act by government. Section 5 provides that proceeding sections 3 and 4 are not applicable, which relates to length of pregnancy and place for the termination of pregnancy, if the action taken by any registered medical practitioner is in good faith. Section 8 also protects the action taken in good faith by any registered medical practitioner. Section 6 and 7 provides for the rule and regulation making powers to the central and state governments, respectively.

(iii) Stage at which pregnancy can be terminated– the MTP Act,[28] regulates clearly the period within which the pregnancy can be terminated. The Act authorizes a registered medical practitioner to terminate the pregnancy of a woman on the prescribed grounds when the pregnancy does not exceed a period of twelve weeks. However, in case of a pregnancy exceeding twelve weeks but not exceeding twenty weeks the concurring opinion of at least two registered medical practitioners is required. These provisions of the Act relating to the length of the pregnancy and the opinion of not less than two registered medical practitioners shall not apply to a case of termination of pregnancy where the registered medical practitioner forms an opinion in good faith, that the termination of such pregnancy is immediately necessary for saving the life of the pregnant woman. Thus in the respect, Act has to this extent upheld section 312 of the IPC which permits miscarriage for the purpose of saving the life of the woman at any state of the pregnancy. The important issue is that can a woman have absolute right to decide whether or not to continue a pregnancy. The Medical Termination of Pregnancy Act does not confer or recognize any absolute right on any person to cause an abortion or termination of pregnancy. Even the pregnant woman cannot terminate the pregnancy except under the circumstances set out in the Act. Even during the first trimester, the woman cannot abort at her will and pleasure.

Abortion as Cruelty under the Hindu Marriage Act, 1955

The MTPA 1971 recognizes the free choice of woman to decide whether and when she will terminate her pregnancy and makes guardian's consent irrelevant in case the woman is of the age of eighteen years or above. The question arises whether woman can terminate her pregnancy without the consent and against the wishes of her husband and if so, whether such action on her part would amount to cruelty under section 13(1) (ia) of the Hindu Marriage Act 1956 and would entitle the aggrieved husband to obtain a decree of divorce against her. This question came for decision in *Satya v. Shri Ram,*[29] in which the High Court observed, "In this sort of a case, the Court has to attach due weight to the general principle underlying the Hindu law of marriage and sonship and the importance attached by the Hindus to the principles of spiritual benefit of having a son who can offer a funeral cake and libation of water to the manes of his ancestors, and held that termination of pregnancy at the instance of wife but without the consent of her husband amounts to cruelty. In this regard the High Court of Delhi,[30] 155 has observed that if however, a wife undergoes abortion with a view to spite the husband then it may in certain circumstances, be contended that the act of getting herself aborted has resulted in an act of cruelty. In *Sushil Kumar Verma v. Usha,*[31] the Court held that aborting the foetus in the very first pregnancy by a deliberate act without the consent of the husband would amount to cruelty. In this case, the wife, who became pregnant within one month of her marriage, got the foetus aborted the following month in a government approved pregnancy termination center with the help of a registered medical practitioner without consulting her husband. The husband was kept completely in dark about the fact of pregnancy as also of its abortion. The husband being aggrieved filed a petition for the grant of a decree of divorce on the ground of cruelty, which was dismissed by the District Court, but the High Court granted it on appeal. Recently in *Samar Ghosh v. Jaya Ghosh,*[32] the Supreme Court ruled that if the wife undergoes vasectomy or abortion without medical reason or without the consent or knowledge of her husband, such an act of the spouse might lead to mental cruelty.[33] Therefore, to keep the matrimonial relation harmonious women may carry foetus obviously not out of her free consent.

The Pre-Natal Diagnostic Techniques (Regulation and Prevention of Misuse) Act, 1994

To preventive menace the central government passed PNDT. This Act provides for the regulation of the use of pre-natal diagnostic techniques for the purpose of detecting genetic or metabolic disorders or chromosomal abnormalities or certain congenital malformations or sex linked disorders and for the prevention of the misuse of such techniques for the purpose of pre-natal sex determination leading to female foeticide; and, for matters connected therewith or incidental thereto. It is more than 12 years since the enactment of the Prenatal Diagnostic Techniques (Regulation and Prevention of Misuse) Act 1994 and it is also at least two years since the more comprehensive, amendment Preconception and Prenatal Diagnostic Techniques (PNDT) Act, 2003, yet enforcing the law has proved to be a major challenge.

The Amendment Act, 2003, covers pre-conceptual techniques and all prenatal diagnostic techniques. The following people can be charged under the Act: everyone running the diagnostic unit for sex selection, those who perform the sex selection test itself, anyone who advertises sex selection, mediators who refer pregnant women to the test, and relatives of the pregnant woman. The pregnant woman is considered innocent under the Act, "unless proved guilty"

All diagnostic centres must be registered with the authorities. They are required to maintain detailed records of all pregnant women undergoing scans there. These records must include the referring doctor, medical and other details of the woman, reason for doing the scan, and signatures of the doctors. These records must be submitted to the authorities periodically.

Penalties under the Act are imprisonment for up to three years and a fine of up to Rs 10,000. This is increased to five years and Rs 100,000 for subsequent offences. Doctors will be reported to the state medical council, which can take the necessary action including suspension. For implementing the Act, "appropriate authorities" are appointed at the state level and work with the director of health services, a member of a women's organization and an officer of the law. At the district level, the appropriate authority is theS medical officer or civil surgeon. Advisory committees consisting of doctors, social workers and people with legal training assist appropriate authorities. Supervisory boards at the state and central levels look at the implementation of the Act. The appropriate authority may cancel the diagnostic centre's registration, make independent investigations, take complaints to court, and take appropriate legal action. It may demand documentation, search premises, and seal and seize material. Courts may respond only to complaints from the appropriate authority.

The rate of conviction under the PNDT Act is abysmally low. In Punjab, out of 88 court cases filed under the Act to prevent pre-birth elimination of the girl child only four have resulted in conviction. Haryana has registered 28 such FIRs but managed only one conviction recently. In March 2006 a court in Faridabad, sentenced a doctor and his assistant to two years in jail and a fine of Rs 5,000 each under the PNDT Act, for carrying out tests to determine the sex of an unborn baby. The arrest and conviction of the duo followed a sting operation by officials empowered to implement the Act. In his judgment, the judge observed: "The convicts do not deserve any leniency. It is due to the illegal acts of persons like the convicts that the sex ratio is declining day by day... The day is not far when there will be no girl-child around. The convicts had orally conveyed the sex of the foetus to the patients, but due to a check on such illegal acts persons like the convicts have worked out their own code for sex-determination." The judge added, "the infamously skewed sex ratio in the country is not just about numbers, though they are quite horrific".[34]

It is unfortunate that law which aims at preventing such practice is not implemented effectively since it came into force in January 1996. Therefore, non-governmental organization approaches the apex court for fresh guidelines. The Supreme Court issued certain directions on the basis of various provisions under the Act[35]

(i) The Central Government is directed to create public awareness against the practice pre-natal determination of sex and female foeticide, through it own programme or central supervisory board (CSB) as provided under section 16 (iii) of the PNDT Act.

(ii) Period between two meetings of advisory committee constituted under sub-sec (5) of section 17 of the PNDT Act to advise the appropriate authority shall not exceed 60 days. It would be seen that this rule is strictly adhered to.

(iii) Meeting of the CSB will be held at least in six months. Section 7 empowers the Central Government to appoint ten members, which includes eminent medical practitioners including eminent social scientists and representatives of women welfare organizations.

(iv) The CSB shall lay down a code of conduct under section 16 (iv) of the Act to be observed by the persons working in bodies specified therein and to ensure its publication so that public at large can know about it.

(v) The CSB shall take action against non-registered bodies operating in violation of section 3 of the Act, inclusive of search and seizure of records.

(vi) All States and Union Territories are disserted to furnish quarterly returns to the CSB giving report on the implementation and working of the Act. It would contains information regarding; survey of bodies, registration of bodies, action taken against non-registered bodies, complaints received and action taken, number and nature of awareness campaign conducted etc.

(vii) The National Monitoring and Inspection Committee constituted by the Central Government for conducting periodical inspection shall continue to function till the Act is effective by implemented. The respect of this committee is placed before central and state supervisory board for any further action.

(viii) Public would have access to the record maintained by different bodies, under rule 17 (3) of the Act.

Relevancy of the Consent of the Women

Causing miscarriage without the consent of woman is illegal. Section 313 of the IPC and MTPA, 1971 provides that no pregnancy shall be terminated except with the consent of the pregnant woman[36]. In other words, consent in an act of reason accompanied with due deliberation, the mind weighing, as in a balance, the good and evil on each side.[37]. At present the abortion is illegal and it cannot be done without the consent of mother. Consent of the mother raises another issue that if a mother wants to miscarry her foetus, can she does that? Answerer according to the present legal system is no. But it could be done under the provisions of MTPA the abortion can be done after having the consent of mother and advice of medical practitioners, if they advise that pregnancy is detrimental to the physical and mental health of the mother.

It may be argued that pregnant woman should have personal liberty to destroy any foetus of her own if she finds it intolerable. An unwanted pregnancy may impose a kind of slavery upon her. It is more important to consider her life and health than that of an early foetus, representing only a child to be which has not yet been fully formed, cannot feel pain, and cannot live outside the womb. According to the Transplantation of Human Organ Act 1994, one may understand that life ends with the brain-stem death, so life starts with development of brain. Daniel Callahan explains in his book "Abortion Law, Choice and Mortality", that the brain structure is essentially complete by the twelfth week. Now, it may be observed, that before that period the woman has the absolute right to decide whether or not to terminate a pregnancy. It is the woman who has to undergo the entire process and therefore, she must be prepared for it both mentally and physically. But absolute right of abortion also throws up the issue of sex determination tests and female foeticide, which are of serious nature. In cases female foeticide the net result is the strengthening of gender bias against woman.[38]

CONCLUSIONS AND SUGGESTIONS

Women play a critical role in the family. The family is the basic unit of society and as such should be strengthened. It is entitled to receive comprehensive protection and support. In different cultural, political and social systems, various forms of the family exist. The rights, capabilities and responsibilities of family members must be respected. Women make a great contribution to the welfare of the family and to the development of society, which is still not recognized or considered in its full importance. The social significance of maternity, motherhood and the role of parents in the family and in the upbringing of children should be acknowledged. The upbringing of children requires shared responsibility of parents, women and men and society as a whole. Maternity, motherhood, parenting and the role of women in procreation must not be a basis for discrimination nor restrict the full participation of women in society. Recognition should also be given to the important role often played by women in many societies caring for other members of their family.

In India, aborting the foetus is legal and this has been effectively and officially used for the various purposes including population control. Therefore the magnitude of the present problem is horrific. It is rightly said that the discrimination against women starts in the womb of mother. In the most of the families girl child is not preferred. Indian Society is a male dominated one and it will remain so, if nothing happens to change it. The age-old attitude of society 'to must have a son' has not changed. The State itself must take a share of the blame, as the records of two premiers national health institutions show. In 1971, the Indian Council of Medical Research undertook a study of the use of amniocentesis, and reported that it was a potent technology for sex detection, and thus useful for population control. Thereafter, the amniocentesis test was made available in government health centres. Some years later, the All India Institute for Medical Sciences made a sample survey of 11,000 pregnant women and found that sex detection motivated women to opt for sex selective abortion. India's Health Ministry then banned the use of amniocentesis and other tests in government hospitals and clinics for sex determination. The private sector meanwhile has gone to town marketing and providing the detection technology, and the abortions. The advent of ultra-sound testing has made action more affordable. The causality of this type of attitude is the mental and physical torture of fair sex. This is the social behaviour, which is unethical and unlawful too. There should be some stringent laws to check this unethical and immoral practice. That's why causing death of a living foetus is being made a crime in IPC. Sections 312-314 deal with miscarriage, subsequently MTPA was passed to check this problem. Recently, PNDT was passed and amended in 2003. It is a problem of social attitude rather than legal one. If society starts preferring girl child then problem shall be solved. To do away with this problem following measures needs to be taken.

(i) The population to some extent has been controlled by the MTPA but child sex ratio has come down therefore the PNDT Act needs to be implemented more forcefully and legal provisions needs to be given more teeth. At the same time, monitoring and surveillance needs to be done. It's not only medical issue, it's a social issue, and government needs to educate the masses. The guidelines given by the Supreme Court needs to be followed strictly.

(ii) Make the girl child in difficult circumstances, aware of her own potential, educate her about the right to health guaranteed to her under all international human rights instruments, including the Constitution and Convention on the Rights of the Child, legislation enacted for her and the various measures undertaken by government.

(iii) For better implementation of the PNDT Act, there should be provision for separate registration of sonography/imaging techniques and genealogical techniques. There is need for a clear and significant role of the police in implementing the Act. There should be elaboration of the process for filing a legal case, specifying the qualifications of officers and the conditions under which the power to search and seize records are delegated to such officers by the Appropriate Authority.

(iv) Set up educational programmes and develop teaching materials and textbooks that will sensitize and inform adults particularly women about the harmful effects of certain traditional or customary practices on girl children in general and female foeticide in particular.

(v) Steps should be taken to prepare girls to participate actively, effectively and equally with boys at all levels of social, economic, political and cultural leadership. All barriers must therefore be eliminated to enable girls without exception to develop their full potential and skills through equal access to education and training, nutrition, physical and mental health care and related information.

(vi) In addressing issues concerning children and youth, Governments should promote an active and visible policy of mainstreaming a gender perspective into all policies and programmes so that before decisions are taken, an analysis is made of the effects on girls and boys, respectively.

(vii) Take steps so that tradition and religion and their expressions are not a basis for discrimination against girls. Eliminate the injustice and obstacles in relation to inheritance faced by the girl child so that all children may enjoy their rights without discrimination, by, inter alia, enacting, as appropriate, and enforcing legislation that guarantees equal right to succession and ensures equal right to inherit, regardless of the sex of the child. In this regard, the Parliament in its wisdom amended the Hindu Succession Act, 1956 by which a daughter is made coparcener and given equal status with the son. This is really a genuine effort. Now the need is to implement it sincerely and enact the similar laws for the other communities.

(viii) Provide an environment conducive to the strengthening of the family in general and protect, respect and promote the potential of the girl child in particular. To do away with the son preference attitude the government should promote couples to adopt the two-child norm for all - may it be daughter or son. I feel that the MTPA has lived its life and to some extent has fulfilled the objective for which it was enacted therefore it may be scrapped.

NOTES

1. Report of the International Conference on Population and Development, Cairo, 5-13 September 1994 (United Nations publication, Sales No. E. 95. XIII. 18), chap. I, resolution 1, annex. I.
2. General Assembly resolution 44/25, annex. Article 2 para 2.
3. Destruction or abortion of a unwanted foetus.
4. Killing of an unwanted infant.
5. B.P. Singh Sehgal, Women, Birth Control and the Law (1993) at 25-26.
6. Devaki Jain, Indian Women (1974) at 90-91.
7. Amruta Rao,Sex Determination (2000) at 164-65
8. http://www.crin.org/docs/resources/treaties/crc.37/India Alliance for Child Rights IACR (The site visited on 3 May 2007
9. http:// www.infochangeindia.org/analysis.121jsp.
10. Only in Kerala and Pondichery the number of females are 1058 and 1001 per 1000 males respectively.
11. Census of India 2001.
12. These two states are home to the 10 districts infamous for the lowest sex ration in the country. These districts are Fatehgarh Sahib, Patiala, Kurukshetra, Gurdaspur, Kapurthala, Bathinda, Mansa, Amritsar, Sonepat and Ambala. There is a correlation between the number of sonography centres in a district and the sex ratio there. The Delhi-based women's group Saheli argues that the government has played a key role in supporting commercially-motivated medical professionals and promoting the diffusion of this technology. For one, it points to the clear link between the liberalisation of import duties on medical electronic equipment and the increase in the number of sonography centres. Second, it notes that ultrasound scanners are much, much more popular than ECG machines, X-ray machines or baby incubators. It would be interesting to study the relative importance of these different machines. Are

they being manufactured or imported according to the need for them, or the market for illegal use– sex' s election.

13. Tara Ali Baig, India's Woman Power (1976) at 89.
14. Whoever voluntarily causes a woman with child to mis carry shall, if such miscarriage be not caused in good faithfor the purpose of saving the life of the woman, be punished with imprisonment of either discription for a term which may extend to three years, or with fine, or with both ; and, if the woman be quick with the child, shall be punished with imprisonment of either discription for a term which may extend to seven years, and shall also be liable to fine. Explanation: A woman who causes herself to miscarry, is within the meaning of this section.
15. Whoever commits the offence defined in the last preceding section without the consent of the women whether the woman is quick with child, or not, shall be punished with imprisonment for life, or with imprisonment of either description for a term which may extend to ten years, and shall also be liable to fine.
16. Whoever with intend to cause the miscarriage of a woman with child, does any act which causes the death of such woman shall be punihed with imprisonment of either discription for a term which may extend to ten years and shall also be liable to fine and the act is without the consent of the woman, shall be punished either with imprisonment for life, or with the punishmen abovementioned. Explanation:- It is not essential to this offence the offender should know that the act is likely to cause death.
17. 1987 Cri.LJ 1106.
18. A.N. Basu, Indian Panel Code (1998) at 1122-1123.
19. Ibid.
20. Modi's Medical Jurisprudence at 300-325. As quoted in Dr. Hari Singh Gour's Panel Law of India.
21. Act 10 of 1897 Sec. 3 (22).
22. Section 52 of Act 45 of 1860.
23. AIR 1975 Bom. 308.
24. Glanville Williams, Text Book of Criminal Law (1999) at 280.
25. ——Statement of Object and Reasons to the Act 34 of 1971. Gazette of India (17 Nov. 1969) Part-II Sec. 2 at 880.

26. Medical Termination of Pregnancy Act 1971 (Act 34 of 1971).
27. 1984 Cri. L J 446.
28. Ibid.
29. AIR 1983 P & H 252.
30. Deepak Kumar Arora v. Sampuran Arora (1983) 1 DMC 182.
31. AIR 1987 Delhi 86.
32. MANU/SC/1386/2007 and 2007(5) SCALE 1.
33. Similarly, if a husband submits himself for an operation of sterilization without medical reasons and without the consent or Knowledge of his wife.
34. www.newindpress.com, March 29, 2006, and www.zeenews.com, March 29, 2006 and Reuters, March 29, 2006.
35. CEHAT v. Union of India, AIR 2003 SC 3309.
36. To understand the importance of theses sections it is necessary to know as to what constitutes consent. Section 90 of the I.P.C. states that a consent is notsuch a consent as is intended by any section of this code, if the consent is given by a person under fear of injury or misconception of fact or under the unsoundness of mind or in intoxicated state, or by child below twelve years of age. Consent is the knowledge or consciousness of the act consented to, which means an active will in the mind of a person to permit the doing of the act complained of.
37. Dr. Hari Singh Gour, Penal Laws of India (2000) at 3175.
38. Santosh Kumar, Abortion: The Law and the Reality, 1998 Cri. L J 171-174.

WOMEN'S RIGHT TO HEALTH: AN OVERVIEW

Varinder Singh & Rachna Arora***

INTRODUCTION

Right to life is considered one of the fundamental rights, and health is one of the vital indicators reflecting quality of human life. In this context, it becomes one of the primary responsibilities of the state to provide health care services to all its citizens. India, despite being a signatory to the Alma Ata Declaration of 1978, which promised, 'Health for All' by 2000, is far from realising this objective. On paper, India has an excellent health care structure that has the potential to reach a large section of the population. Yet, despite this elaborate structure and the rapid advancement of medical sciences, the reality is deplorable. The percentage of population actually covered by the public health care services is reportedly a mere 30 per cent. Although programmes are being constantly reviewed and revised, the problems persist and continue to worsen.

Women's health is not only a manifestation of biology but also a reflection of socio-political, economic and religious context of women's lives. Combination of early childhood discrimination in food, nutrition, health care, coupled with

* Lecturer, Department of Laws, Guru Nanak Dev University Regional Campus, Basti Nau, Jalandhar, Pb.

** Lecturer, V.M.S. College of Laws, Batala, Gurdaspur (Punjab) neglect in adolescent girls and teenage pregnancy, repeated pregnancy, malnutrition in adult female and poor health care services contribute to poor health status of women. Other factors influencing/resulting in poor health status of women are inadequate safe drinking water and sanitation facility, poor hygiene and housing condition particularly in rural and poor urban areas; disproportionate work load, physical violence, mental stress and harassment etc[1].

In India, women's lives are intersect with each other in complex ways to intensify women's subordination. These vexed realities make it an imperative to analyze women's health needs within a broader socio-political and economic context. The campaign for women's health and health-rights has been primarily geared towards the demand for better health services and facilities, protest against coercive tactics that endangers women's health and their human rights, and demand for overall wellbeing of women.

WOMEN'S HEALTH STATUS IN INDIA

Women's access to health services is much less in comparison to men. The underlying reason being their lower status in the family and lack of decision-making power regarding ill health, expenditure on health care and non-availability of health care facilities prevent them from seeking medical help. Women's lack of time due to existing unequal division of labour and the socially sanctioned 'feminine' quality of 'sacrifice'. Besides, the perceptions of acceptable levels of discomfort for women and men lead to gender differences in willingness to accept that they are sick and seek care. Women wait longer than men to seek medical care for illness. This is partly due to their unwillingness to disrupt household functioning unless they become incapacitated[2].

The National Health Policy 2002 promises to ensure increased access to women to basic health care and commits highest priority to the funding of the identified programmes relating to women's health. During the Ninth Plan period, several new initiatives were taken as part of the Reproductive and Child Health (RCH) Programme (1997), in order to make it broad-based and client-friendly. All the interventions of the erstwhile programme of Child Survival and Safe Motherhood (CSSM) became part of RCH. During this period, the focus shifted from the individualized vertical interventions to a more holistic integrated life-cycle approach with more attention to reproductive health care. This includes access to essential obstetric care during the entire period of pregnancy, provision of emergency obstetric care as close to the community as possible, improving and expanding early and safe abortion services and provision for treatment of Reproductive Tract Infections/Sexually Transmitted Infections (RTI/STI) cases at the sub-district level.[3] There are various important factors which affect the women health status in India:

Women and Communicable Diseases

In addition to the poor nutritional status, heavy work burden and maternal and perinatal ill-health, communicable diseases including Malaria, Tuberculosis, Encephalitis, Kala Azar, Dengue, Leprosy, etc. contribute significantly to the heavy burden of disease faced by women.

Communicable diseases remain the most common cause of death in India. Despite the arsenal of diagnostics, drugs and vaccines that have been developed during this century, medical researchers and practitioners continue to struggle against an ever-growing number of emerging infectious diseases such as HIV and hepatitis etc.[4] Structural inequalities of gender and economic resources enhance the risk of communicable diseases among poor. Although both men and women are equally exposed to communicable diseases, there are concrete evidences to show that women suffer far more than men in terms of decision making and access to treatment and services. If one considers that women constitute approximately 70% of the poor, then the interaction between poverty and gender may represent the most important risk factor to be addressed in efforts to arrest communicable diseases There exist crucial linkages of communicable diseases- particularly TB and Malaria, perhaps they are so common - with issues related poverty, the environmental degradation and the change of lifestyles and food habits, etc.

Women and Mental Health

Estimates of mental health show that about 10 million people are suffering-from serious mental disorders in India. Approximately 15% of all women suffer from mental illnesses against 11% of all men.[5] The social roots of women's mental health problems are overlooked owing to gender insensitivity and increasing medicalisation of mental health problems of women Mental health care has been given very low priority and, consequently, mental health services are in an abysmal state in India.

Violence Against Women

Violence against women and girl children at the household and community levels has deep impacts on their survival, dignity, self-esteem, and overall health. Research evidences point out that globally one of the major contributors to women's mortality and morbidity is violence. Women have to confront violence in all spheres of her social life, which constantly propagates and strengthens the unequal relationship between men and women in an attempt to control women's labour, mobility, reproduction and sexuality.

Violence against women refers to a range of acts varying from physical abuse, psychological abuse, sexual abuse, to a host of other ways by which a woman's personal security may be seriously compromised. Women also face financial abuse, if the husband/'bread-earner' abandons the wife and children, or does not allow her access to any money by retaining all financial control. In this context, violence is one of the tools used to reinforce women's subordinate status– to control the oppressed or disempowered.

Women and Occupational Health

The working environment for women, both at home and at work place, affects her physical conditions. These include inadequate lighting, insanitary conditions, absence of any toilet facilities, poor airflow and ventilation, to name a few. Sexual exploitation, harassment at work place are regularly experienced by almost all sections of women in both formal and informal sectors. The most common occupational hazard for women is over-work. Over working has further grave implications on the health of women.

In rural areas, where women work as agricultural labourers, they are exposed to pesticides and chemical fertilizers that can cause diseases of the liver and nervous system, cancer, blindness or deformities. The tasks performed by women are usually those that require them to be in one position for long periods of time, which can adversely affect their reproductive health.

In urban areas, where 80% of the women workforce are in unorganized sector like household industries, building construction and other petty trades, the hazardous work environment and absence of security and welfare mechanisms make women prone to serious health consequences, rape and other forms of sexual harassment.

NATIONAL AND INTERNATIONAL REMEDIES FOR WOMEN'S RIGHT TO HEALTH

There are various Constitutional provisions, policies, laws in the Indian context and International instruments, treaties, conventions to safeguard and promote women's right to health. But it is important to first analyse the concept of right to health.

The Concept of Right to Health

Health and human rights are interconnected and their promotion fundamentally and inextricably intertwined. The effects of violations of dignity and physical integrity on health are as crucial as the effects of poor health on dignity. The linkage of health and human rights refers to the understanding that health status is in a large measure determined by the degree to which human rights are enjoyed. The realization of other rights is not possible if an individual cannot maintain his/her own health. Poor health and inadequate health care are often related to human rights violations. And violation and underfulfillment of human rights are often due to poor health and lack of access to health care.[6] The right to health has clear links to many other rights. The realisation of the Right to Health requires the fulfillment of several interconnected rights of a range of determinants, such as food, education, environment, housing, working conditions, poverty, health care and so on.

Unless all these determinants are also addressed, it is not possible to ensure the right to health. The denial or enjoyment of the rights mentioned above can impact a person's ability to achieve the highest attainable standard of health, and conversely, the health status determines the enjoyment of other rights, i.e. a person who is not 'healthy' may not be able to participate fully and actively in economic, social or political activities in society.

CONSTITUTIONAL PROVISIONS

The Constitution of India does not explicitly recognize health as a Fundamental Right. However, it recognizes the right to life, freedom of speech, expression and opportunity and to seek judicial redress for enforcement of these rights as fundamental rights. Right to Health is included in Article 47 of the Directive Principles of State policy.

The *Preamble* to the Constitution highlights some of the core values and principles that guide the Constitution of India. In the light of the preamble, the Supreme Court of India has held that the objectives of justice, liberty, equality and fraternity stated in the preamble constitute the basic structure of the Constitution. The Preamble directs the state to initiate measures to establish justice, equality, ensure dignity, etc. which have a direct bearing on women's health.

Fundamental Rights Related to Women's Right to Health

Right to Equality and Freedom *(Articles 14-17 and 19)* ensure the right to equality before the law and equal protection of the law, prohibition oi the basis of sex, caste, religion, race or place of birth, equal opportunity in matters of employment and abolition of untouchability. However, the right to equality does not take away the right of the State to initiate or provide special provisions for women and marginalized communities (especially women from scheduled castes and tribes). In the context of health, any form of discrimination, be it gender or practice of untouchability, has severe implications for health, preventing or limiting access to basic needs and opportunities that impact health and access to health care.

Right to Protection of Life and Personal Liberty *(Article 21) ensures* that no person shall be deprived of his/her life or personal liberty, except according to the procedure established by law. While the provision of health services is essential to ensure good health, there are several others factors that influence a person's health. The Supreme Court first recognized this in *Bandhua Mukti Morc.ha vs. Union of India,*[7] a case concerning living and working conditions of stone quarry workers in Haryana and whether these living and working conditions deprived them of their right to life. "The court held that humane working conditions were essential to the pursuit of the Right to Life. It lay down that workers should be provided with medical facilities, clean drinking water and sanitation facilities so that they may live with human dignity".

Right against exploitation *(Articles 23-24)* secures a person or persons against prohibition of traffic in human beings and forced labour, employment of children in factories, mine, or in any other hazardous employment

The Directive Principles of State Policy

Right to Health in the Indian Constitution is contained in Article 47, which is consigned to the Directive Principles of

State Policy. With regard to health and health care, Article 47 states that it is *the Duty of the State to raise the level of nutrition and the standard of living and to improve public health*.

The State must try to ensure that its policies are based on people's (men and women equally) right to an adequate means of livelihood; ensure equitable distribution of wealth and prevent the concentration of wealth and means of production; equal remuneration regardless of sex; ensure that the existing system do not abuse the health and strength of men and women, and children and that they are not pushed by economic necessity to work in occupations that is detrimental to their age.[8]

The State should try to

- provide opportunities and facilities to children to develop in a healthy manner, in the absence of exploitation
- make effective, within the limits of its economic capacity and development, provision for securing the right to work, to education and to public assistance in cases of unemployment, old age, sickness and disablement, etc.[9]
- provide just and humane conditions of work and maternity relief, secure wages by ensuring a decent standard of life and full enjoyment of leisure and social and cultural opportunities, including participation in the management of organizations[10]
- protect marginalised groups like Scheduled Castes and Tribes against exploitation and ensure that their right to justice is protected[11]

INTERNATIONAL CONVENTIONS

The Right to Health is recognised by several International Conventions. In the context of Women's Right to Health, discrimination on the basis of sex is prohibited in the Universal of Declaration of Human Rights and in Article 2 of the two most significant International Covenants -on Civil and Political Rights and on Economic, Social and Cultural Rights.

The Women's Convention or CEDAW is the UN treaty that clearly brings together civil, political and economic, social and cultural rights. In addition, since its inception, the committee established under CEDAW has issued a number of General Recommendations(GR) that elaborate on the articles of the Convention. The one that is most critical to health is the GR *24* that elaborates Article *12* of the Convention.[12]

Convention on the Elimination of Discrimination Against Women (CEDAW), 1965

CEDAW's Article 12 establishes the obligation to adopt adequate measures to guarantee women access to health and medical care, with no discrimination whatsoever, including access to family planning services. It also establishes the commitment to guarantee adequate maternal and child health care.

Article *12 (1)* states that governments shall take all appropriate measures to eliminate discrimination against women in the field of health care to ensure, access to health-care services, including those related to family planning.

Article *12 (2)* ensure to women appropriate services in connection with pregnancy, confinement and the post-natal period, granting free services where necessary, as well as adequate nutrition during pregnancy and lactation. States Parties are encouraged to address the issue of women's health throughout the woman's lifespan. The articles of the convention are applicable to women, including girls and adolescent.

The CEDAW Committee, in its (Twentieth session, 1999) elaborated a general recommendation *(24)* on Women and Health on Article *12* of the Convention.[13] It says that State Parties should implement a comprehensive national strategy to promote women's health throughout their lifespan. This will include interventions aimed at both the prevention and treatment of diseases and will ensure universal access for all women to a full range og high quality and affordable health care, including sexual and reproductive health services.

The International Covenant on Economic, Social and Cultural Rights (ICESCR), 1966

Article 12 (1) of the ICESCR recommends that States Parties recognise the right of everyone to the enjoyment of the highest attainable standard of physical and mental health. Article 12 (2) of the Covenant lays down several steps that should be taken by the States Parties to achieve the full realisation of this right.

Child Rights Convention (CRC), 1989

Articles 23 and 24 of the CRC recognise the right to health for all children and identify several steps for its realisation. Article 23 ensures the rights of a mentally or physically disabled child to dignity; to enjoy a 'full and decent life'; to special care and encourages the promotion of self-reliance so that the child may actively participate in the community.

Article 24 also ensures appropriate pre-natal health care for mothers, ensures access to information particularly of parents and children, access to education and are supported in the use of basic knowledge of child health and nutrition, the advantages of breast-feeding, hygiene and environmental sanitation and the prevention of accidents. States Parties will promote and encourage international co-operatives with a view to achieving progressively the full realization of the right recognised in the present Article, in keeping with particular -needs of developing countries.

Other Instruments that guarantee Right to Health are:

- The International Convention on the Elimination of All Forms of Racial Discrimination;
- The Convention relating to the Status of Refugees;
- The International Convention on the Protection of the Rights of All Migrant Workers and members of Their Families;

- The Declaration on the Protection of Women and Children in Emergency and Armed Conflict;
- The Standard Minimum Rules for the Treatment of Prisoners;
- The Declaration on the Rights of Mentally Retarded Persons;
- The Declaration on the Rights of Disabled Persons;
- The Declaration on the Rights of AIDS Patients.

DECLARATIONS

The Universal Declaration of Human Rights (UDHR) 1948

Article 25 (1) of UDHR affirms that everyone has a right to a standard of living adequate for the health of himself and his family, including food, clothing, housing and medical care and necessary social services, and the right to security in the event of unemployment, sickness, disability, widowhood, old age or other Lack of livelihood in circumstances beyond his control.

Declaration of Alma-Ata on Primary Health Care, 1978

Governments at Alma-Ata reiterated Health for All by 2000 and committed to ensuring comprehensive, primary health care. This Declaration is not binding on governments but it reiterated the commitment of the governments/states towards achieving the right to health.

The Declaration highlighted that:

- Health is a fundamental right and its realisation requires the action of many other social and economic sectors. The current gross inequality in health status is politically, socially and economically unacceptable.
- People have a right and duty to participate individually and collectively in the planning and implementation of their health care.

- Primary Health Care includes in the least, health education, promotion of food supply and proper nutrition, an adequate supply of safe water and basic sanitation, maternal and child health care, including family planning, immunisation against the major infectious diseases, prevention and control of locally endemic diseases, appropriate treatment of common diseases and injuries and provision of essential drugs.

Helsinki Declaration[14]

The Declaration developed by the World Medical Association, lays down ethical Principles to provide guidelines to doctors and other participants in medical research involving human subjects, including research on identifiable human material or identifiable data. It emphasises that the 'knowledge and conscience' of doctors and other participants in such research must protect the life and dignity and promote and safeguard the health and rights of the people. It states that the well being of the person (s) involved in such research should take precedence over the interests of science and society.

INTERNATIONAL (UNITED NATIONS) CONFERENCES

The Women's Right to health has been included in several International Instruments, as seen above. Apart from these Instruments which maybe binding on States Parties who have signed, ratified them, the Women's Right to health is also elaborated in the:

The International Conference on Population and Development Programme of Action (The ICPD Programme of Action, 1994);

- The Fourth World Conference on Women - Platform for Action (The FWCW Platform, 1995);
- The World Conference for Human Rights (WCHR) 1993;
- Vienna Declaration and Programme of Action of 1993;

The Fourth World Conference on Women - Platform for Action (The FWCW Platform) 1995

Paragraph 89: Women have the right to the enjoyment of the highest attainable standard of physical and mental health. Health is a state of complete physical, mental and social well-being and not merely the absence of disease or infirmity.

Paragraph 92: Women's right to the enjoyment of the highest standard of health must be secured throughout the whole life cycle in equality with men.

Paragraph 96: The human rights of women include their right to have control over and decide freely and responsibly on matters related to their sexuality, including sexual and reproductive health, free of coercion, discrimination and violence.

Paragraph 106: Governments [should] ... (g) Ensure that all health services and workers conform to human rights and to ethical, professional and gender- sensitive standards in the delivery of women's health services aimed at ensuring responsible, voluntary and informed consent; encourage the development, implementation and dissemination of codes of medical ethics as well as ethical principles that govern other health professionals.

Paragraph 108: Governments [should] ...(c) Encourage all sectors of society ... to develop compassionate and supportive, non-discriminatory HIV/AIDS-related policies and practices that protect the rights of infected individuals.

The World Conference on Human Rights (WCHR) 1993

Paragraph 41: The World Conference on Human Rights recognises the importance of the enjoyment by women of the highest standard of physical and mental health throughout their life-span... The World Conference on Human Rights reaffirms, on the basis of equality between women and men, a woman's right to accessible and adequate health care and the widest range of family planning services, as well as equal access to education at all levels.

Vienna Declaration and Programme of Action

(Adopted by the World Conference on Human Rights on 25 June 1993)

The human rights of women and of the girl-child are an inalienable, integral and indivisible part of universal human rights. The full and equal participation of women in the political, civil, economic, social and cultural life, at the national, regional and international levels, and eradication of all forms of discrimination on grounds of sex are priority objectives of the international community.

The human rights of women should form an integral part of the United Nations human rights activities including the promotion of all human rights instruments relating to women. The World Conference urges governments, institutions, inter-governmental and non-governmental organisations to intensify their efforts for the protection and promotion of human rights of women and the girl-child

CONCLUSION

While some rights have been accepted as fundamental by both the international conventions as well the Indian laws, the .'Right to Health' has yet to be acknowledged as a fundamental right in India. Women's groups, health and human rights activists in the country have been campaigning for several years for Health to be recognised as a constitutional guarantee. In this ongoing struggle, women along with these groups and activists have played a critical role in the process of formulating their health rights - in deciding what their rights should be, the content of these rights and the processes by which these rights can be claimed. These processes have also witnessed application of existing international conventions to hold the State accountable for violating these rights.

The understanding and scope of women's Right to Health is constantly evolving as women participate more actively in these processes, causing changes in attitudes towards women and their health, bringing about change in the way laws are formulated and interpreted.

Combined efforts are required now, more than ever, to demand and ensure the recognition of Right to Health as a fundamental right.

NOTES & REFERENCES

1. www.nrcw.nic.in visited on 06-03-2007.
2. "Women's Right to Health", National Human Rights Commission, New Delhi, p. 33.
3. "Health" available on www.nrcw.nic.in visited on 10-03-2007.
4. Supra note 3, p. 36.
5. Davar, Bhargavi V. (2002) "Dilemmas of Women's Activism in Mental Health" in Renu Khanna, Mira Shiva & Sarala Gopalan (ed) Towards Comprehensive Women's Health Programme and Policy. SAHAJ for Women & Health.
6. "Health and Human Rights are inextricably intertwined" available on www.expresshealthcaremgmt.com visited on 15-03-2007.
7. AIR 1984 SC 802.
8. Article-39, Constitution of India.
9. Article-41.
10. Article-43, 43A.
11. Article-46
12. Circle of Rights: Economic, Social and Cultural Rights-A Training Resource, IHRIP & Forum Asia, 2000.
13. www.umn.edu/humanrts
14. Adopted by the 18th World Medical Assembly, Helsinki, Finland, June 1964, amended by the 29th World Medical Assembly, Tokyo, Japan, October 1975, and the 35th World Medical Assembly, Venice, Italy, October 1983.

WOMEN EMPOWERMENT IN INDIA: A SYNOPTIC VIEW OF LEGISLATIVE PROVISIONS AND JUDICIAL ATTITUDE

*Sanjay Sindhu**

INTRODUCTION

Human Rights are inherent, inalienable, basic fundamental natural rights for existence of human beings in society. The Constitution of India has ensured equal status to all i.e. not only between men and men, women and women but also between men and women. But the basic question is that how far we have been able to achieve the objectives provided by the Constitution.[1] In view of this an attempt has been made to acquaint the Indian women with the constitutional and legal protection to them, so that they can fight for the rightful cause or for justice.

The Preamble of the Constitution speaks of securing to all citizen equality of status and of opportunity as well as justice – social, economic and political. Further the Directive Principles of State Policy under the same document declares that State should not make discrimination on the ground of sex and that it should direct its policy towards securing justice equally to both men and women. A number of other special legislations have been enacted to raise the position of women.[2]

* Asstt. Professor, Department of Laws, H. P. University, Shimla–171005.

CONSTITUTIONAL PROVISIONS REGARDING EMPOWERMENT OF WOMEN IN INDIA

The Constitution of India guarantees to all its citizen equality before the law and the equal protection of law within the territory of India.[3] All men and women are equal before the law and therefore law protect them all. United Nations Declaration of Human Rights used both the expression,[4] i.e. 'equal protection of law' and 'equality before law', taken together, aim at establishing 'the equality of status' as has been envisaged by the Preamble of the Constitution.

The principle of equality does not, of course, require that every law must have universal application, for the varying needs of different classes of persons often require separate treatment.[5] The classification permissible must be based on some real and substantial distinction bearing a just and reasonable relation to the objects sought to be attained and cannot be made arbitrary and without substantial basis.[6]

Article 14 of the Constitution prohibits class legislation but permits reasonable classification. It is essential that classification must be based on intelligible differentia and should have a rational nexus with the object sought to be achieved by the Act or legislation. Keeping this in view such classification must have the basic object that women can be treated as a class and special laws can be made in their favour.[7]

Article 15(1) of the Constitution prohibits the State from making discrimination against any citizen on the ground of religion, race, caste, sex, place of birth or any of them. Article 15(2) provides that no citizen shall, on grounds only of religion, race, caste, sex, place of birth or any of them, be subject to any disability, liability, restriction or condition with regard to any access to shop, restaurants, hotels, and place of entertainment.[8] Article 15(3), being the exceptional clause of Article 15(1) and 15(2), declares that nothing under the provision shall prevent the State from making any special provision for women and children.[9] In the case of Anjali Raj Vs. State of West Bengal,[10] the court held that Article 15(3) enables the State to make special provision favouring women, it cannot be interpreted in a manner so that it denies the right already guaranteed to them under Article 15(1).[11]

Keeping this in view, provision of Article 15(3) for women cannot be challenged on the ground that there is no reasonable basis for the classification having regarding to the object of the legislation. Hence, provision which confer special privileges to women have been held valid.[12] Even the courts in India have served as a stimulus for the Indian legislation to enact new laws or bring the changes in the existing legislation with a view to afford better and effective protection to the women.

Article 16(1) provides equality of opportunity in matters relating to employment or appointment to any office under the State. Article 16(2) provides special grounds on which citizens are not to be discriminated against each other in matter of opportunity and office under the state. In the case of C. B. Muthamma Vs. Union of India,[13] Justice Krishna Iyer observed:

We do not mean to universalize or degomatise that men and women are equal in all occupation in all situation and do not exclude the need to pragmatise where the requirements of particular employment, the sensitivities of sex or the handicaps of either sex may compel selectivity, but save where the difference in demonstrable, the rule of equality must govern.[14]

The interpretation of Articles 23 and 24 lays down the fact that the founding fathers were concerned not only to protect the interest of women but also to ameliorate the condition of this lot in totality.[15] The Supreme Court in the case of Bandhwa Mukti Morcha Vs. Union of India,[16] observed that the Central Government is bound to ensure observance of various social welfare and labour laws[17] enacted by the Parliament for the purpose of seeking to the workmen a life of basic human dignity in compliance with the Directive Principles of the State Policy.[18] It is the duty of the State to ensure that the health and strength of workmen (men and women) and the tender age of children are not abused and that the citizen are not forced by economic necessity to enter vocations unsuited to their age and strength.[19]

The Directive Principles of State Policy in Part IV of the Constitution lays down certain economic and social goals to be achieved by the Government whether it is Central Government or the State Government. The moral rights embodied in Part IV are equally an essentially feature of it.[20] Article 37 lays down that the Directive Principles are nevertheless fundamental in governance of the country and it shall be the duty of the State to apply these principles in making laws. Further Article 38(2) provides that the State shall, in particular, strive to minimize the inequalities in income, and endeavour to eliminate inequalities in status, facilities and opportunities, not only among individuals but also amongst groups of people residing in different areas or engaged in different vocations. Article 39 is another manifest declares which provides that the State shall, in particular direct its policy towards adequate mean of livelihood, equal pay for equal work , health and strength of workers, men and women and the tender age of children are not abused.[21]

Keeping in view the objectives laid down in these Articles or provisions, various labour laws passed from time to time.[22] Article 40 of the Constitution further lays down that the State shall take steps to organise village panchayats and endow them with such powers and authority as may be necessary to enable them to function as units of self government. Reservation of seats for women in panchayats and municipalities have been provided in Article 343-A and Article 343-T of the Constitution of India.[23] Another Article 44 protects the interests of women, accordingly, it lays down that the State shall endavour to secure for the citizen a uniform civil code throughout the territory of India.

In Part IV-A, the Constitution deals with the Fundamental Duties.[24] Article 51-A(e) relate to women. It lays down that it shall be the duty of every citizen of India to promote harmony and spirit of common brotherhood amongst all the people of India transcending religion, linguistic and regional or sectional diversities to renounce practices derogatory to the dignity of women.

SPECIAL LEGISLATIONS VIS-À-VIS WOMEN EMPOWERMENT

Besides the constitutional provisions other provisions have been made under various legislations. The Child Marriage Restraint Act, 1929 (popularly known as Sarda Act) raises the age for marriage of a girl to 18 years from 15 years and that of a boy of 21 years. The Prevention of Child Marriage Bill 2006 has been passed by the both Houses of Parliament. Repealing and replacing the Sarda Act of 1929, the new legislative measure of 2006 makes some remarkable changes in the law on child marriage. While the minimum age for marriage remains 18 for girls and 21 for boys, every under-age marriage will not be voidable at the option of the minor party. Under the new law a court nullifying such a marriage is to provide ancillary relief by directing the parties to restore to each other all the money, valuables, ornaments and other gifts received at the marriage, directing the male party or his guardian to pay maintenance to the female party until her re-marriage and making suitable arrangements for the custody of children, if any, who will remain legitimate despite the nullification of their parent's marriage.[25]

The Minimum Wages Act, 1948, guarantees that minimum wages to worker will be the same all over State. The low status of women in large segments of Indian society cannot be raised without opening up of opportunities of independent employment and income for them.[26]

The Factory Act, 1948 makes such provisions for empowerment of women. Every factory wherein more than 30 women workers are ordinarily employed, is to maintain a suitable room or rooms for the use of children under 6 years of age. Such room shall be hygienic and a trained women to look after the children in to be employed. Similarly provision occur in the Plantation Labour Act, 1951, Mines Act, 1952, and Beedie and Cigar Worker (Condition of Employment) Act, 1966. However, the labour legislation also prohibits working late night except when the State Government may slightly vary the limit. The Mines Act, 1952 prohibits women working below ground in mines.

The Hindu Adoption and Maintenance Act, 1956 provides that subject to the provisions of the Act, a Hindu wife whether married before or after the commencement, shall be entitled to be maintained by her husband during her lifetime. Moreover, Code of Criminal Procedure, 1973 makes provision for maintenance under section 125-128 of the Code. Under these provisions, it is obligatory on the part of every man, having sufficient means, to provide proper maintenance to his wife if she is not able to maintain herself.

The Suppression of Immoral Traffic in Women and Girls Act, 1956 was amended in 1986 to makes the sexual exploitation of female a cognizable offence. It was renamed as 'The Immoral Traffic (Prevention) Act, 1986. Further, an amendment brought in 1984 to the Dowry Prohibition Act, 1961 made women's subjection of cruelty a cognizable offence. The second amendment made in the same legislation in 1986 makes the husband or in-laws punishable, if a women commits suicide within 7 years of her marriage and it has been proved that she has been subject to cruelty.

The Maternity Benefit Act, 1961 aims at improving the status women. Maternity benefits were provided even before this Act and the Act was Employees' State Insurance Act, 1948. It was based on some kind of insurance on the part of employee or the employer. Only then one was eligible for the benefit under the Act. The present Act puts no such conditions.

The Equal Remuneration Act, 1976 provides for equal pay to men and women for equal work. The grant of equal pay for equal work has been extended to most of the sectors of work including plantation, agriculture, mines, construction, etc.

The Medical Termination of Pregnancy Act, 1971 legalised abortion by qualified professional on humanitarian or medical grounds. The Act provides for termination of pregnancy if it has not exceeded 12 weeks or 20 weeks in which event two registered medical practioners would have to vouch for it. The practioners must believe that the pregnancy if continued would cause grave physical or mention injury to the mother or if the child is let to be born would suffer from abnormalities that would handicap it.

In 1994, the Government of India passed the Pre-Conception and Pre-natal Diagnostic Techniques (Prohibition of Sex Selection) Act for preventing female foeticide. The implementation of this Act was not very fast. It was later amended and replaced in 2002 by the Pre-natal Diagnostic Techniques (Regulation and Prevention of Misuse) Act. The sex selective foeticide is banned under the law. According to this Act, an act to provide for the prohibition of sex-selection, before or after conception and for regulation of pre-natal diagnostic techniques for the purposes of detecting genetic abnormalities or metabolic disorders or chromosomal abnormalities or certain congenital malformation or sex linked disorders and for the preventing of their misuse for sex determination leading to female foeticide and for matters connected therewith or incidental thereto.

Several Commissions have been set-up by the government to look into the matter of status of women in the Indian society. Realising the need of setting up an agency to fulfill the needs, the government decided to set up a Commission for women and enacted the National Commission for Women Act, 1990. The Central Government has enacted another important Act i.e., the Protection of Human Rights Act, 1993. The Act gives a very wide and comprehensive definition of human rights as right relating to life, liberty, equality and dignity of the individual guaranteed by the Constitution. The Government of India, keeping in view the spirit of the Constitution has enacted several legislations,[27] which deals with women. These legislations seek to protect the rights of women against the oppression, unfair treatment and discrimination.

JUDICIAL ATTITUDE

The judiciary all over the world has been playing a great role in protecting the rights of women. The rights of women have been recognized locally and by the National Constitutions. The Indian Judiciary led by the Supreme Court has exhibited a welcome judicial activism in recognizing, popularizing and enforcing these rights. Where there is no direct provision prescribed, the judiciary is contributing a lot by recognizing the workmen's rights. The Supreme Court in State of Maharashtra Vs. Madhukar Narian[28] without referring to Article 21, held that even a women of easy virtue is entitled to privacy and that no one can evade her privacy as and when he likes. In State of Punjab Vs. Gurmit Singh[29] the court has consistently maintained that the offence of rape is violation of the right to privacy of the victim. The Apex Court observed that:

> It is a sad reflection on the attitude of indifference of the society towards the violation of human dignity of the victim of sex crimes. We must remember that a rapist not only violates the victim's privacy and personal integrity, but inevitably causes serious psychological as well as physical harm in the process. Rape is not merely a physical assault. It is often destructive of the whole personality of the victim. A murderer destroys the physical body of his victim, a rapist degrades the very soul of the helpless female.[30]

The Supreme Court in a number of cases held that right to economic empowerment of women is a human right. In the case of C. Masilmami Mudaliar Vs. Idol of Sri Swamina Thaswami Thirukoil,[31] the Supreme Court has recognized, highlighted and conferred the rights to economic empowerment of women as fundamental right under Constitution of India.[32]

In Vishaka Vs. State of Rajasthan,[33] the Supreme Court laid down a number of guidelines to remedy the legislative vacuum. The court has defined, having regard to the definition of women's right under section 2(d) of the Protection of Human

Rights Act, 1993, sexual harassment includes any unwelcome sexually determined behaviour like physical contact and advances, a demand or request for sexual favour, sexually coloured remarks, showing pornography and any other unwelcome physical, verbal or non-verbal conduct of sexual nature. As a result of judgement in the instant case, any women employee who is subjected to sexual harassment of any kind can take recourse to initiating criminal proceedings, disciplinary action and also seek compensation from the guilty employer and other persons responsible for the harassment.

As a landmark judgement, the Supreme Court has demonstrated great judicial activism while coming to the rescue of the working women even at the cost of resorting to judicial activism under Article 141 of the Constitution. The broad guidelines of the Vishaka case has set a new trend in the Protection of human rights to dignity of working women in the country like India.

The Supreme Court in Delhi Domestic Working Women's Forum Vs. Union of India,[34] suggested the formulation of the scheme of awarding compensation to rape victims. The court suggested the setting up of Criminal Inquiries Compensation Board under Article 38(1) of the Constitution. It was also held that the trial of rape case in camera should be the rule and an open trial as an exception. The Supreme Court awarded compensation of ten lacks to an alien women under Article 21 of he Constitution who has been a victim of rape.

It is clear that in the absence of enacted law to province for the effective enforcement of the basic human rights to gender equality and guarantee against sexual harassment and abuse, more particularly against sexual harassment at work place, the judiciary laid down guidelines and norms for due observance at all work places or institution, until a legislation is enacted for this purpose.

In Ningammar Vs. Chikkaiah,[35] compulsory blood test to determine paternity was held to be violative of fundamental rights of life or liberty. In Chairman, Railway Board Vs.

Chandrima Das,[36] the Apex Court held that where a Bangladeshi women was gang-raped compensation can be granted under public law for violation of fundamental rights on the ground of domestic jurisprudence based on constitutional provision and human right jurisprudence.

In CEHAT Vs. Union of India,[37] the Supreme Court referred to the repercussion of unhindered female infanticide effecting overall sex ratio in various States. The Court issued the direction to Central Government, State Government, Union Territory and appropriate authorities for the implementation of the enacted Act. Further in CEHAT and others Vs. Union of India and others,[38] the Supreme Court made the registration of the clinics with ultra sound machines mandatory and directed the State Governments to take suitable action for creating awareness in public.

In this way, the judiciary has acknowledge the concept of gender empowerment and equality. The legislature and judiciary has been doing its job in a responsible way but lot has to be done and that too in an effective way.

RECENT TRENDS FOR EMPOWERMENT OF WOMEN

It is very important to mention here that for the constitutional protection of women in India, the judiciary make it abundantly clear that the courts have played the role of catalyst in ensuring their position in an effective manner. Recently, the Protection of Women From Domestic Violence Act, 2005 has come into effect, where women bruised and battered physically and emotionally by their husbands and in-laws will have a protective shield at their command. Their number may run into lakhs, if not crores.[39] Earlier women could use only section 398-A of the Indian Penal Code, 1860 to file a complaint against an abusive spouse. In Delhi, on an average 137 cases of 304-B, IPC (deaths due to dowry) and 1728 cases of 406 IPC and 498-A, IPC (demand of dowry and violence for dowry) are registered in a year.[40] But the law was not comprehensive enough to enforce her right to say on in her matrimonial home or to demand a maintenance if thrown out or seek protection from the abusive partner. Keeping in view that helplessness, the new legislation comes into existence.

In the new legislation it is not only physical or sexual abuse which constitutes domestic violence but also 'verbal and emotional abuse'[41] that includes insults, ridicule humiliation, name calling and insults or ridicule, specially with regard to not having a child or a male child. It is further pertinent to note that all this is not being said to underestimate the ordeal of the sufferance of domestic violence, but to ensure that there is no misuse of the law either.[42] A similar kind of things are still happening under the Anti Dowry Act.[43]

Besides this another notable feature of the Act is that under this legislation an aggrieved person is not only the wife, but any women who is or has been in a domestic relationship[44] with the respondent and who alleges to have been subjected to any act of domestic violence by the respondent.

It is further important to mention here that domestic violence is not confined to only one character of women i.e. wife. It also includes mothers, daughters, sisters, widows, divorced women living in the home as well as those who are in an informal relationship with the accused, including a bigamous relationship. It covers all domestic relationship in a 'shared household'.[45] Apparently the Act would also cover a man who abuses or beats up a sex worker with whom he has had a long standing relationship, such a pimp or an ongoing sexual relationship, though the scope of this provision would need to be tested in the court.

The intention of law-makers here apparently is to ensure that the guilty husband is not able to escape responsibility by merely denying that the complainant is his wife. Where the criminal law provision dealing with dowry focus on incarceration, the Domestic Violence Act gives women an opportunity to keep the perpetrator at a distance, but not in jail. Women can no longer be evicted from their homes by the abuser, and can seek an order to reside in the same house or be allotted a part of it for her personal use.

The first case decided under the Protection of Women from Domestic Violence Act, 2005 took 57 days only.[46] At least for the time being, the new law seems faster and more effective in giving relief to women victims. In the instant case, the complainant demanded stopping of violence, custody of children, shelter in husband's house,[47] monthly maintenance and stopping husband from selling his property.[48] The court was forthcoming in granting the temporary custody of the child below 5 years to the complainant till the disposal of the petitioner filed separately under Hindu Marriage Act for custody of children. The court utilized section 21 of the new Act, which override all other laws and enables the court to grant temporary custody of the child to the mother. In real sense, section 21 is a very important tool in the hands of the court to deliver speedy justice to victim. Moreover, section 20 of the Protection of Women from Domestic Violence overrides all other existing laws[49] and can be used to grant monthly maintenance to the separated wife. The court was forthcoming, in ordering under section 18 that husband and in-laws be restrained from repeating any act of domestic violence. The court wished to ensure this by probability husband and in-laws from any form of communication with the wife.[50]

It can be concluded that the Domestic Violence Act represents a landmark in empowering the women to achieve equality at par with men. The legislation provides civil law relief for domestic violence which is recognized as occurring for all sorts of reasons, across every class, religion and caste, in rural and urban areas.

The constitutional philosophy, special legislations, innovative active role of judiciary and recently passed Domestic Violence Act provides special favour to women and direct the State to treat the women at par with males equally. But unfortunately, still in the country like India women are subject to all kinds of discrimination and humiliation. It is now right time to give proper considerations to these issues to uplift the status of women in the country like India.

NOTES

1. The Constitution of India, 1950, Articles 14, 15(1), 23, 39-A and 42.
2. Sachidananda and Sinha, Ramesh, P., Women 's Rights : Myth and Reality, (1984), p. 28.
3. The basic principle enshrined in the Article 14 is that all persons living within the territorial limits of India are equal before the law irrespective of their race, religion, caste, sex, place of birth or nationality.
4. For details see U. N. Declaration of Human Rights, 1945 – Article 4 : All are equal before the law and are entitled without any discrimination to equal protection of the law.
5. Chiranjitlal Vs. Union of India, (1950) SCR 869
6. Quoted from Bair, M. A.A., The Constitution of India vis-à-vis Women, Indian Socio-Legal Journal, Vol. XXI, Nos. 1 and 2 (1995), p. 30.
7. Various provisions under different legislations have been declared valid and within the framework of the Constitution where women have been given special treatment. The court declared such provision as the permissive classification not violating the principle of equality under Article 14 of the Constitution.
8. The concerned Article further prohibits any discrimination with regard to use of well, tank, bathing, place of public resort, etc.
9. The basic reason behind Article 15(3) is that women 's physical structure and performance of maternal function place her to a disadvantage in the struggle for subsistence and her physical well being becomes an object of public interest and care in order to reserve the strength of the race.
10. AIR 1952 Cal. 825
11. Ibid., as per Justice Bose.
12. A number of laws have been enacted relating to prohibition of female infanticide, dowry, exposure of women in advertisement, female child marriage, atrocities and molestation, abduction

and rape, maternity benefits, medical termination of pregnancy, prohibition of prosecution and trafficking in women, etc.

13. AIR 1979 SC 1868
14. Ibid. at 1870
15. Shastri Madhu, Status of Hindu Women, (1990) at p. 94.
16. AIR 1984 SC 802.
17. For example, The Factories Act, 1948; The Minimum Wages Act, 1948; The Bounded Labour System (Abolition) Act, 1976; The Mines Act, 1952; The Merchant Shipping Act, 1958; The Motor Transport Workers Act, 1951; The Beedi and Cigar Workers (Conditions of Employment) Act, 1966; The Apprentices Act, 1961; The Plantation Labour Act, 1951, etc.
18. For more details see Bandhwa Mukti Morcha Vs. Union of India, AIR 1984 SC 802 at p. 812.
19. The Employment of Children Act, 1938; Sec. 3 of the Act prohibits employment of children below 15 years of age to work in any occupational concern with the transport of passengers , goods by mail, by railways, etc.
20. The only difference being that the moral rights are not specifically enforceable as against the State by citizen in a court of law in case State fails to implement its duty but, nevertheless, they are fundamental in the governance of the country and all organs of the State including the judiciary, are bound to enforce those directives.
21. For more details see Article 39 of the Constitution.
22. The Equal Remuneration Act, 1976; The Bounded Labour System (Abolition) Act, 1976; The Factories Act, 1948; The Mines Act, 1952; The Plantation Labour (Amendment) Act, 1981 and many other statutes.
23. Part IX and IXA have been added to the Constitution by the Constitutional Amendment Act, 1992 ad the Constitution (74th Amendment) Act, 1992 popularly known as the Panchayat and Nagarapalika Constitution Amendment Acts, with Articles 243, 243-A to 243 D and Articles 243 P to 243 ZQ; for more details see Myneni, S. R., Women and Law, (2002) at p. 20.
24. Article 51-A newly added to the Constitution by 42nd Amendment 1976. This Article for the first time specified a code of ten commandments for a citizen.

25. For more details see The Times of India, January 17, 2007, p. 16.
26. Chaudhary, B. R., Problems of Working Women, Patriot, Dec. 16, 1983, p. 6-7.
27. The Medical Termination of Pregnancy Act, 1972; The Hindu Adoption and Maintenance Act, 1956; The Maternity Benefits Act, 1961; The Equal Remuneration act, 1976; The Prevention of Immoral Traffic act, 1986; The Hindu Marriage Act, 1955; The Special Marriage act, 1954; The Dowry Prohibition Act, 1961; The Child Marriage (Restrain) Act, 1933; The Hindu Succession Act, 1960.
28. AIR 1991 SC 207
29. AIR 1996 SC 1393
30. Ibid.
31. AIR 1996 SC 1696
32. In the instant case Justice K. Rama Swamy, noted that as per the United Nations Report, 1980, women constitute half of the world population,.performs nearly 2/3 of work hours, receives 1/10 of the world's income and own less than one hundredth percent of the world's property.
33. AIR 1996 SC 1697
34. (1995) 1 SCC 14.
35. AIR 2000 Karnataka 50
36. AIR 2000 SC 988
37. AIR 2001 SC 2007
38. AIR 2002 SC 3689
39. According to National Crime Record Bureau, 2005, 40 percent of Indian women are victims of domestic violence. A crime is committed against a women in India every three minutes, for more details see Report of National Crime Record Bureau, 2005.
40. The Hindu, February 25, 2007, p. 16.
41. It includes not providing food, clothes and medicines for one's children, preventing a child from attending school, college or any other educational institution, forcing a person to get married when he or she does not want to, or preventing a person from marrying the person of his or her choice.

42. Since the definition of domestic violence in the new Act is much wider than that provided in the IPC, the number of complaints under the new definition can be expected to be far more than the complaints under the IPC as given above.
43. The Prohibition of Dowry Act, 1961; under this legislation a large number of fictitious complaints are being filed against in-laws only to settle scores with them.
44. Complaints can be filed by neighbours, social workers or relatives on behalf of the victim.
45. A shared household is very broadly defined to include one where the abused person lives singly or with the abuser.
46. For more details see The Hindu, February 25, 2007, p. 16.
47. The complainant also demanded the shelter in husband's house which was not granted on the plea that she had been living separately for one and a half year.
48. Regarding stopping the husband from selling his property, the court did not give any relief to the complainant saying that the relevant documents had not been placed on record to prove the property was owned by the husband.
49. In the instant case the court declined to grant monthly maintenance under the new law saying that such prayer is already pending before a separate court under the Hindu Marriage Act, 1956
50. The Hindu, February 25, 2007, p. 16.

COMPARISON OF MARRIED AND NEVER MARRIED WOMEN IN RELIGIOUS COMMUNITIES IN INDIA

*Nahid Sarikhani**

INTRODUCTION

Marriage is an important social phenomenon that it is approved as a social institution, by law and customs. It admits men and women into a family life. Like many social institutions, the institution of marriage is dynamic in nature. It holds not only the function of social control but it also play major role as a vehicle of social change by influencing behaviour, beliefs and values. A study of the origin and development of the institution of marriage at all levels of culture reveals that the institution has undergone a number of changes through the ages. (A Team of Experts, 2004).

Therefore, marriage is one such way to regulate and control sex and ensure healthy procreation and mutual love among men and women. In fact, the primary aim of marriage is healthy "development 'of one's personality. So, for achieving to healthy and safe society need to attend to this major institution.

Different religions also have emphasized to it. As, marriage among Hindus is called as a "sacrament"; among

* Department of Sociology, Mysore University, Manasagotri, Mysore, Karnataka, India.

Muslims it is known as a "contract"; (Sharma and Thapa, 2003) and among Christian it is sacred institution, it has been blessed by God and it is a natural thing (A Team of Experts, 2004), Sikhs are encouraged to marry, and marriage is called 'Anand karaj', which means ' the ceremony of happiness (Bashir,2004), among Jains marriage is largely a worldly event. It is recommended to all Jain Shravakas (unless they have taken a vrata of Brahmacharrya) and Marriage is a public declaration of a couple's intent to be together for life, and it is a declaration of the community's support for the couple (Yashwant ,2005) and others religions have expressed to it's importance. It has certain rites and rituals attached to it. These rites have varied from religion to religion, place to place, caste to caste, etc.

Some time, peoples couldn't perform these rituals. As a result, number of single peoples will increase. It creates problems for single population especially single women.

On the one hand, an individual who remains single and never marries feels out of place, socially and culturally. Remaining single is more acceptable for men than it is for women. When a woman is not married, it is assumed that there is something wrong with her; she may be very difficult to get along with, she may be uncompromising, and therefore she is single.

Indian single women also experience a multitude of problems in the social arena. For example, Single women are not allowed to participate in religious festivities and marriage celebrations because it is considered unlucky, unholy, and inauspicious; Moreover, they are hesitant to make friends with men (either single or married) because the friendliness might be misinterpreted to mean that the woman is frivolous, immoral, and sexually permissive; And also parents who could not find a suitable match for their daughters were ostracized and looked down on. (Rao and Rao, 1976).

On the other hand, Single women were supposed to be the responsibility of the extended family, and this tradition still continues; as there are families where the parents and other members of the family are totally dependent on the income of the young girls. They are mightily afraid of the girls getting married. They avoid setting their marriages on one excuse or the other. The young girls, emotionally attached with the parents, feel guilty in settling and neglecting the parent's responsibility. The marriageable age passes away. (Dak, 1988).

In general, there are various reasons in India that girls have to remain single that these factors according to previous studies are consisted help to family's income, high cost of dowry system, don't find suitable person, head of family by girls, etc.

Additionally, the rise in the age of marriage might have been the cumulative effect of a number of factors like education of women, engagement of girl in economic pursuits, urbanization, westernization and modernization etc. (Sharma and Thapa, 2003).

In the study, the author attributes analyzing comparison of Married and Never Married Women in different religion from the scope of statistical center of India. The data were reflected by general census of 2001 in India. In this report was explored sex ratio of Married and Never Married women; married age among different religion; number of never married women according to Act 1929 in India; relationship between Never Married women and head of households.

FINDING

India has younger population in the world, as 35.3% of the population of the country has been in the age 14 years and less in the census 2001.

Census 2001 data on marital status of persons show that 34.7 % population of 10 years and above are 'Never Married' and 45.6% are Married in the country.

According to census 2001 in India 468,593,016 population (45.6%) age of 10 years and above have reported as 'Married'. Sex ratio among them is 1021 for all religions. It presents early marriage among females; irrespective of any religious affiliations is reflected in the data.

According to census 2001 in India, at the national level, the proportion of married females to total number of females is reported to be 47.7%. The proportion is highest in case of Jains (53.4%) followed by Sikhs (50.9%) and Hindus (48.7%). The proportion is lowest in case of Muslims, whose percentage is 42.4. But based on, 'the Child Marriage Restraint Act, 1929' (Rajashekara, 2005) we can state 11,741,755 married population are under lawful age of marriage in India. In the other words, under this Act Married female less than age of 18 years are 4,869,803 population and males less than age of 21 years are 6,871,952 populations. The rise in number of Married population probably present a number of factors like poverty and the poor awareness level of families, dominated traditional culture in society, etc.

Census 2001 data on Married women show that 0.6% them have been in the age group 10-14 years, 1.5% populat has been in the age group 15-17 years, 33.5%poeples has been in age group 18-29 years and 64.4% of them have been in the age 30 years and above. The statistical above indicate early marriage is visible in the age-group 10-17 years among all religious communities in the country.

While comparing the proportion of currently married females among different religious communities by age group10-17 years, it is interesting to note the differentials in the proportion among different religious communities. While in case of Hindus, about 0.6% of the females in the age-group 10-14 years and 1.5% of them in the age-group 15-17 years are married; in case of Muslims, the rate were 0.6% and 1.6% respectively. In case of Sikhs 0.5% of the female in the age-group 10-14 years are married. The proportions for Christians, Buddist and Jain in the age –group10-14 were comparatively very low, these being 0.3%, 0.3% and 0.2% percents respectively. In the age-group 15-17 years, the rate for Christian is 0.7%, Sikh is 0.6%, Buddist is 0.8% and Jain is 0.4%.

Hence, results of above indicate early marriage is higher among Muslims and Hindu than others religious communities at the national level. On the other hand, as per census 2001, the mean age at marriage for females, who married in the last five years, has been 19.6 years. Among females the mean age at marriage varied from 17.8 years (Rajasthan) to 24 years (Goa).(Census and you, 2005).

More over, the data presents of the total married women 5,408,958 or 27.1% returned as" household heads". 13% of them are reported from the younger age group" less than 30 years", 56% of them are in age group 30-49 years and 31% of married women of households heads are in the oldest age group. Therefore a majority of married women were recognized as 'Head of the household'. As a matter of fact, majority of them which may be due to husbands living away from the family on account of business, employment, husband's silk, etc.

Mean while, according to census 2001 in India 273,903,685 population (34.7%) age of 10 years and above have reported as 'Never Married'. Sex ratio among them is 652 for all religions. But based on, 'the Child Marriage Restraint Act, 1929' (Rajashekara, 2005) we can state actual statistics Never Married population is 65,246,394 population in India. In the other words, under this Act Never Married females age of 18 years and above are 26,612,624 population and males age of 21 years and above are 38,633,770 populations. The rise in number of Never Married males than to Never Married females probably present a number of factors like poverty and low-income men, higher education in men, urbanization, westernization and modernization etc. while these factors among Never married girls consist poverty and low-income family, dowry system, to be head of household of women, education of women, engagement of girl in economic pursuits, etc.

Census 2001 data on Never Married women show that 41.1% of them (10,950,112 females) have been in the age group 18-19 years, 46.4% population (12,344,793 females) has been in the age group 20-29 years, 4.8%poeples (1,264,663 females) has been in age group 30-39 years and 5%of them(1,340,950 females) have been in the age 40 years and above. Moreover, a majority of Never Married women (68.9%) in the country are living in the rural areas.

On the on hand, table 1 shows, the highest Never Married Women rates over 9 per cent has been returned from Uttar Pradesh (11.6%), Maharashtra (9.9%) and Tamil Nadu (9.7%) respectively. The lowest Never Married rate of women less 3 per cent has been recorded in 22 states and Union Territories. The rest of Never Married women of over 3 per cent to 8 per cent have been recorded in 10 states and Union Territories. Besides, with regard to the results, there is a wide gap between the number of never married women in rural and urban areas.

On the other hand, the data presents of the total never married women 689,947 or 2.6% returned as "household heads". Additionally, 64.7% of them are reported from the younger age group "less than 30 years", 19%of them are in age group 30-49 years and 16% of never married of households heads are in the oldest age group. In the other words, only less than one and fifth of never married of household heads have reported persons in the age of 50 years and above. Hence, a majority of younger age group of never married women were recognized as 'Head of the household'.

Table 2 shows number of never married women of age 18 years and above at the national level. The percentage distribution of never married women by religious communities in census 2001 reveal the highest percentage of them reported in Hindu communities (75.5%) and the lowest percentage has been recorded in Jain communities (0.7%). Of course, comparison of all Religious communities in India indicate after Hindu communities , the rate of Muslim, Christian, Sikh, Buddhist and Jain communities were respectively 13.5%, 5.7%, 2.7%, 1% and 0.7% among never married women age of 18 years and above.

Table 1
Never Married Women Rate by Residence and State in India, 2001

State	*Total*	*%*	*Rural*	*%*	*Urban*	*%*
Jammu & Kashmir	497741	1.87	342890	2.30	154851	1.32
Himachal Pradesh	236137	0.89	204511	1.37	31626	0.27
Punjab	906126	3.40	558366	3.74	347760	2.97
Chandigarh	37495	0.14	1579	0.01	35916	0.31
Uttaranchal	278265	1.05	180298	1.21	97967	0.84
Haryana	423111	1.59	227564	1.53	195547	1.67
Delhi	481950	1.81	20151	0.14	461799	3.95
Rajasthan	718654	2.70	360368	2.42	358286	3.06
Uttar Pradesh	3099142	11.65	1758479	11.78	1340663	11.47
Bihar	976726	3.67	730684	4.90	246042	2.10
Sikkim	27560	0.10	23614	0.16	3946	0.03
Arunachal Pradesh	35341	0.13	26885	0.18	8456	0.07
Nagaland	163651	0.61	140837	0.94	22814	0.20
Manipur	176936	0.66	125526	0.84	51410	0.44
Mizoram	56118	0.21	22049	0.15	34069	0.29
Tripura	113222	0.43	84280	0.56	28942	0.25
Meghalaya	105213	0.40	71612	0.48	33601	0.29
Assam	1061497	3.99	868664	5.82	192833	1.65
West Bengal	2103184	7.90	1037865	6.96	1065319	9.11
Jharkhand	556114	2.09	328460	2.20	227654	1.95
Orissa	1384064	5.20	1097465	7.35	286599	2.45
Chhattisgarh	432207	1.62	271675	1.82	160532	1.37
Madhya Pradesh	951756	3.58	425661	2.85	526095	4.50
Gujarat	1378923	5.18	709602	4.76	669321	5.73
Daman & Diu	5484	0.02	2095	0.01	3389	0.03
Dadra & Nagar Haveli	4144	0.02	3134	0.02	1010	0.01
Maharashtra	2639555	9.92	1036645	6.95	1602910	13.71
Andhra Pradesh	1604079	6.03	827082	5.54	776997	6.65
Karnataka	1784098	6.70	964988	6.47	819110	7.01
Goa	99335	0.37	54060	0.36	45275	0.39
Lakshadweep	2311	0.01	1277	0.01	1034	0.01
Kerala	1637308	6.15	1163535	7.80	473773	4.05
Tamil Nadu	2570176	9.66	1225620	8.21	1344556	11.50
Pondicherry	48897	0.18	13783	0.09	35114	0.30
Andaman & Nicobar Islands	16104	0.06	10686	0.07	5418	0.05
India	26612624	100.00	14921990	100.00	11690634	100.00

Source: C2 Table, India, Census of India 2001.

Table 2
Population and Proportion of Never Married and Married Women by All Religious Communities

Religious Communities	*never married*		*married*				
	18 years and above	*%*	*All Age*	*18 years and above*	*%*	*less than 18*	*%*
All Religious Communities	26,612,624	100	236772617	231,902,814	100	4,869,803	100
Hindu	20,091,134	75.5	194068084	189,990,450	81.9	4,077,634	83.7
Muslim	3,592,369	13.5	28313808	27,679,961	11.9	633,847	13.0
Christian	1,516,292	5.7	5370956	5,317,280	2.3	53,676	1.1
Sikh	713,756	2.7	4613704	4,562,845	2.0	50,859	1.0
Buddhist	268,764	1	1762397	1,743,216	0.8	19,181	0.4
Jain	188,432	0.7	1093297	1,086,253	0.5	7,044	0.1
Oth-reli-comm	210,558	0.8	1392876	1,369,148	0.6	23,728	0.5
Not-stated	31,319	0.1	157,495	153,661	0.1	3,834	0.1

Source: C3 Table, India,Census of India 2001.

DISCUSSION

Results have indicated marriage is very important among Indian people. As pervious studies have revealed for Indians, there's no way to escape thinking about marriage, eventually. It wouldn't be a stretch to say that *shaadi*, the word for marriage in many Indian languages, is the first word a child understands after *mummy* and *papa*. To an Indian, marriage is a matter of karmic destiny. There are many happy unions in the pantheon of Hindu gods—Shiva and Parvati, Krishna and Radha. (Jain, 2005).

Mean while, all religious communities have emphasized on it. Hence, it has created problems for people especially women. If you see to data of census 2001, near to half (45.6%) of population age of 10 years and above are Married in the country. Sex ratio among them is 1021 for all religions. It presents early marriage among females. Besides, 11,741,755 married populations are under lawful age of marriage in India. In the other words, part of population has ignored 'the Child Marriage Restraint Act, 1929'. Under this Act Married female less than age of18 years are 4,869,803 population and males less than age of 21 years are 6,871,952 populations. As a result, a large group of them are still unemployed, and suffering due to economic dependence to their families.

According to table 3, among religious communities, early marriage was observed more among Hindus and Muslim families. Because, Marriage is also discussed in the Hindu religious as a social religious duty which has three main aims, Dharmas (duty), Praja(Progeny), rati (Sensual Pleasures), (Sharma and Thapa, 2003). It creates problems in acquiring education and suitable jobs. Moreover, Pre-puberty marriage for girls a must in the traditional Hindu society were firstly high regard for the chastity of women and secondly the idea, as pointed out by Kapadia, that the girl may not be mature enough to question the authority of her husband's domination under which she is shifted from the domination of her father after marriage. (Sharma and Thapa, 2003) Among Muslims, according to "Hidaya" Muslim scripture, the age of puderty is 12 and 9 in the case of boys and girls respectively. Boys and girls can accept the marital contract after attaining the age of puberty.(Sharma and Thapa, 2003).In spite of, among Sikhs Child marriage is taboo, but we can observe early marriage; because it presents in other part "When a girl becomes marriageable, physically, emotionally and by virtue of maturity of character, a suitable Sikh match should be found and she be married to him by Anand marriage rites". Hence, probably the difference has created this problem between Sikh's communities. (Anand Sanskar, 2007).

Mean while, early marriage between Christian and Jain are low. The institution of marriage among the Christian families, is not indictable, not an absolute imperative or necessity according to Christianity. The highest ideal of human life is a life of celibacy. (A Team of Experts, 2004) moreover, in the choice of life-partners, Christians provide ample freedom to boys and girls, unlike the arranged marriages among Hindus. (A Team of Experts, 2004) Among Jains, marriages are mostly conducted by the Jain pundits only (community center), hence, these communities probably can control early marriage relatively.

Therefore, the data of above show the age of marriage of women among the religious communities varies from place to place, caste to caste and sometimes from family to family. However, traditionally, the culture and attitude of head of family affect in the determination of the marriageable age of the girls before the attainment of puberty.

On the other hand, results census 2001 in India have revealed 273,903,685 populations (34.7%) age of 10 years and above have reported as 'Never Married'. Sex ratio among them is 652 for all religions. Whereas, Based on 'the Child Marriage Restraint Act, 1929' (Rajashekara, 2005) we can state actual statistics 'Never Married population' is 65,246,394 populations in India. In the other words, under this Act Never Married females age of 18 years and above are 26,612,624 populations and males age of 21 years and above are 38,633,770 populations. The rise of number of never married population can increase the HIV/AIDS pandemic in the society. As results one of study have indicated In India, there has been a sudden surge of interest during the last decade, mainly on account of threat of the HIV/AIDS pandemic, in studying the matters related to sexuality and sexual behaviour among special groups in general and among never-married youth in particular. (Narayanaswamy and Audinarayana, 2005).

In additional, there are various factors that it expresses reasons of never married women. The most important they are poverty family and help to supplement of family's income, to be head of household some girls, dowry system.

Results show 2.6% of women returned as head of household. In the other hand, they have to accept responsibility of managing affairs of the household and also the decision making on behalf of the household. As a matter of fact, this group of persons probably have accepted Head of the Household to reasons like poverty of family, father's death, mother's divorced mother, father's sick, etc.

Mean while, the prevalence of Dowry system' between Indian peoples. Unlike it was prohibited based on Act of 1986(Dowry Prohibition Act OF 1961, this has been amended in 1984, 1985and 1986), also According to it: giving and taking of dowry in any form is a crime; makes both the giver and taker of dowry culpable in the crime; it protects the complainant from being implicated in the crime (Rajashekara, 2005); and harassment by way of unlawful dowry demands of the woman or her relatives also comes under this definition; (Hindustan Times, 2006) but a majority of Indian families demand it from girl's families. One study was revealed the actual cost of dowry to a parent depends upon the social and economic position of the family and the education of the bridegroom. As per the findings of Srinivas in one of his studies in certain parts of south India, the bridegroom price viz. dowry is standardized with the academic qualifications of the boy. (Sharma and Thapa, 2003).

Therefore, Table 3 shows number of middle age (30-49years) and old age (50years and above) never married

Table 3

Comparison of Married and Never Married Women by Religious Communities and Age in India, 2001

Age Group	*All*		*Hindu*		*Muslim*		*Christian*		*Sikh*		*Buddist*		*Jain*		*Other*	
	Count	*%*	*Count*	*%*	*Count*	*%*	*Count*	*%*	*Count*	*%*	*Count*	*%*	*Count*	*%*	*Count*	*%*
							Married Women									
Total	236772617	100.0	194068084	100.0	28313808	100.0	5370956	100.0	4613704	100.0	1762397	100.0	1093297	100.0	1392876	100.0
10-14	1407581	0.6	1186300	0.6	169217	0.6	15825	0.3	21751	0.5	5506	0.3	2585	0.2	5301	0.4
15-17	3462222	1.5	2891334	1.5	464630	1.6	37851	0.7	29108	0.6	13675	0.8	4459	0.4	18427	1.3
18-19	7853582	3.3	6500797	3.3	1098354	3.9	76907	1.4	70317	1.5	47619	2.7	8277	0.8	45820	3.3
20-29	71477143	30	58526151	30	9134104	32	1355201	25	1203942	26	530389	30	265035	24	415957	30
30-39	66964078	28	54639648	28	8121255	29	1616628	30	1308181	28	502720	29	320642	29	413197	30
40-49	42878989	18	35102007	18	4884942	17	1140586	21	906727	20	315053	18	239807	22	263672	19
50+	42267176	18	34840063	18	4393218	16	1119728	21	1063991	23	345348	20	250397	23	229012	16
Age not stated	461846	0.2	381784	0.2	48088	0.2	8230	0.2	9687	0.2	2087	0.1	2095	0.2	1490	0.1
							Never Married Women									
Total	26612624	100.0	20091134	100.0	3592369	100.0	1516292	100.0	713756	100.0	268764	100.0	188432	100.0	210558	100.0
18-19	10950112	41.1	8379488	41.7	1604484	44.7	416631	27.5	298919	41.9	107301	39.9	68349	36.3	67864	32.2
20-29	12344793	46.4	9231110	45.9	1591292	44.3	819567	54.1	363683	51.0	131520	48.9	103441	54.9	95805	45.5
30-39	1264663	4.8	938163	4.7	147672	4.1	121369	8.0	13220	1.9	14206	5.3	6524	3.5	22241	10.6
40-49	505506	1.9	375972	1.9	50086	1.4	55444	3.7	5684	0.8	5036	1.9	3461	1.8	9229	4.4
50+	835444	3.1	605781	3.0	102588	2.9	87976	5.8	13646	1.9	7249	2.7	4438	2.4	12833	6.1
Age not stated	712106	2.7	560620	2.8	96247	2.7	15305	1.0	18604	2.6	3452	1.3	2219	1.2	2586	1.2

Note: population of Never married women based on 'the Child Marriage Restraint Act, 1929' (population of age 18 year and above) was estimated.

Source: Source:C3 Table Appendix, India, Census of India 2001.

women are considerable in India. According to census 2001, 6.7%never married women are middle age and 3.1% are old age. Comparison among religious communities reveal the highest of middle and old age never married women recorded in Christian communities and the lowest of middle and old never married women reported in Sikh communities.

As a matter of fact, results above indicate to need that government rises level of aware people than to suitable age of marriage in society and among religious communities. Besides, provide conditions for women who are in age of marriage.

REFERENCE

Anand Sanskar (2007), Sikh Matrimonial Ceremony and Conventions. www.allaboutsikhs.com/sikh-way-of-life/anand-sanskar-sikh-matrimonial-ceremony-and-convent.html.

A Team of Experts (2004), Modern UGC NET/SLET: Sociology. New Delhi. LTD. 90.

Bashir,Bilkiss (2004), Sikhmarriage,www:ngfl.ac.uk/re/sikhmarriage.html.

Census of India 2001.2004. C2 Table. New Delhi: registrar general & census commissioner.

Census of India 2001.2004. C3 Table. New Delhi: registrar general & census commissioner.

Census of India 2001.2004. C3 Table appendix. New Delhi: registrar general & census commissioner.

Census of India 2001.2004. HH-6 Table. New Delhi: registrar general & census commissioner.

Census of India 2001.2004. HH-7 Table. New Delhi: registrar general & census commissioner.

Census and you (2005), Series India. New Delhi: registrar general & census commissioner.

Community Center. Jain Wedding. Janakpuri. C-62. New Delhi-58 (India).www: India.mapsofindia. com/culture/indian-weddings/jain-wedding.html.

Dak, T.M. (1988), Women and Work in Indian Society. Delhi. Discovery publishing House.226-227.

Jain, Anita (2005), Is Arranged Marriage Really any Worse than Craigslist? www: svt.typepad.com/arian/ 2005/03/arranged.html

Narayanaswamy and Audinarayana (2005), Sexual Behaviour and its Determinants among Young Never-Married Male Factory Workers in a South Indian Knit City.India. TamilNadu. BharathiarUniversity.

Rajashekara, H. M. (2005), Understanding the Indian Constitution, university of Mysore, 74.

Rao, V. V. and Rao, V. N. (1976), Arranged Marriage: An Assessment of the Attitude of the College Students in India. *Journal of Comparative Family Studies* 7: 433-453.

Sharma, Vidya Dhar and Thapa, Vandana (2003), Jupiter Series: Sociology Manual (Paper- I I & III). New Delhi. R. E.G. D. 183-200.

Yaswant, K. (2005), JainMarriageRituals/Procedures, *www:cs.colostate.edu / malaiya / jainmarriage.html*

INDEX

D

I

Islamic Countries, 245
Islamic Countries, 245

J

K

L

M

N

O

P

Q

R

S

T

U

V

W